Josette Baer

Revolution, Modus Vivendi or Sovereignty?

The Political Thought of the Slovak National Movement
from 1861 to 1914

With a foreword by Dušan Kováč

Josette Baer

REVOLUTION, MODUS VIVENDI OR SOVEREIGNTY?

The Political Thought of the Slovak National Movement
from 1861 to 1914

With a foreword by Dušan Kováč

ibidem-Verlag
Stuttgart

Bibliographic information published by the Deutsche Nationalbibliothek
Die Deutsche Nationalbibliothek lists this publication in the Deutsche Nationalbibliografie; detailed bibliographic data are available in the Internet at http://dnb.d-nb.de.

Bibliografische Information der Deutschen Nationalbibliothek
Die Deutsche Nationalbibliothek verzeichnet diese Publikation in der Deutschen Nationalbibliografie; detaillierte bibliografische Daten sind im Internet über http://dnb.d-nb.de abrufbar.

Cover picture: The Danube, viewn from Devín, the ruins of a medieval fortress unfar from the capital Bratislava. © Josette Baer, Bratislava 2009

ISBN-13: 978-3-8382-0146-7

© *ibidem*-Verlag / *ibidem* Press
Stuttgart, Germany 2010

Table of contents

Slovak political thought as discovery

In science, discoveries are being made all the time. It doesn't always have to be the theory of relativity. Even a small discovery is a discovery.

In the history of political thought, however, we cannot rely too much on discoveries. These post-modern times often have a sense of *déjà vu* about them: everything is known, everything was there before and everything repeats itself. From time to time, however, we encounter a work about which we can say that it genuinely offers new insights. Such a work is the new book by Josette Baer: Revolution, modus vivendi or national sovereignty? The political thought of the Slovak national movement from 1861 to 1914.

One can view the book as a place of discovery firstly from the perspective of the international context. Slovakia has existed as an independent state since 1993, and since 2004 as a member of the European Union. Until then, Slovakia had been something of a terra incognita, even for many experts; a country whose existence was certainly known, but which nevertheless remained anonymous. When Slovakia was part of Czechoslovakia, many saw it as united with the state, which was perceived as Czech. Only a very limited circle of distinguished experts was aware of the particularity of Slovakia, and hence also the particular nature of Slovak history and Slovak political thought. At the beginning of the 21st century, this new member of the European Union aroused a natural curiosity in many people. To travel to Slovakia and get to know the country, the cities, the people – this could be done in a matter of days, or weeks. To understand Slovak history, culture and hence also the country's intellectual character, however, is quite impossible without well-informed, expert work.

One can also discover and appreciate the work of Josette Baer in a purely Slovak context. There are many expert works about various epochs of Slovak history and culture. It is a pity, though, that few are written in a world language. And among those, regretfully, only a small number fulfil the demanding criteria of expert study. It is also surprising that in the Slovak intellectual environment there are so few expert studies which are committed to the history of Slovak political thought. This is partly due to the fact that political science was not promoted as an academic field during the years of communist totalitarianism. We can, of course, learn something about Slovak political thought in historical studies, but these are mainly focussed on a particular historical context, less on political theory.

That is why Josette Baer's study is also a contribution to the current discourse in Slovakia and is sure to attract the interest of Slovak experts. In her study, the author, who teaches at the University of Zurich, also provides an interesting insight into the European background. From this perspective, Slovak political thought is seen not only in Slovak terms, but integrated into a wider European context.

The study covers the years from 1861 to 1914, though in some parts, it inevitably exceeds this time-frame. These were important years for Slovakia. The Slovak political programme, whose central tenet was the demand for Slovak autonomy within the political framework of Hungary – ultimately, the programme of the federalization of Hungary on the basis of ethnicity – emerged during the revolutionary years of 1848–1849. The programme was mainly the Slovak reaction to European nationalism and its idea of a 'national state'. This programme was basically in contradiction with the Magyar political programme, which, though stemming from the very same ideas, claimed to be a transformation of the whole Hungarian multi-ethnic kingdom into a 'Magyar national state'. Neither the Slovak nor the Magyar programme could be successfully realized during the revolutionary years; in the epoch of so-called Neo-absolutism, Vienna did not wish to change anything in this regard. That was the reason the Slovaks expressed their wishes again after the end of Neo-absolutism, with almost exactly the same programme as in the revolutionary years; this time, however, the programme was called the *Memorandum of the Slovak nation*, which was adopted in 1861. This remained as the official Slovak 'Magna Charta' until the beginning of WWI, when the Slovak political and cultural elites acceded to the building of the Czecho-Slovak state.

This is the chronological time-frame of Josette Baer's study. However, during this epoch, there was a dramatic event: the Austrian-Hungarian compromise (*Ausgleich*) of 1867. The compromise gave almost all the political power of the Kingdom of Hungary to the Magyars, who started to realise their political dreams: the transformation of Hungary into a Magyar national state. For the Slovaks, this meant a time of depression and harsh assimilation, which culminated in 1907 with the so-called Apponyi laws that magyarized the schools. As an immediate consequence, the Slovaks lost their primary schools, which hitherto trained children in their Slovak mother tongue. From the viewpoint of the international context, however, there is another important factor: the emergence of the *Zweibund* (Dual Alliance) in 1879, which united Germany and Austria-Hungary. This alliance greatly reinforced the Magyar position and the Magyar centralist aspirations. Not only Bismarck's Germany, but also the Germany of Emperor William, were united in supporting the politics of the Magyars, particularly against "liberal and decadent Vienna".

In these conditions, the Slovak political programme of federalization of the Hungarian kingdom could not be realised. This affected the Slovaks and their political thought; the consequence was desperation and a feeling of loss on the part of the Slovaks; on the other side, however, there was also an interesting international orientation shown by the Slovaks, who were looking for a solution in the changing international situation.

Josette Baer's study deals with this dramatic epoch of the Slovak national movement. In this sense, the attentive reader can find in her book motifs that are characteristic of the development of nationalistic political thought at the turn of the 19th to the 20th century, and in the general history of Europe, but also sketches that are characteristic of the particular Slovak conditions.

Her study is therefore an interesting contribution to a deeper knowledge of Slovakia, Central Europe and the context of European political thought in which the Slovak representatives appear as unique intellectual figures, but also in the sense of *pars pro toto*.

In that sense, this volume represents a discovery and a contemporary enrichment of knowledge about one part – perhaps a small one, but nevertheless not uninteresting and not to be neglected – which until now was missing from our mosaic of political thought.

Dušan Kováč, July 2010, Bratislava, Slovakia

Acknowledgements

The present volume is the result of my interest in Slovak intellectual history, which began more than ten years ago, while doing research for my PhD on Masaryk and Havel in the Clementinum in Prague in 1994. After completion of my PhD, I became aware of the painful lack of studies by 'Western' scholars about Slovak political thought of the 19th century. On my first research stay in Bratislava in 1998, I explored the town, walked down Michalská ulica and saw a bookshop that had a rather eclectic offering: religious monographs, bibles and literature. Today, the bookshop is gone and the thoroughly renovated shop sells women's clothes. There, I found Tibor Pichler's *Národovci a občania*, which made me want to do more research on Slovak thinkers. Pichler's portraits of Slovak intellectuals of the national movement and his concise analysis of their thought aroused my interest to learn more about Slovak history in general, and Slovak intellectual history in particular. While the political and economic histories of Slovakia have been established, the currents of political thought remain concealed to the non-Slovak speaking academia and public.

This study attempts to present a first and therefore necessarily limited overview of Slovak political thought of the second half of the 19th century, including the debates surrounding the *memorandum* of 1861, also known as the *Vienna memorandum* and the currents of *Russophilia* and *Czechoslovakism*. I selected six intellectuals and politicians, who entered Slovak history as *narodovci* (nation builders and awakeners), owing to their specific contributions to the nation's identity, culture and politics. Ján Francisci, Ján Palárik, Štefan Marko Daxner, František Sasínek, Svetozár Hurban Vajanský and Vavro Šrobár had different views and ideas and pursued different goals. Francisci's diplomatic talent made him concentrate his efforts on managing and administering the early national movement's activities while holding an administrative position with the Hungarian government. Palárik and Sasínek were Catholic priests personifying the opposition of liberalism and conservatism in the movement. Daxner was an advocate and the legal expert of the movement; he made higher education his area of expertise. Hurban Vajanský, a poet and writer, spoke out for a Russophile direction that was based on Ľudovít Štúr's late and desperate Panslavism; he linked the issue of Slovak national survival to the Russian Empire's influence in Europe. Šrobár, a medical doctor, eventually opted for Czechoslovakism, whose main principle consisted in the promotion of democratism against the rule of the aristocracy and clergy. He was the co-founder of the *Hlas* group, whose intellectual perspectives, methods and goals were influenced by Masaryk's *Realism*. The six shared one common interest: to strengthen the Slovak nation in its attempts at securing the autonomy of their culture and language – and with that, their political rights. Some took part in the 1848 revolution pursuing the goal of an autonomous Slovak district, others opposed this idea and opted for a *modus vivendi* with the ruling Magyars. A third possibility was a common state with the Czechs as the highest possible level of autonomy, short of sovereignty.

The introductory chapter provides basic information about Slovak political history in Upper Hungary, and the crucial events of the revolution of 1848 and the *memorandum* of 1861. For a Hungarian and Austrian perspective of 19th century history, I refer to the volumes of *Die Habsburger Monarchie 1848 – 1918* listed in the bibliography. The essential issues in Slovak intellectual history that the thinkers dealt with were *Magyarisation,* the *okolie, historiography, Russophilia and Czechoslovakism*; these concepts will be explained in the following chapters. I tried to analyse the political thought of the six intellectuals according to their political goals and their legitimating explanations. The analysis focussed on the influence of Western ideas of liberalism and constitutionalism, as well as on what one could call 'intra-Slavic' currents of thought emerging with the Slavic renaissance of the late 18th and early 19th century, for example *Panslavism* and *Slavophilia*. My intention was further to let the political atmosphere appear through the voices of the six *narodovci*, who all had the intellectual abilities that enabled them to publish extensively. The chapters appear in chronological order according to the dates of birth of the thinkers. The names of locations, towns and cities appear according to their historical names in the subject period, i.e. Turčiansky Svätý Martin instead of the 20th century Martin and Pressburg/Pozsony instead of Bratislava, the new Slavic name of the capital of Slovakia in 1918.

A brief remark on references: All authors referred to contemporary ideas, texts and influential persons. To illustrate the political contexts of the subject period, I tried to provide as much information as possible about individuals, works and popular sayings referred to by the authors. If not referred to otherwise, I found this information on *Encyclopaedia Britannica Online* and *COTOJE Online. Encyklopedie Universum. Ottová Encyklopedie. Malá Československá Encyklopedie.* I trust that the reader can verify this information by consulting the mentioned online resources, as I wanted to avoid a bulk of references to the same sources.

A not so brief but nevertheless important remark on the issue of Jews and Roma in 19th century Slovakia: All intellectuals were Christians; some were Catholic, some Lutheran. They referred to their Jewish and Roma fellow-citizens mostly when addressing the life in the countryside or the harshness of the Magyar assimilation. Scrutinising their texts, I did find expressions that to us and in our times sound racist and anti-Semitic. However, we should be careful not to rush into general conclusions and judgements: in the 19th century, Slovaks, Austrians and Hungarians, as well as the entire Christian world, adhered to the 'usual' Christian anti-Semitism promoted by the churches. Joseph II rule of law state ended *de iure* institutional discrimination against the Jews, but most people still considered them second-class citizens. I refer to the Hilsner Prozess in Austria in 1899, which, thanks to Masaryk, who organised the new forensic science to prove Hilsner's innocence, saved the Jewish *clochard* from the gallows; see Steven Beller's article, listed in the bibliography. The Jewish citizens in the empire were loyal to the ruling Austrians in Cisleithania and the Magyars in Transleithania – because this was the means of their economic survival. They had to speak German and Hungarian to protect their sources of income. As *entrepreneurial minority*, the Jews had to fear more oppression than the Christian national minorities if they did not express loyalty to the ruling. They were shopkeepers, worked in trade and owned inns and pubs; business demanded that they comply with the administration, which implied the maintenance of smooth relations with the authorities. They adapted, but were not yet assimilated. In the context of Magyarisation in 19th century Hungary, to speak of Jewish assimilation would be to create confusion, since the concept of "assimilation" did not mean the same to the Slovaks as it did to the Jews. Magyarisation attempted to create a Hungarian political nation that was understood as Magyar, hence creating a homogeneous Magyar-speaking citizenry. Most of the Jewish citizens spoke Hungarian – whether they adhered to their faith at home in private or converted was of no concern to the Hungarian government. Express allegiance to Hungary was essential. The particular Jewish term "assimilation" was a method and current of thought that projected civic equality with the gentiles. Jews in the German-speaking countries thus assimilated in order to enjoy equal civil rights by converting to Christianity or abstaining from the religious life of their community. The alternative to assimilation for the European Jews was Zionism and emigration to Palestine. For a detailed analysis of Jewish assimilation, I refer to Hanna Arendt; for a historiography of persecuted entrepreneurial minorities, see Dan Chirot, both listed in the bibliography.

None of the six intellectuals expressed their anti-Semitic bias, if they adhered to it, repeatedly and profoundly. They were, to put it bluntly, occupied with more important issues such as the future of the national movement, high-school education and publishing. From their texts, I did not have the impression that they were significantly more anti-Semitic than intellectuals in France or England at that time. The Dreyfus Affair occurred in 1894 in France. For a detailed picture of the situation of the Jewish and Roma minorities, I refer the reader to volume III of *Die Habsburger Monarchie 1848 – 1918* and the works of Steven Beller. For 20th century history of the Jews in Slovakia I recommend the works of Ivan Kamenec, listed in the bibliography.

I should like to thank the following colleagues, friends and institutions for their support, helpful suggestions and comments. I am greatly indebted to SAIA, the Slovak Academic Information Agency that financed my research stays in Bratislava from March 2008 to August 2008, and from March 2009 to July 2009 with two generous stipends. My further thanks go to Gabriela Dudeková, Roman Holec, Daniela Kodajová, Ivan Kamenec, Elena Mannova, Slavomír Michálek and Tibor Pichler at the Slovak Academy of Sciences SAV. The staff of the library of the SAV UKSAV in Bratislava, the University library at Bratislava (Univerzitná Knižnica) and the Slovak National Library SNK in Martin were extremely helpful, in particular Ľudmila Šimková, Elena Hanzelova, Karin Šišmišova and Magdalena Brinckova. Adam Bžoch and Markus Giger helped with the translation of Slovak poetry, while Yannick Hill proofread the manuscript. Lastly, I am honoured that Dušan Kováč supervised my research and agreed to write the preface; his critical comments were invaluable.

The errors and shortcomings of this volume are my own.

Josette Baer
Bratislava, Slovakia, and Zurich, Switzerland, July 2010

X. Introduction

From a letter of the governor of Bohemia count Max Coudenhove to k.k. Minister President Ernst Seidler von Feuchtenegg and k.k. Minister of internal affairs count Friedrich Toggenburg, Vienna, 12 July 1917:

> "Your Excellency! In view of recent political developments in Bohemia, I consider it my duty to submit a report to your Excellency's attention, concerning the present rather disquieting situation ... Everywhere, anti-Austrian tendencies are being expressed in open fashion ... two anonymous publications, recently discovered, spoke in drastic terms of 'the death throes of Austria' ... reports about the war, especially in the *Narodni Listy*, give the impression that Bohemia does not belong to Austria, and the friendliness toward the Entente ... is being concealed less and less ... The current thinking of the decisive political circles of the Czech nation ... must therefore be considered revolutionary."[1]

Count Coudenhove could not have foreseen that Bohemia's independence would be achieved through the diplomatic efforts of Thomas Garrigue Masaryk[2], a professor of philosophy, rather than through revolution. Nor was the governor aware of the crucial importance of the idea of *Czechoslovakism* that should successfully legitimate Slovakia's integration to the common state. In 1918, two nations of Western Slavic origin merged into Czechoslovakia. Their recent historic developments were quite different in socio-economic, cultural and political terms[3], but their languages were close. The Czechs living in the socio-economically more developed Austrian part of the Habsburg empire accomplished their nation building process[4] with the creation of

---

[1] Quoted after Zdeněk Šolle, *Masaryk a Beneš ve svých dopisech z doby pařížských mírových jednání v roce 1919*, vol. I (Praha: Archiv AV ČR, 1993), pozn. 52, 85, 88, 89. Please note that all translations from Slovak, Czech, Russian and German into English are mine, if not quoted otherwise. Passages I wished to emphasise are indicated with 'italics JB'.

[2] For an analysis of Masaryk's political thought see my *Politik als praktizierte Sittlichkeit. Zum Demokratiebegriff von Thomas G. Masaryk und Václav* (Sinzheim: Pro Universitate, 1998).

[3] On the formation of German, Czech and Slovak national identities see Jiří Kořalka, "Nationsbildung und nationale Identität der Deutschen, Österreicher, Tschechen und Slovaken um die Mitte des 19. Jahrhunderts," in *Ungleiche Nachbarn. Demokratische und nationale Emanzipation bei Deutschen, Tschechen und Slovaken (1815-1914)* (Essen: Klartext, 1993), 33-48; for a detailed historical analysis of Czech and Slovak relations from the Middle Ages until the dissolution of the state in 1993 see Dušan Kováč, *Slováci. Češi. Dějiny* (Bratislava: Academic Electronic Press AEP, 1997).

[4] For the periodisation of the phases of Czech nation building and state building I drafted a model, whose essential element is the development of Czech intellectual history from late 18th century to early 20th century, i.e. the building of the Czechoslovak Republic. My model is largely based on

the common state, which was *de iure* a union of two nations. Yet, the Czechs *de facto* dominated the union, due largely to the fact that the Slovaks, living in the Northern part of the Hungarian kingdom, also called Upper Hungary, had been subject to Magyarisation, a policy to assimilate them to Magyar culture and language. Assimilation had protracted their economic development. Over almost a century, expressions of their cultural and national identity were oppressed, sanctioned and punished. The following figures illustrate the results of Magyarisation: in 1900, the Slovaks represented 10.4% of the Transleithanian population, yet Slovak students or rather, students who considered themselves Slovaks, made up only 1.4 % of the kingdom's total student body. Slovak representation in public services and state administration amounted to 0.4%, in educational institutions 0.9%, in industry, trade and banking 1.2% and in clerical institutions 2.9%[5].

What were the reasons for these low figures? For a clearer picture of the historic context this book is based upon, the following sections present a brief introduction to the development of the Slovak national movement from the 1848 revolution to the outbreak of WWI in 1914.

X. 1.   The Hungarian reform period and illegal Magyarisation

The Slovak-Magyar relationship in Northern Hungary[6], the territory of today's Slovakia, differed in many ways from the Czech-Austrian one in Bohemia. In the

---

Miroslav Hroch's seminal periodisation. He defined nation building of the small nations in Central Europe in three phases. Miroslav Hroch, *Die Vorkämpfer der nationalen Bewegungen bei den kleinen Völkern Europas: Eine vergleichende Analyse zur gesellschaftlichen Schichtung der patriotischen Gruppen* (Prag: Acta Universitatis Carolinae, 1968), 24-26. For details on Czech intellectual history development see my "Czech national identity – an exit factor from Totalitarianism?" in *Totalitarismus und Transformation* (Göttingen: Vandenhoeck & Ruprecht, 2008).

[5] L'udovít Holotík, "Die Slovaken," in *Die Habsburgermonarchie 1848–1918*, Vol. III, Die Völker des Reiches (Wien: Österreichische Akademie der Wissenschaften, 1980), 775-800; 792, 785.

[6] Slovak settlement in the kingdom of Hungary included the following counties (*comitatus, župy*) adjacent to Galicia in the North and East and Moravia and Lower Austria in the West. The counties are referred to in Hungarian and Slovak: Abauj-Torna – Abovská-Turňanská župa; Arva – Oravská ž.; Bars – Tekovská ž.; Gömör – Gemerská-Malohontská ž.; Hont – Hontianska ž.; Lipto – Liptovská ž.; Nograd – Novohradská ž.; Nyitra – Nitrianska ž.; Poszony – Přesporská (Bratislavská); Saros – Šarišská ž.; Szepes – Spišská ž.; Turoc – Turčianska ž.; Trencsen – Trenčianska ž.; Ung – Užská ž.; Zemplen – Zemplínská ž.; Zolyom – Zvolenská ž., Laszlo

decades before the revolution, the early Slovak national movement focused on language and cultural rights. A central figure was the Lutheran pastor and teacher Ľudovít Štúr[7] (1815 - 1856). The movement, adhering to an early nationalism of romanticist origin, was numerically too weak to effectively block Magyar pressure; they failed to retain the use of the Slovak language in schools and church services. The distinguished historian Daniel Rapant aptly described the attempts to assimilate Hungary's non-Magyar population prior to the Austro-Hungarian *Ausgleich* (compromise) of 1867 as "illegal Magyarisation"[8]. The fight against the measures violating their language rights led to the creation of the written Slovak language in 1843. As important was the decision of the Austrian Slavs to support Vienna against the revolutionary Hungarians in 1848. The Slovaks, in particular, hoped that their loyalty to the emperor would result in the effective re-implementation of their language rights. A Slovak autonomous county or *okolie*, ruled directly by Vienna bypassing Magyar rule, was not yet an issue. It would become the central theme of the national debate surrounding the *Slovak memorandum of 1861.*

The words of Lajos Kossuth (1802 - 1894), the leader of the Hungarian liberals and, for a short time, president of the revolutionary government, capture the very essence of the problematic relationship the Magyars were creating with the non-Magyar national groups in the Hungarian kingdom:

"Since the expression 'nation' for the modern state means much more than the knowledge of this or that language, I hereby proclaim that never, but never shall I recognize in the

---

Szarka, "The Slovak National Question and Hungarian Nationality Policy before 1918", *The Hungarian Quarterly 35*, no. 136 (1983): 98-114; 98-99. See also "Nationalitätenkarte der österreichisch -ungarischen Monarchie nach den Sprachen-, bzw. Konfessionserhebungen vom Jahre 1910", map in the appendix of *Die Habsburgermonarchie 1848–1918*, Vol. III. For the establishment of the Slovak *župy* in the first half of the 14th century see Dušan Kováč, *Dejiny Slovenska* (Praha: Nakladatelství Lidové Noviny, 2007), 34, 37, map on 37.

[7] For a detailed analysis of the thought of Štúr see my "Ľudovít Štúr - Nationalism and Panslavism in Slovakia," in *Slavic Thinkers or the Creation of Polities. Intellectual History and Political Thought in Central Europe and the Balkans, 19th Century* (New Academia Publishing: Washington D.C. 2007), 45-77; a shorter and earlier version is "National Emancipation – not the Making of Slovakia. Ľudovít Štúr's Conception of the Slovak Nation." *Postcommunist Occasional Papers 1*, no. 2, 2003, http://www.stfx.ca/pinstitutes/cpcs/studies-in-post-communism/

[8] Daniel Rapant, *Ilegalná Maďarizácia 1790-1840* (Turčiansky Sv. Martin: Matica Slovenská, 1947).

framework of the Holy Hungarian Crown another nation or nationality than the Magyar one. I know there are races and peoples here who speak other languages. The nation, however, here is only one."[9]

The so-called *spring of nations* of 1848 epitomised the culmination of the Magyar reform project that had started as a reaction against Austrian centralism around 1790[10]. The reform project was in essence a revival of the Hungarian language, literature and science; it gained momentum thanks to the stipulations of the post-Napoleonic continental order. In 1815, the European empires under the leadership of Prince Clemens Wenzel von Metternich (1773 - 1859) had re-established the system of a balance of power that was based on the empires' sovereignty and, above all, the stability of their foreign and internal affairs. To obtain internal stability, a functioning administration was required. Already in the previous century, the Habsburg Empire

---

[9] Daniel Rapant, *Slovenské povstanie 1848-1849*, I, dokumenty (Turčiansky Sv. Martin, 1950), 38, quoted in Joseph A. Mikuš, "Slovakia within the kingdom of Hungary (907-1918)," in *Slovakia. A Political and Constitutional History (with Documents)* (Bratislava: Slovak Academic Press, 1995), 11-28, 31. Kossuth was born to Slovak-German parents of impoverished nobility and Lutheran faith. He became involved with politics as a substitute delegate sent to the diet in Pressburg in 1832. Acquainted with Hungarian politicians of the Reform period, he published his radical liberal views in the reports from the diet and was widely read. In 1837, he was arrested, but freed in the amnesty of 1840 and appointed editor of the journal *Pesti Hirlap* (Pest News). He polarised the moderate Hungarian reformers and the Slovaks, Croatians and Romanians alike with his radical views about Hungarian superiority and an entitlement to unchallenged rule. After his dismissal from the journal in 1844, Kossuth was elected delegate for Pest and soon assumed leadership of the opposition. When the revolution broke out in Paris in February 1848, he swiftly used the opportunity to set up a declaration of national autonomy, which a majority of the parliamentarians supported. At the request by the Imperial government, the Croatian army invaded Hungary in September 1848. Kossuth was appointed head of the committee of national defence. In April 1849, the diet proclaimed Hungary's national independence and elected Kossuth as governor. With the arrival of the Russian army led by general Pashkevich, he fled to Turkey. In his last years, Kossuth never ceased to lobby for the Hungarian cause in the USA, France and Italy. His idea of a Danubian federation, uniting Hungary, Croatia, Serbia and Romania, was not well received, probably due to a lack of political realism. He published his *Memories of My Exile* in English in 1880 and died in Torino, Italy. His hot temper, magnetic charisma and revolutionary views made him a symbol of Hungarian national independence.

[10] Ludwig von Gogolák, "Die historische Entwicklung des slowakischen Nationalbewusstseins," in *Die Slowakei als mitteleuropäisches Problem in Geschichte und Gegenwart* (München: Oldenbourg, 1965), 50. Gogolák speaks of " a linguistic and national unification of the old feudal Hungarian body politic to resist the centralisation and amalgamisation carried out by the House of Austria [Domus Austriaca]."

had enacted administrative reforms to govern its poly-ethnic population more effectively. In the spirit of *Enlightened Absolutism*, Joseph II set up the rule-of-law state, which granted legal equality to all citizens, while his educational reforms were meant to facilitate communication between the imperial administrative bodies. While the *Edict of Tolerance* of 1781 granted freedom of religion, the *Imperial Act* of 1784 made German the only administrative language of the empire, much to the chagrin of the Hungarian nobility, who used Latin. As a reaction against Vienna's centralism, the magnates increasingly started to communicate in Hungarian.

The nobility had always been poly-ethnic, loyalty to the Habsburg dynasty being the pillar of the empire, not ethnic origin, language or emerging national feelings. On the eve of the 19th century, the intellectual movements of liberalism and nationalism began to change the feudal Hungarian society into a constitutional nation state. Language, ethnic descent and the commonly shared culture became a new and one might say, more democratic facets of identity. These changes resulted in a shift of loyalty from the Habsburgs to the nation, which gave the term "Hungarian" a double meaning that consisted of a historical and a linguistic-ethnic aspect[11]. First, 'Hungarian' was applied to every individual nobleman living on Hungarian territory, i.e. the lands of the medieval kingdom of Saint Stephen. Every *nobleman* belonged to the *natio hungarica*, regardless of his mother tongue or ethnic descent. Then, the French nation state theory, developed in the aftermath of the 1789 Revolution, had a de-aristocratising and democratising influence: "Hungarian" referred to every *citizen* of the Hungarian nation state, regardless of aristocratic or ethnic origins. The second meaning emerged during the last phase of the Magyar reform period that was increasingly intertwined with the liberal views of the *Vormärz*; it lasted from approximately 1825 to 1848. The declared goal of the movement was Magyar leadership in Hungary:

> "It was a romantic and fantastically unrealistic idea in itself, as the Magyar ethnos did not even amount to half the population."[12]

Now, the concept a "Magyar" referred to a person of Magyar ethnic descent and culture, while the term "Hungarian" designated the nationality of a person living on

---

[11]   Lászlo Katus, "Die Magyaren", in *Die Habsburgermonarchie 1848–1918*, Vol. III, 411-488; 411-413.

[12]   Kováč, *Dejiny...*, 111.

Hungarian territory. All intellectuals involved this investigation were therefore Hungarian Slovaks or Hungarian citizens of Slovak ethnic origin.

Weaker in numbers and influence, the Slovak nobility had joined the Magyar nobility in its reform movement opposing Viennese centralism. Led by Lajos Kossuth, the movement focused on the historic imagination of the medieval kingdom of Saint Stephen connecting Hungarian self-determination to the feudal concept of *natio hungarica.* The political elite saw national homogeneity as the only guarantee for the survival of the Magyars, a numerical minority in their own lands[13]. National homogeneity was to be achieved through loyalty towards Magyar rule and the exclusive use of Hungarian as state language. The terms "Hungarian" and "Magyar" began to merge, since transforming the kingdom's estates to a modern, bureaucratic state administration required effective hence homogeneous communication. Hungarian directly opposed the hegemony of German, but the idea of making it the kingdom's only language was also based on liberal and nationalist considerations: communication in Hungarian would allow a more effective integration of the lower social classes[14], who, unlike the nobility, did not speak Latin. Hungarian citizenship demanded absolute allegiance to the project of the Magyar state, its constitution, language and laws, and determined the national status, while ethnic origins and communication in other languages were considered a private matter.

Except for its democratising and anti-aristocratic aspects, the goals of the Magyar reform project were indeed similar to those of Joseph II's *Enlightened Absolutism*: a centralised administration would establish effective government of the rule-of-law state, which granted citizens' equality in front of the law. The liberal reforms further targeted the socio-economic privileges of the Hungarian magnates, which distinguished the Magyar project from *Enlightened Absolutism,* with its essential idea of aristocratic leadership. The liberal reformers deemed the abolition of the privileges of the aristocratic landowners as much a prerequisite for their projected state as linguistic homogeneity.

---

[13] Gogolák, "Die historische Entwicklung... ", 51.

[14] Ludwig von Gogolák, "Ungarns Nationalitätengesetze und das Problem des Magyarischen National- und Zentralstaates", in *Die Habsburgermonarchie 1848–1918*, Vol. III, 1207–1303; 1242.

From the perspective of the political thought of the Magyar liberals, national minorities or national groups did not exist, since their understanding of nation *qua* citizenship did not take the ethnic aspect into account. There was only one political nation in Hungary: the Hungarian, read Magyar. The liberals strived for Vienna's recognition of their political supremacy and statehood, but their reforms presented a serious threat to the language and culture of the non-Magyar population.

X. 2. The early Slovak national movement

In the early to mid-19th century, two processes began to overlap that mutually excluded each other: *Hungarian state building and Slovak nation building*. Due to the crucially important status of language, these processes were irreconcilable. Hungarian state building, or "the Magyar-nationalist conception of the Hungarian state,"[15] required national homogeneity based on Hungarian as the language of communication, while Slovak national identity centred on the Slovak language – in a fashion quite similar to the Hungarian renaissance at the turn of the century. The synergy of liberalism and nationalism, of political-economic modernisation and ethno-nationalist power-accumulation became the basis of the state and resulted in increasing efforts to assimilate the Hungarian non-Magyars. The oppressiveness of Magyarisation would peak after the *Ausgleich* of 1867, which provided the Magyars with constitutionally granted dominance over the kingdom. In regard to their relations with the nationalities, the compromise practically issued the Magyars a *carte blanche*. The language law the Hungarian parliament adopted in 1868, a couple of months after the compromise was in effect, would unleash an even harsher wave of assimilation.

The Magyars justified their demands for self-determination by citing the *historic state rights* of the lands of the crown of Saint Stephen; in analogy, the Czech liberals laid claim to the historic rights of the lands of the crown of Saint Wenceslas. The Slovaks, by contrast, lacked such a historical entity or *historical-political individuality*[16]. Their identity was based only on language and culture. In times of

---

[15] Kováč, *Dejiny...*, 111.

[16] A historical-political individuality represented a historically grown entity that had enjoyed territorial sovereignty before it was incorporated into the Monarchy, i.e. the kingdom of Hungary. A crownland was either a constitutive element of a larger individuality, such as Silesia

emerging national awareness, the existence of a historical territory was accompanied by the fact that it had included a constitutional guarantee of autonomy in the past. The territory became as important and legitimate a factor as the reference to medieval constitutional rights, for both were issues of a legal nature on the basis of state law. The treaties and agreements deriving from such historic past were the basis for negotiations with the emperor. Before Magyarisation started, Slovak identity had also entailed Hungarian citizenship, i.e. the status of being a citizen of the Hungarian kingdom and gravitating politically towards Buda. But the absence of a historic territory had two profound consequences for Slovak nation building: First, the Slovaks lacked a strong and independent nobility to represent them in the Hungarian diet and the *Reichstag* (Imperial council) at Vienna. Second, the Slovak language became key to Slovak identity as the least common denominator, since confessional lines divided the population into Protestants, mostly Lutherans, and Roman Catholics[17]. Intellectuals of both confessions were crucially involved in the national movement and would only join forces in 1863 with the foundation of the cultural association *Matica slovenská*[18]. We shall come back to this important national foundation later.

One of the goals of Magyarisation was to merge the Slovak Lutheran with the Hungarian Calvinist church, as uniting the nation's Protestants in one church would create social cohesion; a further benefit was the abolition of the Slovak language in a central institution so crucial to Slovak identity. In 1840, Count Karol Zay, the general inspector of the Lutheran church, issued a new decree in the diet of Pressburg (Pozsony, Prešporok, from 1919 on Bratislava); it declared Hungarian the official language in the Protestant churches of the Slovak *župy* (counties). The members of the early national movement viewed the decree as a direct assault on their national

---

within the lands of the Bohemian crown or a historical-political individuality on its own, such as Moravia. Robert A. Kann, *Das Nationalitätenproblem der Habsburgermonarchie*, vol. I Das Reich und die Völker (Graz, Köln: Böhlau, 1964), 46. The historic state rights referred to the former sovereign status of the individuality or the crownland, respectively, and became a crucial instrument for Slavic autonomy claims. Palacký, as an example, referred to the Czech citizens in the lands of the St. Venceslas Crown as Bohemians, not as Czechs, to stress, as he believed, the historically legitimate dominance of the Czechs in Bohemia, and push through the integration of the German ethnos in Bohemia; Jiří Kořalka, "Nationsbildung...", 41.

[17] Kováč, *Slovaci...*, 32f.
[18] Kováč, *Dejiny...*, 132.

and cultural existence, as it ran counter to the provisions of the imperial constitution, which protected the autonomy of confessional institutions[19]. The decree abolished the autonomy of the Slovak Protestant clerical institutions, while the Catholic Church was not subject to the decree, since its liturgical language was Latin. The Slovak Lutheran clergy reacted with a petition, the *Slovenský prestolný prosbopis*. Štúr was crucially involved in the draft. In June 1842, he and Ján Kollár (1793 - 1852), the famous poet of *Slavy dcera* and author of the idea of *Slavonic reciprocity*, submitted the petition to Chancellor Metternich. Signed by two hundred clergymen representing approximately half a million of the faithful, the *prosbopis* asked for minimal cultural and language rights: a chair for Slovak language at Pest University and a separate censorship bureau for Slovak books. It also demanded the reopening of Slovak schools and suggested using Latin instead of Hungarian in church documents[20]. These measures were meant to reverse the ongoing illegal Magyarisation. Vienna ignored them.

Together with Michal Miloslav Hodža (1811 - 1870) and Jozef Miloslav Hurban (1817 - 1888), Štúr worked on the creation of a Slovak literary language, whose norms they standardised in 1843. Calling themselves Hegelians, they followed the thought of the German philosopher Georg Wilhelm Friedrich Hegel (1770 - 1831) at least in one important issue: they identified their Slovak national spirit as being a part of Hegel's universal *Weltgeist*, which was the ultimate expression of human reason that was moving toward freedom[21]. Freedom, in their rather superficial Hegelianism, was not synonymuous with a sovereign state, which would have been an absurdly unrealistic claim anyway. Independent statehood was not their goal. They focussed their efforts on cultural freedom. In other words: if the Slovaks wanted to be a nation, they had to have a national spirit, a *metaphysical and physical expression of*

---

[19] Gogolák, "Die historische Entwicklung...," 53.

[20] Kováč, *Dejiny...*, 106.

[21] Dmitrii Chizhevskii is still the most informative source on Štúr's reception of Hegel's philosophy, "Hegel bei den Slowaken," in *Hegel bei den Slawen* (Darmstadt: Wissenschaftliche Buchgesellschaft, 1961 (2)), 397-411. He speaks of Štúr's thought as a "free variation of Hegelian topics", 404.

their existence. The physical expression of the national spirit was a codified written language distinguishing them from other nations[22].

The importance of language as a feature of identity was the great intellectual legacy of the romantic philosopher Johann Gottfried Herder (1744 - 1803). His thought had a crucial influence on the Central European nations and their emerging cultural and national identities. In his famous section on the Slavian nations, Herder praised the Slavs as a peaceful, hospitable and industrious nation, committed to trade and agriculture and incapable of defending themselves against violent enslavery by other nations[23]. Kollár took Herder's defence of diversity to a linguistic level and created the idea of *Slovanská vzájemnost (Slavonic reciprocity)*[24]. Linguistic research, the initiating theme of Slavic renaissance, had delivered proof of the common descent and kinship of all Slavic tribes. Kollár defined Czecho-Slovak as one language, which resulted in the intellectual movement of *Czechoslovakism* that, firstly, promoted the *cultural union* of Czechs and Slovaks. In that union, the Czechs had a naturally superior status thanks to the higher level of their grammar and lexica. Linguistic superiority, perceived and promoted by Czech intellectuals, then turned into the belief that the Czechs were also culturally and politically more advanced than the Slovaks. Some one hundred and sixty years later, Masaryk would re-formulate Kollár's linguistic-cultural definition of Czecho-Slovak cultural unity as a political programme he called *Czechoslovakism*. The idea of *political Czechoslovakism*

---

[22] Interestingly, Tibor Pichler touches on Hegelianism in his explanation of the 'movement' from "nation building to state building thought or civil political thought"; Tibor Pichler, "Dejiny a pohyb ideí v slovenskom politickom myslení", *Filozofia 58*, č. 10 (2003): 684-698.

[23] Johann Gottfried Herder, *Outlines of a Philosophy of the History of Man*, transl. from the German *Ideen zur Philosophie der Geschichte der Menschheit* by T. Churchill (New York: Bergman Publishers, 1980), 483.

[24] Johann Kollár, *Ueber literarische Wechselseitigkeit zwischen den verschiedenen Stämmen und Mundarten der slawischen Nation* (Pesth: Trattner-Karolyi, 1837). For an English translation of the most important chapters see my *Preparing Liberty in Central Europe. Political texts from the Spring of Nations 1848 to the Spring of Prague 1968* (Stuttgart: ibidem, 2006). On Kollár's influence on the Slavic nations see the excellent collection of essays *Ján Kollár a slovanská vzájomnosť. Geneza nacionalizmu v strednej Európe* (Bratislava: Spoločnosť' pre dejiny a kultúrú strednej a východnej Európy SDKSVE, 2006). On reception and development of Slavic identity see the equally recommendable Andreas Moritsch, ed., *Die slawische Idee* (Bratislava: Slovak Academic Press, 1993).

legitimated a common state of both kin-nations and justified the creation of the Czechoslovak Republic.

If the Slovaks considered themselves a nation in the sense of Hegel's spirit and Herder's language, if they considered themselves adherents of the values of the Enlightenment and subject to natural law, then folk songs and countryside customs would not suffice. The values of *Romanticism* and *Enlightenment* merged. The romantic idea of cultural diversity justified to demand for the right for one's own culture. As romantic reaction against the universalism and rationalism of the Enlightenment, diversity anticipated pluralism[25] as effective tolerance towards other cultures, while the wish to join the community of nations was a value of the Enlightenment. Herder and Štúr's *romantic pluralism* was essentially a-political: Reconciliation of different cultures and values is impossible, so is the idea of the unity of mankind. On the contrary: to promote the universal validity of one belief system would gravely violate natural diversity – and with that the divine plan. Romantic pluralism valued the cultures of Magyars, Slovaks and Czechs as being different – therefore the three nations should not merge. These considerations focussed on cultural issues, but soon led to political repercussions. Had the Magyars abstained from their assimilation, acknowledging the natural right of the nationalities to their culture and language, they could have concentrated their efforts on cultural development while pledging political allegiance to the Hungarian state project. While national identity and defensive nationalism were not entirely caused by Magyarisation, they were certainly accelerated by it.

The Slovaks had to have a codified written language to prove that they were, indeed, a nation, a civilised and cultured member of the community of mankind – not just a tribe of folks men living in the Upper Hungarian countryside.

> "Language is ... the most obvious sign of the existence and individuality of every nation. Like an individual person, the nation's *inner being* appears through its language, its *spirit* is ... embodied in its language."[26]

---

[25] Isaiah Berlin, "Herder and the Enlightenment," in *The Proper Study of Mankind. An Anthology of Essays* (London: Pimlico, 1998), 359-435; 368.

[26] Štúr, "Ponosy a žaloby Slovanóv" (1843), in *Dielo v piatich zväzkoch* (Bratislava: Slovenské vydavateľstvo krasnej literatúry, 1954-56); vol. I, 1954, 116–125, 117, italics JB.

The Slovaks shared cultural customs and beliefs and adhered to the two largest Christian confessions, but spoke in three dialects. What dialect should be codified? This was as much a linguistic as a political issue.

X. 3. Codification, revolution and the congress of the Slavs

Štúr and the members of *stará škola* (old school)[27], the early generation of the national movement, agreed, after some debate, on the Middle Slovak variant, which was politically neutral and linguistically accessible. The newly codified language helped to unify the national movement, which had traditionally been divided into three factions: first, the Protestants, who were mostly adherents of the idea of a Czechoslovak cultural unity, among them Kollár and the Slavist and literary critic Pavel Jozef Šafárík (1795 - 1861); second, the Catholic faction with the adherents to the priest and linguist Antonín Bernolák (1762 - 1813) and the poet Juraj Fandlý (1750 - 1811). The Slovak Protestant *intelligentsia* were the third and youngest faction that wanted to separate from the unionist Czechoslovakist view; they supported Štúr's Lutheran faction. Štúr's coinage was not the first one; Bernolák had undertaken an earlier attempt at the standardisation of Slovak grammar and orthography in 1787.

Cultural and religious contact between Czechs and Slovaks had always been close – although, in the eyes of Štúr and his adherents, not so close that it justified a union at the expense of the Slovaks. Czech Hussite Protestants, persecuted by the re-Catholisation of Bohemia in the aftermath of the lost *battle at the White Mountain* (*Bilá hora*) in 1620, had fled to Slovak villages in Upper Hungary, where they could freely express their religious beliefs, thanks to the fact that a considerable part of the ruling Hungarian nobility was of Calvinist faith. The liturgical language of the Slovak Catholics was Latin, while the Lutherans held their services in the Czech liturgical language of the *Bible of Kralice,* which strengthened the ties with the Bohemian Protestants[28].

For Štúr, the Bernolák codification was culturally and politically too close to the Western Slovak dialect that itself was based on the Czech variant used in the

---

[27] For a detailed account of the thought of the *stará škola slovenská* and the *nová škola slovenská* see the chapter about Ján Palarík.
[28] Kováč, *Slováci...*, 38.

Bible of Kralice. To him, this variant immediately connoted the cultural and political unity of Czechs and Slovaks in linguistic, political and also psychological terms. Due to the Czech claim for supremacy, the union was not an option, as it would simply replace Magyar linguistic dominance with Czech. The Eastern Slovak dialect, on the other hand, was linguistically too distant for the majority of the population. Štúr and his followers therefore chose the vernacular spoken in the central region, which was a clear sign of autonomy to both the Czechs and Magyars. The Czechs favoured the Czecho-Slovak union they could dominate; they also believed that the union would enhance the influence of the Slavs at the Imperial court in Vienna. The Magyars perceived Slovak nation building as a direct threat to their future state and, deliberately or not, mis-interpreted it as part of the political movement of Panslavism[29].

The revolution of 1848 proved to have a crucial influence on Štúr, Hurban, Hodža and the younger adherents to the *stará škola* such as Ján Francisci (1822 - 1905) and Štefan Marko Daxner (1822 - 1892). First, they considered supporting the Magyars against Vienna, hoping this would halt and reverse the assimilation. Yet, as soon as the revolutionary government declared Hungary's independence and adopted the March laws, the pressure of Magyarisation increased, with a complete absence of guarantees for the rights of the nationalities[30]. The Slovaks reacted with the *Declaration of the Slovak nation* (*Žiadosti slovenského naroda*), adopted on 11 May 1848 in Liptovský Svätý Mikuláš. The document was a revolutionary national programme and consisted of the following demands: equality of Hungary's nationalities; autonomous diets on the district level for every nationality; proportional representation of the nationalities in Hungary's parliament, and recognition of Slovak as the language of administration in the Slovak counties[31]. Further demands, some of which they shared with the Magyar liberals, were the abolition of serfdom, re-

---

[29] Good introductions are: Hans Kohn, *Pan-Slavism: Its History and Ideology* (New York: Vintage Books, 1960), Leon Poliakov, *Moscou, troisième Rome: les intermittences de la mémoire historique* (Paris: Hachette, 1989), Frank L. Fadner, *Seventy Years of Pan-Slavism in Russia: Karamzin to Danilevskii, 1800-1870* (Washington: Georgetown University Press, 1962) and Wilhelm Goerdt, "Teil II Russland und Europa", in *Russische Philosophie. Grundlagen* (Freiburg, München: Karl Alber, 1995 (2)), 262-304.

[30] Kováč, *Dejiny...*, 116.

[31] Kováč, *Dejiny...*, 117.

distribution of land to the peasants and the universal right to vote. The demands for autonomy and representation of the nationalities were of course diametrically opposed to Kossuth's plans for a constitutional Hungarian nation state. In need of support, Štúr approached the Croatian governor, *banus* Josip Jelačić (1801 - 1859), to discuss a future co-operation against the Magyars, since the Croats faced a very similar situation in their lands.

The *Congress of the Slavs*[32] took place in June 1848 in Prague. Initiated and chaired by the Czech liberal František Palacký[33], the gathering promised to offer an opportunity for future anti-Magyar co-operation. All delegations tried to find solutions for their specific political problems and discussed various possibilities: a compromise between Poles and Ruthenians in Galicia, with the creation of a bi-lingual province that would grant the Ruthenian minority proportional representation; autonomy status and recognition of the Croatian triune kingdom, including Dalmatia – then governed by Austria – and recognition of the historic rights of the St. Wenceslas crown[34]. The enthusiasm of the hour even brought promises of a new

---

[32]   Very recommendable about the Slovak participation in the four congresses of the Slavs is Daniela Kodajová's "Slováci na slovanských zjazdoch – sny, realita a sklamania slovenského rojčenia (1848, 1867, 1908, 1910)", in *Stredoeurópske národy na križovatkách novodobých dejín 1848-1918. Zborník venovaný prof. PhDr. Michailovi Danilákovi, CSc. k jeho 65. narodeninám* (Prešov, Bratislava, Wien: Filozoficka fakulta Prešovskej university, Spoločnosť pre dejiny a kultúru strednej a východnej Európy pri SAV v Bratislave, Österreichisches Ost- und Südosteuropa-Institut in Wien), 1999; 87-96.

[33]   On Palacký see Jiří Kořalka, *František Palacký (1798-1876): Životopis* (Praha: Argo, 1998); Richard G. Plaschka, "The political significance of František Palacký." *Journal of Contemporary History 8*, no. 3 (1973): 35-55; Joseph F. Záček, ed., *East European Quaterly 15*, no. 1 (1981), entire issue dedicated to Palacký.

[34]   Robert A. Kann, *A History of the Habsburg Empire 1526-1918* (Berkeley: University of California Press, 1974), 305. The Czech liberals used the historical rights of the Bohemian Crown (*státní právo*) to legitimate their claims for an autonomy status equal to that of the Hungarians. The ancient lands of the St. Wenceslas Crown, Bohemia, Moravia and Silesia, formed a historically grown, constitutional unit within the Empire. The reforms of enlightened absolutism started under the reign of Maria Theresa in 1749, sought to centralise and modernise the medieval administration and cut down the old privileges of the local nobility. The Bohemian lands were united with the Hungarian and Germans lands. With the intention of establishing administrative efficiency, the language reforms undertaken by Emperor Joseph II made German the sole language of communication. On the historic rights see also Jörg K. Hoensch, *Geschichte Böhmens* (München: Beck, 1987); Robert A. Kann, *Das Nationalitätenproblem der Habsburgermonarchie*, vol. I *Das Reich und die Völker*, vol. II *Ideen und Pläne zur*

European order based on the equality of nations[35]. In this revolutionary atmosphere, a *Zeitgeist* friendly to liberal and democratising reforms, the Slavs' most pressing demand was full equality with the Austrians and Magyars. Equality, in turn, called for federalisation. But differences separating the delegations and the pre-mature ending due to the revolutionary turmoil precluded the adoption of a common political programme. The only achievement of the Congress was the *manifesto,* with its clear commitment to the ideals of the French Revolution and, equally important, the demand for federalisation according to the territorial principle, i.e. territorial settlement of Austria's nationalities[36]. Loyalty to the monarchy was a conservative idea, while federalisation was a liberal one; *Austroslavism* promised to be a realistic compromise that would work to the benefit of the Slavs. The majority of the delegates voted for it, since they hoped that their support against the Magyar liberals would be rewarded with increasing influence in Vienna. This could in turn pave the road toward extended autonomy rights.

After the congress, Palacký became crucially involved in the *Kremsier draft constitution,* named after Bad Kremsier (today's Kroměříž) in Moravia, where the *Reichstag* had moved because of the fighting in Vienna. The draft constitution was a compromise between federalism and centralism, preserving the administrative order of the crown lands, extending local autonomy to the communities and assigning the crown only a suspensive veto[37]. Although the issue of territorially dispersed minorities was not solved, the theoretical construction of a more liberal empire based on the will of its people would have been a chance for the Habsburgs to re-gain their legitimacy. But the reaction would not let the constitution come into being.

The Hungarian government released warrants of arrests against Štúr, Hodža and Hurban in May. The Slovak representatives, first opposed to supporting Vienna, voted for Austroslavism and drafted cooperation-agreements with the Croats, the

---

Reichsreform (Graz: H. Boehlaus, 1964 (2)); Robert A. Kann and Zdeněk V. David, *The peoples of the Eastern Habsburg Lands, 1526-1918* (Seattle: University of Washington Press, 1984).

[35] Josef Macurek, "The Achievements of the Slavonic Congress," *The Slavonic and East European Review,* 1947/48, no. 26, 329-340. Some 350 delegates of all Slavic nations, except the Bulgarians, met in Prague from 2nd to 12th June. The meeting was not merely a gathering of the Austrian Slavs to promote Austroslavism, but a consequence of the preceding decades of Slavic renaissance and also an idealistic manifestation of Slavic reciprocity.

[36] Macurek, 330.

[37] Kann, *A History...,* 311, 312.

Vojvodina Serbs and the Ruthenians. The recruitment of voluntary troops started. On 16 September 1848, Štúr, Hurban and Hodža proclaimed the foundation of the *Slovak National Council* (*Slovenská národna rada*) as the most powerful political and military organisation of the Hungarian Slovaks. Croatian and Slovak troops joined *ban* Jelačić. On 19 September, the *národna rada* convened in Myava, declared the Hungarian government in Pest as illegal and called for a national uprising. Until its final defeat in the battle of Világos in August 1849, the Hungarian army was quite successful. The revolutionary government established a reign of terror in Hungary and a better part of the Slovak volunteers were driven to Moravia. Štúr, Hodža and Hurban were declared traitors and stripped of their civic rights; they fled to Prague.

X. 4.   Neo-Absolutism, the October diploma and the *memorandum*

In March 1849, while the fighting in Hungary was still going on, the Slovak representatives approached Emperor Francis Joseph I with a petition for an autonomous Slovak district. It would be ruled directly from Vienna and have its own diet. The language of communication and administration would be Slovak. Their demands seemed realistic, because the general expectations of territorial and political reforms – which would solve or, at least, accommodate the monarchy's nationality problem – were nourished by Palacký's draft federation[38]. Yet, the dissolution of the Kremsier *Reichstag* some days later put an end to the liberal and national hopes the *spring of nations* had set forth. Emperor Francis Joseph I adopted the conservative *Stadion* constitution, named after its author count Franz Stadion (1806 - 1853). The constitution initiated a decade of dynastic restoration that would become known as the era of *neo-Absolutism*, headed by prince Felix of Schwarzenberg (1800 - 1852)[39] and minister Alexander Bach (1813 - 1893)[40]. A centralist administration, strict

---

[38]   Kováč, *Slovaci...*, 45.

[39]   Minister President Schwarzenberg was the chief figure in planning the abdication of the feeble-minded and epileptic Emperor Ferdinand I (1793-1875) in December 1848 and the following enthronement of Francis Joseph I. Ferdinand I had been placed on the throne by Metternich and was the last crowned king of Bohemia (1835-1848), where he spent most of his life and was referred to as "Ferdinand V, the Benign". Schwarzenberg led the government as imperial chancellor until his death in 1852.

[40]   For a detailed account of the centralist measures of the Schwarzenberg-Bach administration see Kann, *A History...*, 320-327. A talented lawyer of middle-class origin, Bach became known in

censorship and the army controlled the empire from 1851 until 1859. Political life came to an immediate standstill. The Slavs' support of the monarchy showed practically no results, and Italy and Hungary were ruled by a military dictatorship. But, for the Magyars

> "...the impetus given in the development of national political life, even through so short a period as the revolutionary one, was not in vain. It left its indelible traces. The political developments after 1867 would have been inconceivable without the vivid memories of 1848."[41]

The October diploma of 1860 was the first of many attempts made by the Austrian government to solve the nationality problem. Each of these attempts – the February patent of 1861, the Austro-Hungarian compromise of 1867, the Austro-Moravian compromise of 1905 and lastly, the general right to vote of 1907 – tried to de-escalate the Hungarian threat of secession, accommodate the Czechs, and maintain the empire's conservative order. While the reactions and protests of the Magyars and the Czechs would have some leverage in Vienna, the Slovaks would lack such influence.

The semi-federalist October diploma of 1860 included autonomy rights for the nationalities, but the elites opposed it as too centralist. Vienna's need to reconcile with the Magyars was not only a result of Austria losing the war against France and Piedmont in 1859; her diplomacy in relations with Bismarck was increasingly failing. The kingdom's territorial size and geopolitical position had secured Habsburg hegemonial power in East Central Europe in the past and was of crucial importance for the Empire's survival[42]. The Magyars and the Czechs opposed Vienna's centralism while the members of the Slovak national movement feared the withdrawal of Austrian control over Hungary that would result in Hungarian

---

March 1848, when he spoke out for liberal ideas and demanded the abolition of censorship and a centralised and democratic Austrian constitution. He even participated in a crowd that attacked the barricades at Vienna castle, which made him the darling of Vienna's revolutionaries. In the meantime, he met secretly with the aristocratic circle of conservative government members around count Felix Schwarzenberg, which planned to establish Francis Joseph as the new Emperor. Schwarzenberg offered Bach the ministry of justice and, in July 1849, the ministry of the Interior and police, which he held until his demission in 1859. From 1859 until 1868, Bach was Austrian diplomat at the Vatican. Rewarded with the title of a baron for his service, he spent his retirement in Vienna and died in 1893. Bach entered Austrian history as an example of a characterless turncoat, only concerned with his own advancement.

[41] Kann, *A History...*, 317.
[42] Gogolák, "Ungarns Nationalitätengesetze...", 1263.

dominance[43]. In the diploma, the emperor declared that any pressure or measures sharpening the opposition between the nationalities would be blocked; this – once again – gave the non-Magyar nationalities the hope that Vienna would intervene on their behalf in the future[44].

The national movement called for an assembly in Turčiansky Svätý Martin in Central Slovakia on 6 and 7 June 1861 to discuss the future of Slovak national politics. The delegates adopted the *memorandum of the Slovak nation*, whose essential demands were almost identical to the petition submitted to the emperor in March 1849. The *memorandum* consisted of four main demands, with the third including eight specific sub-demands[45]. First, a constitutional bill of law that granted the individuality of the Slovak nation [osobnosť národa slovenského... zakonom pozitívnim...uznaná] and the recognition of the Slovak language as language of communication [vlastenkosť reči slovenskej]; second, regarding of the region of its interest, i.e. of its settlement, the recognition of Slovak national individuality under the name of the Upper Hungarian county [pod menom hornouhorského slovenského okolie]; third, equality and freedom of nations and languages, with eight specific sub-demands to be realised in the *okolie*; fourth, regarding the solidarity with all non-Magyar nations, freedom for all citizens and oppressed nations in Hungary, in particular the Ruthenians, Romanians, Serbs and Croats[46]. The most important sub-demands were: recognition of Slovak as administrative language [úradná reč slovenská] in the *okolie*; the abolition of the laws that had enacted the abolition of the rights of the Slovak language, art 16:1791; 7:1792; 4: 1805; 3: 1836; 6: 1840; 2: 1844; 5. §3: 1848 ab 16 lit.e). Further sub-demands were a chair for Slovak at Pest University and the freedom of association in national-cultural groups and

---

[43] Kann, *A History...*, 327-328.

[44] Martin Vietor, "Die Beschaffenheit der Ausgleichsgesetze," in *Der österreichisch-ungarische Ausgleich 1867. Materialien (Referate und Diskussion) der internationalen Konferenz in Bratislava 28.8.-1.9. 1967* (Bratislava: Verlag der Slowakischen Akademie der Wissenschaften, 1971), 299-314; 299.

[45] "Memorandum národa slovenského", in *Z prameňov národa. Na pamiatku stodvatsiateho piateho výročia vzniku memoranda slovenského národa z roku 1861* (Martin: Matica slovenská, 1988), 257-261.

[46] "Memorandum...", 258-261.

communities[47]. The petition ended with the slogan "For a united, free and constitutional country, and in it freedom, equality and brotherhood of all nations!"[48]

New was the territorial issue or rather, the issue of autonomy within the given territory that should have a new name, the Upper Hungarian *okolie* or county integrating all Slovak *župy*. The demand for the *okolie* with Slovak as the official language of administration led to criticism within the movement. Many opposed the *okolie*, fearing it would create an obstacle to vital Slovak interests. Nonetheless, for the sake of unity, most of the opponents signed the petition that became known as the *Vienna memorandum (Viedenský memorandum)*. The Slovak leadership first submitted the petition to the Hungarian diet, which, instead of an answer, reacted with a public campaign, carried out by the urban administrative institutions[49]. A second version with more elaborate demands for territorial and administrative autonomy and a clear time frame for implementation was presented to the emperor on 12 December 1861, taking advantage of the dissolution of the Hungarian diet by Francis Joseph I in August[50]. The petition failed. The national assembly, however, was the first open gathering of Slovaks after 1849, and it played host to a wide range of opinions about how to deal with Magyar assimilation. An important result was the *Matica slovenská*, the cultural organisation founded in Turčiansky Sv. Martin in 1863. One could therefore say that the October diploma gave the national movement a crucial impulse that led to a differentiated debate. Many articles dealing with national issues would appear in the newspaper *Peštbudinské vedomosti (Budapest news)*, founded by Ján Francisci in 1861.

The February patent of 1861, drafted by Prime Minister Anton Schmerling (1805 - 1893), limited the power of the local diets while assigning legislative power to crown and imperial council, which was a step back to centralism. The Magyars, Croats, Czechs and Slovenes reacted with a boycott of the *Reichstag* in 1863. The Magyars, in particular, rejected the patent that infringed Hungary's status as kingdom. While the October diploma recognised the kingdom as being of similar legal importance as the Austrian *Erblande* – the hereditary Austrian lands – the

---

[47] "Memorandum...", 260-261.
[48] "Memorandum...", 262.
[49] Kováč, *Dejiny...*, 130.
[50] Kováč, *Dejiny...*, 130.

February patent reduced Hungary's legal status to a mere province[51]. For the leaders of the Slovak national movement, however, the February patent seemed to promise Vienna's renewed control of Hungary, – and with that a possible restitution of their language rights, if not an improvement of their legal status toward greater autonomy. The *okolie* never came into being, nor were even the most modest demands for language rights. After Austria had lost the war against Prussia and left the German confederation in 1866, she could no longer afford not to reconcile with the Magyars.

X. 5.   The *Ausgleich*, the *Matica Slovenská* and the nationality law of 1868

The *Ausgleich* of 1867 was in essence rather a personal reconciliation of the emperor with the Magyar elite than a constitutional compromise, since Austria had never ruled nor completely incorporated Hungary into her lands[52]. Neither had the Magyar aristocracy endured re-Catholisation and expulsion like the Bohemian nobility. The *Ausgleich* divided the empire into *Cis-* and *Transleithania* and granted the Magyars the highest amount of autonomy short of the sovereign nation state. Francis Joseph I was Austrian emperor and Hungarian king in personal union. Both states had a common foreign policy and diplomacy and also shared the ministry of defence and finances. From the viewpoint of the Hungarian nationalities, the *Ausgleich* represented Vienna's complete withdrawal and determined their fate, placing them at the mercy of the Magyars. For the empire, however, the compromise presented a much-needed arrangement:

> "... the main point in the interrelationship between the national question and the Compromise pertains neither to the differences in its handling in Austria and Hungary, nor even to their causes. ... the national problems were extraneous to the chief object ... In other words, what most writers consider a particular shortcoming of the Compromise in regard to national justice was from the standpoint of its creators and supporters a fully intended and quite well designed asset to preserve the power structure of the monarchy in domestic and foreign relations."[53]

The compromise confirmed *ex-post* not only the moral and political accuracy of the Hungarian reform period, its measures and general direction. Far more, the Magyars'

---

[51]   Friedrich Walter, "Kaiser Franz Josephs Ungarnpolitik in der Zeit des Neoabsolutismus," in *Der österreichisch-ungarische Ausgleich von 1867* (München: Oldenbourg, 1968), 30-31.

[52]   Gogolák, "Ungarns Nationalitätengesetze...", 1267.

[53]   Robert A. Kann, "The Austro-Hungarian Compromise of 1867 in Retrospect. Causes and Effect," in *Ausgleich, Materialien,* 24-44; 32.

insistence on hegemony over their historic lands stood in direct relation to the legacy of 1848: The efforts of Kossuth and the liberals had not been in vain. The compromise granted Vienna's non-involvement to the kingdom's inner affairs hence the Magyar ruling elite free hands in the organisation of their state. That they declared themselves the state building nation, in the sense of state founding, was one issue. Quite another was the technique of *divide et impera* they now applied in dealing with the nationalities – an effective and feared method of Austrian statecraft, whose theory and practice they had experienced themselves in 1848/9[54]. In other words: although, in theory, there was but one Hungarian nation, the moderates Ferenc Deák (1803 - 1876) and baron Joseph Eötvös (1813 - 1871) made concessions to the Croats that resulted in the *Hungarian-Croatian compromise* (*Nagodba*) of 1868[55], realising one of the stipulations of the Austro-Hungarian *Ausgleich*.

In his insightful speech at the Hungarian diet on 13 May 1861, which would prove a blue-print for Magyar politics in the years following the *Ausgleich*, Deák had not only confirmed Kossuth's goal of the identity of the Hungarian polity and nation, i.e. the legal continuity of the Hungarian political nation. He had defined the literal

---

[54] Gogolák, "Ungarns Nationalitätengesetze...", 1269.

[55] Kann, *A History....*, 363-364. Deák graduated in law and entered political life in 1843 as member of parliament. He joined the reform movement, but held a moderate position during the revolution. From 1849 to 1854 he retired from politics protesting against the neo-absolutist regime. His knowledge of the law and his formulation of Hungary's conditions made him the principal architect of the *Ausgleich*. In 1873 he retired due to ill health, but his commitment and moderation made him one of Hungary's most important politicians of the 19th century. He is referred to as the "Sage of the Country" (*A Haza bölcse*).

Eötvös became known to the Hungarian public as novelist, educator and statesman. He studied in Buda and a stay in England crucially influenced his thoughts about literature, society and the establishment of a modern Hungary. In his novels *A falu jegyzoje* (1845; The Village Notary) and *Magyarország 1514-ben* (1847; Hungary in 1514), he critisised Hungary's feudalism, calling for the abolition of serfdom and reforms of Hungary's legal institutions. Appointed minister of education by the revolutionary government, he soon came into personal conflict with Kossuth and resigned. He wrote his grand work *A tizenkilencedik század uralkodó eszméinek befolyása az álladalomra* (1851-54; The Influence of the Ruling Ideas of the 19th Century of the State) in Munich, combining ideas of Enlightenment and the French Revolution with English constitutional practice. After his return to Hungary in 1851, he published extensively and was again appointed minister of education from 1867-1871. His draft of a moderate nationality law in 1868, which was not realised, foresaw a federation of the historic entities with an administration based on the ethnic principle on county and community levels. In his last years, Eötvös committed himself to academic and educational issues.

exception that confirmed the rule: Croatia had to be treated as a nation, not as a nationality.

> "...Croatia has a territory of her own which has a special position and was never incorporated into Hungary, but stood at our side ... If Croatia now wishes to participate in our legislation as a state [Land] ... if she wishes to *relate to us nation to nation*, we shall not reject her, but require only that she shall not be hindered from sending her delegates to our assemblies ... to provide her and us with the means and the opportunity to begin the work of understanding on the legal basis of our state [staatsrechtliche Grundlage]."[56]

The quintessence of *divide and impera,* as seen from Pest, meant that special treatment of Croatia would prevent her future co-operation with the other nationalities. The lesson of the Slavic co-operation of 1848 had been learnt. In the eyes of the Magyar elite, Deák's considerations bore testimony of his statesmanlike foresight: legitimating Croatia's special treatment in Hungary with her own claim of the autonomy of the Triune kingdom[57] de-escalated the tense Magyar-Croatian relations. The strict focus on what Magyars and Croats had in common, namely the historic state rights, elevated the Croats' legal status while simultaneously distancing them from the other nationalities. This was a clear message to the Slovaks, Romanians and Ruthenians that their autonomy claims lacked a legal basis, since they had no historic state rights at their argumentative disposal. In other words: Croatia had to be treated differently as she fulfilled the legal requirement of the historic-rights-status, while the autonomy extended to the nationalities, in theory, was not understood as a collective right, but as an individual right[58]. With the exception of Croatia, where Croatian was the inner language of communication, this legal provision practically banned the use of any other language than Hungarian in the private realm, dissolving the nationalities into a mere sum of individuals and denying their declared common identity. From the viewpoint of Hungarian state law, the claims of the Slovaks, Ruthenians and Romanians were simply irrelevant.

---

[56] *Der Ungarische Reichstag I,* 233ff; Deák, *Konyi VI,* 14ff, 284, quoted after Gogolák, "Ungarns Nationalitätengesetze ...," 1263-1264, italics JB.

[57] The demand for the *Triune kingdom,* i.e. the union of Croatia, Slavonia, Dalmatia, Bosnia-Herzegovina and parts of Slovenia, was based on the Croatian historic state rights, an essential element in the programmes of all political parties.

[58] Ľudovít Holotík, "Der österreichisch-ungarische Ausgleich und die Slowaken," in *Ausgleich, Materialien,* 727-745; 742.

Yet, Croatia's elevated status did not bring the expected outcome. Deák's suggestion was a strategic move that proved skilful in theory but disappointing in practice. Croatia's constitutional rights on paper and the way the government of count Gyula Andrássy[59] (1871 - 1879) and Deák realised the stipulations were two completely different things. In the 1870s, the influence of the moderates, Deák and Eötvös, was vanishing. The Magyar majority in the Hungarian parliament was eager to gain control, which rendered the Hungarian-Croatian *subdualism*[60] avoid of its original intentions. It worked – but to the advantage of the Magyars. While the Austro-Hungarian compromise was a union of two equal states, the Hungarian-Croatian was a union of two unequal states. Croatia could send her delegates to the Hungarian parliament, but the Magyar majority could outvote them anytime[61]. Croatia's autonomy extended to her internal administration, education and judicial affairs, with the *banus* appointed by the Hungarian king Francis Joseph I. According to the constitution, the *banus* reported to the Croatian *sabor* (assembly). But the king's decision had to be approved by the Hungarian parliament, which usually chose a Magyar[62]. The Croats enjoyed *de iure* the status of a nation, but, as regards effective rights, there was not much of a factual difference between them and the Slovaks, Romanians and Ruthenians. After the moderates Deák and Eötvös retired, the pressure on the nationalities reached an unprecedented level.

With regard to the Slovaks, one could describe the *Ausgleich* as the finishing touch on a portrait of disappointed hopes. In the years immediately preceding the compromise, Vienna had established a provisory government in Hungary, the so-called *provisorium*, which although not absolutist anymore, was centralist enough to take away the sharpness of Magyarisation pressure. The concessions to Slovak education and national culture had been modest, but they gave rise to hopes that a relatively independent national life, the spreading of literature and the use of

---

[59] Andrássy (1823-1890) joined the revolutionary government in 1848 and went into exile in 1849. He was amnestied in 1857 and returned to Hungary, where he supported Ferenc Deák and became one of the architects of the *Ausgleich*. In 1867 he was appointed Hungarian prime minister and defense minister. He created the Austro-German alliance with Bismarck in 1879.

[60] Gogolák, "Ungarns Nationalitätengesetze... ", 1266.

[61] Kann, *A History...*, 363.

[62] Kann, *A History...*, 363.

language would be possible[63]. The preparations for the foundation of the *Matica slovenská* illustrate these hopes:

"The committee in charge [of preparing the foundation, add. JB] took advantage of the favourable political situation, setting up the statutes in a relatively short time and submitting them to the Hungarian governor on 1 August 1861. At the same time, fund-raising for the Matica slovenská was going on all over Slovakia. It was a grand undertaking that bore testimony to the level of national awareness of the Slovaks and demonstrated that all social strata, at least in some regions, were already integrated into the national movement. There were not many wealthy persons ... that was why the collecting of funds took place on the level of groschen [penny, add. JB] In the event, however, even the most humble Slovak workers proved eager to sacrifice a groschen of their meagre salary to support the national cause."[64]

The opening ceremony of the *Matica* took place on 4 August 1863, and the persons elected to the leading positions demonstrated the organisation's national character that united the two largest confessions: the Catholic bishop Štefan Moyses was the first chairman, while the Protestant pastor Karol Kuzmány was vice-chairman[65]. The dissolution of the *Matica* on 6 April 1875 would prove the full and, at the end of the day, counter-productive strength of the government of Kálmán Tisza (1875 - 1890)[66]. The Kossuth legacy of the one-nation-state theory was so powerful that no other political conception would gain importance. We could say that the experience of Austrian rule characterised Magyar nationality policy to a considerable extent. The psychological legacy of Austrian statecraft culminated in the conservative attitude, arrogance of power and fear to loose that power. Magyar intransigence would seal the fate of Hungary in Trianon.

Preparations for the nationality laws of 1868 started already in April 1866. The Hungarian diet established a committee to draft a law bill on the equality of nationalities. At the very beginning, the positions of the committee and the parliament on the one hand, and the leaders of the nationalities on the other were irreconcilable. The majority of the delegates adhered to Kossuth's one-nation-theory,

---

[63] Holotík, "Der österreichisch-ungarische...", 734.

[64] Kováč, *Dejiny...*, 131. The favourable political situation Kováč refers to was the temporary dissolution of the Hungarian diet by the emperor in 1861.

[65] Kováč, *Dejiny...*, 132.

[66] Tisza was a member of the parliament in the 1848 revolution and went into exile after 1849. After his return to Hungary, he supported the compromise and assumed the premiership in 1875. Under his government, Hungary underwent social, political and economic reforms.

while the nationalities insisted on the right to use their language as the official language in their territories. The committee's task was

> "to draft a law bill, according to which the nations [Völker] can freely develop their national life – *within the inalterable limits* set by the political unity of the state, that is the territorial integrity, and the unity of legislation and government [Einheit der Gesetzgebung und Staatsführung]."[67]

The nationality leaders could not accept the one-sided Magyar definition of 'political unity' that set 'inalterable limits'. They sent their comments and critiques, which did not result in negotiations, since the committee did not take them into consideration. The power of definition was with the Magyars, who had no intention to threatening the procedure through a serious dialogue, let alone negotiations. The parliamentarians dominated the entire legislative procedure from the very beginning with no possibilities left for the nationality leaders to participate expressing their viewpoints. The law on the equality of the nationalities was sanctioned by the emperor on 7 December 1868 and consisted of the preamble about the political unity of the state and twenty-nine paragraphs. An important point of critique was the complete absence of guidelines for implementation and interpretation of the law; the text lacked regulations or sanctions about how to proceed in cases of violation[68]. This enabled the Magyar administrators and politicians to unleash an unlimited wave of Magyarisation measures.

X. 6. The political situation until WWI and the emerging of the Slovak citizenry

The Magyar adherence to the anachronistic method of *divide et impera* at a time when the idea of equality of nations was most appealing to the Slavic nations governed by foreign powers, would lead to the loss of what they so desperately tried to maintain: control of the non-Magyar nationalities and the monarchy's territorial integrity. Trianon can be seen as the result of decades of unnecessary oppression; a policy that could easily have been altered by granting the nationalities their basic cultural rights without loosing effective control. With the benefit of hindsight, it is easy to condemn Hungarian politics *ex post* as national chauvinism. However, the

---

[67] Gogolák, "Ungarns Nationalitätengesetze...", 1271, italics JB.
[68] Gogolák, "Ungarns Nationalitätengesetze...", 1283.

dissolution of the *Matica slovenská* in 1875 seems to us an unnecessary step in a chronology of anachronistic measures. Magyarisation pushed a considerable part of Slovak citizens into emigration and could not completely root out the national consciousness of those who stayed. It would strenghten Slovak-Czech relations in the first years of the 20th century. How did Slovak national identity survive under these conditions? Here, a short excursion into a few data on the composition of the social classes urban development and the party landscape can give us important insights.

Magyarisation in conjunction with the agrarian character of the country and the population's social conservatism were decisive factors for the protracted development toward a strong and conscious civil society, or better, urban citizenry, that had developed in Western Europe[69]. Elena Mannová speaks of "distinctly different configurations of the economic system, the legal system, property and civil and minority rights", attesting the population "pre- or un-civil tendencies such as confessional fundamentalism, refusal of democratic and liberal ideas, anti-Semitism and provincialism"[70]. Only in the 1950s did the communist government start a coherent industrialisation and urbanisation – albeit totalitarian in conduct and scope. The following figures[71] illustrate the dominance of the agrarian sector in Slovakia's economy, compared to England, Germany and the Czech lands (Bohemia, Moravia and Silesia): In 1900, 8.0% of the English labour force worked in the agrarian sector; 37.5% in Germany; 47.6% in the Czech lands and 67.9% in Slovakia. In 1930, Slovakia's population was still concentrated in the agrarian sector with 62.5%,

---

[69] In this context, the term "civil society" (*bürgerliche Gesellschaft*) is rather misleading, since on the one hand it can refer to the post-1989 developments that aimed at the establishing of a 20th century liberal civil society opposed to the values of Marxism-Leninism. On the other hand, "civil society" may also refer to the tradition of Western liberalism and its historic development of citizens' rights, a process that started at the end of the 18th century leading to the revolution of 1848 and the significance of the bourgeois middle class in Germany, France and Austria. To describe the situation in Slovakia, we shall use the terms "citizenry" (*Bürgertum*), "thin citizenry" (*schmale bürgerliche Schicht*), "urban citizenry" (*städtisches Bürgertum*), "lower citizenry" (*Kleinbürgertum*), the more neutral "middle class" and combinations of these terms, respectively.

[70] Elena Mannová, "Entwicklungsbedingungen bürgerlicher Schichten in der Slowakei im 20. Jahrhundert", in *Bürgertum und bürgerliche Gesellschaft in der Slowakei 1900-1989* (Bratislava: Academic Electronic Press AEP, 1997), 11–18; 11.

[71] Ján Svetoň, *Obyvateľstvo Slovenska za kapitalizmu* (Bratislava: Slovenské vydavateľstvo politickej literatúry, 1958), 113; quoted after Mannová, "Entwicklungsbedingungen ...", 12.

compared to England with 5.6%, Germany with 28.9% and the Czech lands with 31.2%. The settlement structure can further account for the pre-industrial conditions: In 1900, there were only 2 towns with more than 20 000 inhabitants, i.e. 3.5% of the population, while 13.7% of the population lived in 38 small towns with no more than 5 000 inhabitants[72]. The specific character of the Hungarian administration can further account for the predominance of the small towns and the lower citizenry (*Kleinbürgertum*): the legal changes in the second half of the 19th century limited the legal status of the municipal towns and directly "affected citizens' mechanisms of self-governance"[73]. These administrative limits led to a significant weakening of the urban citizenry's economic and political status.

It is problematic, indeed, to use the term "Slovak society". Questioning its existence in Hungary before 1918, Tibor Pichler distinguishes between a "linguistic" and a "political nation", since

> "Slovak nationhood [Slowakentum] existed in multi-local identities with the ethnic Slovak mother tongue as their common denominator. ... The beginnings of a Slovak standard culture [Standartkultur], a continuously developing literature and ... the efforts for an institutionalisation of the nation ... were existing. ... however, a distinct cohesion, generally reflected upon and generally supported, was missing. The leap from the Slovak speaking local communities to the establishing of a Slovak society had still to be taken."[74]

The citizenry's process of developing into an urban middle class progressing from a political and national awareness toward the modern identity of citizenship coincided with the emerging of political parties. Ľubomír Lipták describes the functioning of the parties in detail:

---

[72] *Encyklopédia Slovenska VI* (Bratislava: Veda) 1982, 189; quoted after Mannová, "Entwicklungs-bedingungen ...", 13.

[73] Ján Pašiak, "Bürgertum im Kontext der Siedlungsentwicklung", in *Bürgertum und...*, 19-35; 23. "Virilism" was a practice and institution that effectively opposed universal suffrage in the regions of the national minorities. Only a distinct number of wealthy tax payers, the so-called virilists, were allowed to participate in the councils of the towns and counties; the representatives were appointed due to their financial weight, not elected. Virilism ensured the political and economic power of the citizens loyal to the Hungarian government and the institution survived until 1918; Ľubomír Lipták, "Elitenwechsel in der bürgerlichen Gesellschaft der Slowakei im ersten Drittel des 20. Jahrhunderts", in *Bürgertum und...*, 67-80; 67, 70.

[74] Tibor Pichler, "Nationaleiferer oder Bürger. Institutionalisierung als Problem," in *Bürgertum und...*, 61-66; 64-65.

"The political parties ... passed through two stages of development in the period 1860 – 1914. Until the beginning of the 1890s they were so-called electoral parties. The most important exception was the Social democrats and their forerunners. The parties mostly entered the public arena only before elections. Apart from this, their members of parliament and the press represented them. The members of parliament formed innumerable regional cliques and groups, mostly from land-owning circles, either from their own ranks or from among the county intelligentsia, or they were appointed from the centre, that is Budapest, on the basis of political agreement. ... Until the beginning of the century and perhaps until 1918, the existence of parties was less apparent in elections to town councils, where family groups, clans and interests generally prevailed."[75]

In the periods between the elections, the parliamentarians' connections with the citizens in their constituencies were minimal. Also, the parties' activities were further determined along "the double triangle of three nationalities: Slovak, Hungarian and German and three religious confessions: Catholics, Protestants and Jews."[76] Due to the assimilation and economic factors, the foundation of political parties in Slovakia was protracted, compared to the party landscape in the Czech lands, Austria and Hungary; the major Czech parties such as the Agrarians, Social Democrats, and Communists emerged in the 1890s and had close contacts to their Austrian and Hungarian sister parties. The two major Hungarian parties were Deák's *Party of Compromise*, after 1875 the *Liberal Party*, which was moderate in nationality issues, while the more radical *Independence Party* pursued the complete separation of Hungary from Austria. The *Liberal Party*, after 1906 the *Constitutional Party* and after 1910 the *National Labour Party*, dominated the party landscape in Slovakia and disposed of "a generally reliable reservoir of support for the government"[77]. The *Slovak National Party* (*Slovenská národna strana*) was founded in 1871 as a result of the split of the national movement; the members of the *nova škola slovenská* opposing the *okolie* were supportive of a compromise with the Magyars and created the short-lived *Slovak Compromise Party* (*Slovenská strana vyrovnania*) in 1872. The *Catholic People's Party* (*Katolická ľudová strana*) formed in 1894 and tried to gain

---

[75] Ľubomír Lipták, "Slovak political parties, societies and political culture up to 1914", in *Changes of changes. Society and politics in Slovakia in the 20ᵗʰ Century* (Bratislava: Academic Electronic Press AEP, Historický ústav SAV, 2002), 125-137; 127.

[76] Lipták, "Slovak political parties...", 127. For detailed analysis of the relationship of the churches, national and ethnic identities and Slovak statehood see Tatiana Ivantyšynová, (ed.), *Národ – cirkev – štát* (Bratislava: SDK SVE a CEP, HU SAV, 2007).

[77] Lipták, "Slovak political parties...", 128.

non-Magyar voters for its conservative, anti-capitalist and populist slogans[78]. In 1905, the *Slovak Social Democratic Party* (*Slovenská socialnodemokratická strana*) was founded; it had close ties to the Austrian and Czech Social Democrats and could not have survived without their organisational support[79]. The peasant farmer's movement formed into the *Agrarian Party* also in 1905; led by Milan Hodža (1879 - 1944), it became the second largest Slovak party apart from the *People's Party* after 1918. The Agrarians understood themselves as a viable alternative to socialism and capitalism promoting a "third way"[80]. The *Hlas* movement, named after the journal *Hlas* (*voice*), emerged in 1898. Young urban intellectuals formed the movement that promoted democratic, socially progressive and a-religious politics inspired by Thomas G. Masaryk, the future founder of the Czechoslovak Republic[81]. The émigré association *Slovenská liga* in Cleveland would support the Czechoslovak exile, led by Masaryk, Edvard Beneš and the Slovak astronomer and pilot Milan Rastislav Štefánik (1880 - 1919), and prove an important factor in the creation of Czechoslovakia in 1918[82]. To conclude, we could summarise that the protracted development and the semi-functional character of the Slovak parties differed from the party landscape in Bohemia and Austria due to the dominant elements of an agrarian country, a legislation that did not favour local self-government, a strict assimilation and the lack of industrialisation and urbanisation that the empire's centres Vienna, Prague and Budapest had at their disposal[83].

---

[78] Lipták, "Slovak political parties...", 131.

[79] Lipták, "Slovak political parties...", 133.

[80] Lipták, "Slovak political parties...", 132.

[81] Interestingly, Masaryk chose Czech as his political and national identity when studying at Vienna university, where he became acquainted with Czech nationalism in the expatriot student circles. Born to a Slovak coachman and a German cook, he grew up in very poor conditions in Hodonín in Eastern Moravia. Although he was interested in the political situation in Upper Hungary, he focussed on formulating his Czech political programme avoiding an open involvement with the *Hlasists*.

[82] Until the end of the 19th century, some three hundred thousand Slovaks, mainly from the poorer regions in Northern and Eastern Slovakia emigrated to the USA and Canada. Some went to Pittsburgh in Pennsylvania, where they worked in the mines and the steel industry. Others emigrated to Canada to work in the woods or on farms. The emigré circle *Slovenská liga* was founded in Cleveland in 1907; Kováč, *Dejiny...*, 143, 144.

[83] On Vienna as melting pot of progressive political ideas and the culture of the Viennese *haute bourgeoisie* see Carl E. Schorske, *Fin-de-Siècle Vienna. Politics and Culture* (New York:

The *Hlinková Slovenská ľudová strana* HSĽS (*Hlinka's Slovak People's Party*) was founded in 1913 by the Catholic priest Andrej Hlinka[84]. Despite being critical of Czech supremacy in the common state, neither the majority of Hlinka's adherents nor of the population pursued independence, which emerged as an option only with the increasing pressure from Hitler Germany[85]. The I. Slovak Republic (1939-1944), governed *de iure* by Cardinal Jozef Tiso (1887 - 1947), was *de facto* a Nazi puppet state that had to adopt the *Führer principle* and the totalitarian administration. The HSĽS gained total control of the state and Slovakia's economy was oriented towards the needs of Germany. The decree on the Slovak version of the Nuremberg racial laws, the so-called Slovak anti-Jewish codex, was declared on 9 September 1941 after the massive discrimination in the preceding months had already isolated the Jewish citizens. The constitutional bill of law of 15 May 1942 stripped them of their civil rights and provided the legal basis for deportation. The Slovak national uprising (*Slovenské národné povstanie*) started on 30 August 1944 in Banská Bystrica, jointly organised by the Czechoslovak exile government, the Slovak Communist Party, partisan units and the Soviet Union. With President Beneš's visit to Košice in April 1945 the post-war reconstitution of Czechoslovakia began. The democracy would survive for only three years.

Before I move on to the first chapter on Ján Francisci, let me introduce the method and the contents of this investigation.

X. 7.   Method, definitions, contents, hypothesis

X. 7. 1.   Method

The present investigation has an *interdisciplinary* focus: it presents an analysis of political and philosophical ideas against the background of established historical facts. It aims to contribute to fundamental research (*Grundlagenforschung*) on the

---

Vintage, Random, 1979). On Prague see the excellent volume by Otto Urbán, *Česká společnost 1848-1918* (Praha: Svoboda, 1982) and focussing on the political parties Otto Urbán, "Die tschechische Frage um 1900", *Österreichische Osthefte 32*, no. 3 (1990): 427-43. For the Hungarian perspective see Istvan Deák, *Assimilation and nationalism in East Central Europe during the last century of Habsburg rule* (Pittsburgh, PA: University of Pittsburgh, 1983).

[84]   James R. Felák, *At the Price of the Republic: Hlinka's Slovak People's Party, 1929-1938* (Pittsburgh: Pittsburgh University Press, 1994).

[85]   Kováč, *Dejiny...*, 217.

intellectual history (*Geistesgeschichte*) of Central Europe. Research on the national movement and Slovak political and economic history has been accomplished by Rapant[86], Gogolák[87], Holotík[88], Bokeš[89], Mikuš[90], Kováč[91], Podrimavský[92] and Holec[93]. Sutherland[94] and Brock[95] focus on poetry and literature, addressing political concepts and their roots in political philosophy only superficially. Pichler's analysis[96] is the first work known to me that establishes the political thought of members of the national movement and delivers an impressive intellectual portrait. A detailed analysis of the main currents of political and philosophical ideas of this period in English is still lacking.

Our investigation covers articles, essays, programmes and memoirs of six Slovak intellectuals, starting with the discussions about the *memorandum* of 1861 and ending with the foundation of the Czechoslovak Republic in 1918. In our analysis we shall use *two paradigmata* that cover *1. the political goals*, and *2. the philosophical / political legitimating*. None of the programmes, suggestions, conclusions and drafts came into being; we shall necessarily deal with political thought that did not effect realisation. Vavro Šrobár's goal of a Czechoslovak union in a democratic state can be seen as an exception, owing to a radical change in international politics caused by WWI.

---

[86] Daniel Rapant, *Ilegálna Maďarizácia 1790-1840* (Turčiansky Sv. Martin: Matica Slovenská, 1947).

[87] Gogolák, "Die historische Entwicklung…"; "Ungarns Nationalitätengesetze…"

[88] Holotík, "Die Slowaken".

[89] František Bokeš, *Dokumenty k slovenskému národnému hnutiu v rokoch 1848 – 1914*, 3 volumes (Bratislava: Historický ústav Slovenské akademie ved, 1965, 1972).

[90] Mikuš, *Slovakia…*

[91] Kováč, *Slováci…* and *Dejiny…*

[92] Milan Podrimavský, *Slovenská národná strana v druhej polovici XIX. storočia* (Bratislava: vydavateľstvo slovenskej akadémie vied, 1983).

[93] Roman Holec, *Poľnohospodárstvo na Slovensku v poslednej tretine 19. storočia* (Bratislava: Veda, 1991); a good introduction to the Slovak trade union is the semi-popular text *150 years of the Slovak cooperative movement. Victories and defeats* (Bratislava: Reetas-Renesans, 1997).

[94] Anthony X. Sutherland, "Studies into the intellectual history of Slovak nationalism (1500s-1914)." *Slovak Studies XXV* (1985): 69-145.

[95] Peter Brock, *The Slovak National Awakening: an Essay in the intellectual history of East Central Europe*. Toronto, Buffalo: University of Toronto Press, 1976.

[96] Tibor Pichler, *Národovci a občania: O slovenskom politickom myšleni v 19. Storoči* (Bratislava: Slovenská Akadémie Věd SAV, 1998).

The ideas, goals and programmes of the *narodovci*[97] (patriots, national awakeners) were, however, not futile in regard to the national discussion: what did it mean to be Slovak, how to halt the assimilation and what circumstances would be required to gain autonomy within the framework of the Hungarian kingdom? Even on the brink of WWI, sovereignty was an unrealistic goal, but the idea of forming a common state with the Czechs gained some support among the elites when the U.S. entered the war. Now, what could an analysis offer that investigates political thought that lacked realisation? Why investigate 'unsuccessful' political thinking?

We deem it crucially important to learn more about the political culture and the intellectual history of a nation that achieved EU membership in 2004, and with that, the specific details of the elite's political thought. The *narodvci* determined what Slovak nationhood meant in the first place, analysed the circumstances that would be favourable for the status of equality within the monarchy and never ceased to oppose the assimilation. The study is elite-based in scope and content. However, we think that our interdisciplinary method can open a window to the political culture of late 19th century Slovakia, in particular the currents of political thought. Therefore, one could classify our investigation also as a study of *contextual biography*[98], a particular method of biographical and historical writing that analyses a historical epoch, its institutions, political atmosphere and power-relations through the 'prism' of a prominent personality's biography. Our interdisciplinary contextual biography method uses intellectuals' actions and political ideas as a 'window' into the historical epoch under scrutiny.

---

[97] The philosopher Tibor Pichler uses the concept "Nationaleiferer" in the sense of "ethnic nationalist" for the concept *narodovec*, according to *the Dictionary of the Slovak language* (Bratislava: vydavateľstvo Slovenskej Akadémie vied, 1960). "Nationaleiferer" corresponds to the English "he who is enthusiast about the nation" or "he who promotes the nation's development" or "patriot". I shall be using "narodovec", "national awakener", "nationalist" and "patriot"; the latter in the sense of enthusiasm about the Slovak nation, not connoting statehood (*patria*); Tibor Pichler, "Nationaleiferer oder Bürger. Institutionalisierung as Problem," in *Bürgertum und bürgerliche Gesellschaft in der Slowakei 1900-1989* (Bratislava: Academic Electronic Press AEP, 1997), 61-66.

[98] Simone Lässig, "Introduction: Biography in modern history – modern historiography in Biography", in *Biography between structure and agency. Central European lives in international historiography* (New York, Oxford: Berghahn books, 2008); 1–26.

Albeit in an abbreviated form suitable to the purpose of our study, the following research outline shall present the relationship between political thought and political culture[99]:

> "The political history of a nation, nationality or ethnic minority > shapes distinct experiences of political rule and affects collective identity> governmental rule affects intellectual elite > elite is the actor responsible for articulation, promotion and legitimating of political ideas in terms of political power > a 'canon' or body of ideas emerges that legitimates or opposes power, identity and ethical values > this body of ideas or currents of thought is disseminated among the populace, forms the basis of collective memory and co-determines, enforces or changes popular attitudes and perceptions of political power and identity(ies) > the population's reception of the ideas of the 'canon' and its experience of governmental rule co-determine party affiliation and national, international or supranational allegiances > elite perceives of popular attitudes and opts for reforms or change of the political system toward democratisation or authoritarian-conservative regime > 'canon' of ideas or parts of it prevail through history, but are being affected by reform, change or sustenance of the political system."

The outline should be understood as an *idealistic* model; however, in regard to the Central European historical peculiarities, political culture is crucially connected to the elites' thought about *identity under foreign rule* – and with that the nation's intellectual history. Naturally, the relationship of political culture and intellectual history is but one factor when considering regime reforms, change or sustenance. Economic, sociological, socio-economic and international factors play further important roles. Yet, compared to Western intellectual history, Central European intellectual history is not only a young but often forgotten research field.

X. 7. 2. Definitions

Our research interest lies in the *formulation of national political goals* and the *philosophical / political legitimating* of these goals. In his seminal study[100], Miroslav

---

[99] For the theoretical assessment, details of the research line, method and deduction of the definitions see the introduction of my *Slavic thinkers...*, 1-13. Note that I developed an outline, method and definitions *to analyse political culture in Central Europe and the Balkans in an inductive fashion* tailored primarily to the specific historical situation of Central Europe and the Balkans. Any comparison to Western European intellectual history would only lead to the already established theorem of economic backwardness. However, we consider 'spill-overs' or the intellectual influence/reception of Western political thought as crucially important, since they present a phenomenon of exchange and inspiration – not a competitive comparison of two separate intellectual entities.

Hroch suggested a chronology of nationalism developing in Central Europe scrutinising the social classes involved:

1. Phase A is the initial period, dominated by scholars. They become interested in the cultural, linguistic and historical roots or attributes of their ethnic community, but are still too isolated and too few to formulate political demands.

2. In Phase B, the circle of scholars is joined by a significant number of citizens who are interested in spreading the new scholarly knowledge of Phase A. They are eager to create a nation based on the historic, cultural and linguistic attributes of their ethnic group.

3. Phase C finally starts when the majority of the population has reached a national consciousness and forms a mass movement, and political programmes are being formulated.

According to this model, we could position the Štúr generation in phase A and the *narodovci* of our study in phase B. Yet, in Slovakia, phase B and C somewhat overlap, in particular considering the formulation of political programmes that are connected to the emerging of mass movement. The beginnings of phase C could be positioned somewhere in the 1920s, when Slovakia was an integral part of Czechoslovakia and the citizens subject to the modernising state theory of *Czechoslovakism*. We are not sure, however, when and if one can speak of a mass movement at all, that is a mass movement in the understanding of a freely evolving movement. Owing to Magyarisation, such a critical mass of nationally conscious citizens was not yet formed in late 19th century. The mass movement starting in the 1950s was imposed by the communist government and did not emerge out of the free will of the citizens.

Let me now present my definition of political culture and its connection to intellectual history:

The political culture of a social entity (nation, nationality, ethnic minority) consists in the system of beliefs about patterns of political interaction and political institutions. Beliefs as sets of norms and values are being changed and shaped by the historical

---

[100] Hroch, *Die Vorkämpfer...*, 24-26. See also the latest and modernised version: Miroslav Hroch, *Das Europa der Nationen. Die moderne Nationsbildung im europäischen Vergleich* (Göttingen: Vandenhoeck & Ruprecht, 2005), 46-47.

experiences of foreign rule and the ideas of Enlightenment, Nationalism, and Liberalism, or the absence thereof.

In short: political culture deals with what people believe about politics, not what is actually happening in politics[101]. Beliefs reflect traditional or new sets of values that were and are subject to historic changes; political culture can therefore never be stagnant as it 'filters' the specific aspects of tradition and change according to a nation's goals and political needs, such as identity formation, including the rights of political, ethnic and confessional minorities, discussions about the type of constitution, hence governmental rule and its perception of various conservative, liberal, international or supranational aspects.

The paradigmatic questions that shall guide us through this investigation concern *A. political goals* and *B. philosophical / political legitimating.*

A. Political goals:

What political goals did the intellectuals pursue and what did they do to achieve these goals? A national revolution, a *modus vivendi* with the Magyars or sovereignty? Suggestions on territorial autonomy or federalisation? Suggestions for constitutional arrangements or amendments, in particular the language law? Definitions of national identity and citizenship? How did they conceive of the status of language? What role did the international situation play and what international contacts or links did they have? How did they interpret natural law? Did they found or support the foundation of a political party?

B. Philosophical / political legitimating:

What philosophical / political arguments did the *narodovci* under discussion use to legitimate their political goals? What thinkers or philosophers did they consult to strengthen their arguments? Did they refer to Herder and Hegel like Štúr did or did they prefer Western political philosophers such as Charles de Montesquieu, Jean-Jacques Rousseau, Immanuel Kant or John Locke? And if they referred to Western political philosophers, how did they adapt their thought to the Slovak situation? Did Czech intellectuals such as Palacký and Masaryk have a direct influence? How did they conceive of liberal, socialist and conservative ideas in their views about

---

[101] Sidney Verba, "Conclusion: Comparative Political Culture," in *Political Culture and Political Development* (Princeton: Princeton University Press, 1965), 516.

nationhood? What influence did the ideas of the Austrian social democrats Karl Renner and Otto Bauer have?

Two key aspects that will be recurring throughout the text, need elaboration and clarification: first, the concept of *natural law* and second, the concept of *human rights*.

1. "Rational Natural Law":

> "As the origins of the idea of equality of nations and individuals, rational natural law is to be understood as a system of rights or justice, which is common to all human beings, since it derives from nature, i.e. the nature of man."[102]

Natural law and, more importantly, its legitimating of who should be sovereign and what powers that sovereign should hold, can be roughly divided into three subfields that correspond to the chronological development of the idea from the early Middle Ages to the 20th century: the anthropological variant as defined by Saint Thomas Aquinas, which focuses on human nature; the religious variant of Jean Bodin, which views natural law as determined by a higher will; and the rational variant, also called the *law of reason*, determined by human reason. Thomas Hobbes, Hugo Grotius, Samuel von Pufendorf, Jean-Jacques Rousseau and Immanuel Kant developed the idea of reason as a law-determining human gift. They were of crucial importance in preparing the legitimating of enlightenment values, which eventually led to the French revolution. In the 19th century, rational natural law became the principal argument against foreign power considered to be illegitimate. One could say that it was used by citizens to contest the power of the *nobility perceived as socially and intellectually illegitimate* and by national groups to challenge the rule by a *government considered as foreign and / or culturally alien*. In this paper we will understand *natural law* always as *rational natural law*, which had had its origins in the 17th century, when confessional features determined natural law theory less and less. The Peace of Westphalia that ended the *Thirty Years War* (1618-1648) had

---

[102] http://www.britannica.com/eb/article-9055045/natural-law; accessed 3 June 2008. "The term natural law designates a system of law that is freely derived from human nature without the need for a legislator to define it. Accordingly, natural law theory assumes that beyond the sphere of positive law there is a higher law from which positive law is deduced and by which it must always be measured"; http://www.lexexakt.de/glossar/naturrecht.php; accessed 3 June 2008.

given the decisive impulse to accommodate the confessional opposition on the European continent. The philosopher Simone Zurbuchen describes this process as follows:

> "He [Samuel von Pufendorf, add. JB] had created, similar to Rousseau, a 'minimal religion' ['Minimalreligion'], the so-called 'natural' religion as a basis for natural law and thus civic morality. At first, the distinction between 'natural' religion and the religious confessions that transcended that minimum by no means included a political definition of religion. The goal of this *differentiation* is not the determination of the function of religion for state and society. The goal is the exclusion of religious doctrines from the spheres of law and politics because it is beyond human ratio to *reason about them*. This *de-confessionalisation of natural law* corresponds with the demand for political tolerance towards the adherents of different Christian beliefs. It is not to lead to a weakening of the influence of Christian religion on society, but to sustain that influence even under the condition of the confessional divide."[103]

2. "Human Rights": We understand individual rights generally as human rights as stipulated in the UN declaration of 1948[104]. There are, of course, differing understandings of the extent of citizens' rights, in particular rights that protect from interference by the state. The 19th century notions of civil rights did not equal democratic rights in the modern sense, but they were certainly based on their liberal forerunners, the civil liberties called for by the French revolution and epitomised in the slogan *liberté – égalité - fraternité*. For the purpose of this paper and focussing on Habsburg conservatism, we can define the concept of 'individual rights' in our subject area as a minimal one: rights covered by basic penal or criminal law that primarily protected the citizen from crime, fraud, and negligence. Montesquieu's separation of powers into executive, judicial and legislative powers, a system so vital to avoiding corruption, interest cliques and nepotism, was non-existent in Austria-Hungary. The conservative Habsburg Empire did everything to prevent this liberal idea from taking root. Censorship, corruption, a state security police and the unchallenged rule of aristocracy, clergy and the army kept the system alive.

---

[103] Simone Zurbuchen, *Naturrecht und natürliche Religion. Zur Geschichte des Toleranzbegriffs von Samuel Pufendorf bis Jean-Jacques Rousseau* (Würzburg: Königshausen & Neumann, 1991), 4; italics by JB.

[104] For an excellent and concise overview of the philosophical development of human rights see http://plato.stanford.edu/entries/rights-human/; accessed 4 June 2008.

X. 7. 3   Contents, hypothesis

It would be too idealist to assume that we shall encounter a clear-cut division of declared goals and legitimating arguments in the texts subject to analysis. We shall try, however, to separate the goals from the legitimating arguments and the critique of other viewpoints. The analysis evolves on a theoretical level; nevertheless, we shall try to assess the texts against a historical background to get a clearer idea of their political potential. How realistic, and how likely to be realised, were the intellectuals' various arguments in the given situation?

The analysis is divided in six chapters according to the six selected intellectuals: Ján Francisci (1822-1905), Ján Palarík (1822-1874), Štefan Marko Daxner (1822-1892), František V. Sasínek (1830-1914), Svetozár Hurban Vajanský (1847-1916) and Vavro Šrobár (1867-1950). Their political argumentation displays the broad spectrum of thought within the national movement. Francisci remained faithful to the idea of Slovak autonomy within Hungary all his life, starting with his participation in the 1848 revolution. He chaired the national assembly in Turčiansky Sv. Martin and signed the *memorandum* of 1861. Palarík signed the *memorandum* too, but favoured a *modus vivendi* with the ruling Magyars to strengthen Buda against Vienna's centralism. Daxner fought with Francisci against the revolutionary troops in 1848, studied law and was responsible for the final edition of the *memorandum*. Sasínek criticised the idealising-romanticist historicism of some members of the movement and above all, the distortions of Slovak history he had believed the Magyars were undertaking for decades. Vajanský chose *Russophilia* as political alternative to the hopeless situation and contributed to Slovak intellectual history by reviving the memory of Stur's desperate panslavism. Šrobár was inspired by Masaryk's Czech *Realism* and later, *Czechoslovakism*; he gave the national movement a new impulse to modernise, since the *Hlas* movement was critical of the *memorandum* generation and offered an exit from Hungary and Austria by a union of Slovaks and Czechs.

In the conclusion, I will attempt to draw an intellectual portrait of the national movement by assessing the thinkers' potential and prospective successes. To some extent, such an undertaking remains speculative. Our intention is, however, to shed light on the most important currents of Slovak political thought when the completion of nation building or national identity was blocked by Magyarisation and state building or sovereignty an unrealistic idea. The results of the investigation will be helping to answer the leading research question:

Why was Andrej Hlinka's People's party HSĽS the most successful after 1918, given the fact that a wide range of political opinions, ideas and intellectual currents existed prior to 1918?

Ján Francisci, © Slovenská Národná Knižnica, Martin (SNK)

I.   Ján Francisci (1822 - 1905). Romanticism and Pragmatism

I. 1.   Political goals

I. 1. 1.   The three falcons and the revolution

It might seem a banality to begin the first chapter of a volume dealing with the political thought of six Slovak *narodovci* with the general statement that Ján Francisci's political goal was Slovak autonomy. Yet the concept of 'autonomy' brings us to the very core of the problem: In what terms did Francisci think of 'autonomy' – and, in what historic circumstances? One could briefly state that his understanding of Slovak autonomy and its changing political connotation through 19th century mirrors the political history of his nation. From his early youth on he was involved in every national event that dealt with autonomy claims. The reasons for this inseparable relation are Francisci's pragmatism and unfaltering engagement.

Also known under his pen names Janko Rimavský, Slavoľub and Vratislav, Francisci was in his twenties when he became a well-known adherent of the early national movement of the Štúr generation. His organisational skills and complete dedication to the nation are impressive. His managerial and editorial activities for Slovak literature, education and journals remind one of Masaryk's *drobná práce* (*the small works*): the method of *small works*, promoted by Masaryk in the 1890s, implied to contributing to the nation's education and self-awareness by self-education. Educating oneself peacefully, continuously and without making fuss about oneself would strengthen the nation's economic prosperity, culture and identity, in particular in unfortunate times and circumstances. *Small works* would eventually prepare the nation for independence, according to Masaryk. Neither Francisci nor his mentor Štúr thought that far ahead. They were focussing on the language issue. Francisci was involved in all spheres and institutions of political significance: as a leader of student protest, military leader, organiser, administrator, founder and editor of journals and even as contact for foreign relations. He protested against Štúr's dismissal from the Pressburg lyceum by leading his students to study at the lyceum in Levoča. As captain of the Slovak volunteer troops he fought the Magyars during the 1848 revolution. After 1849, he accepted high positions in the Austro-Hungarian administration and was, at the same time, one of the founders of the *Matica slovenská*. His contacts to Russian slavophiles more than once enabled young

Slovaks to get higher education in Russia and secured the continuity of journals in Slovak that never really ceased to be in financial trouble. The questions we shall try to answer in this chapter are: What are the philosophical foundations of Francisci's notion of national identity? How does one explain the noticeable descrepancy between his ideals and his actions, and his support of Slovak autonomy while holding high positions in the Hungarian administration?

No movement claiming for a goal of national or universal significance can survive without individuals, who are willing to dedicate a considerable amount of their time, if not their life, to the cause. In our times, we first think of the people working at the EU, UN and the OSCE as the principal international organisations that promote peace, mutual understanding, economic development and protection of minorities. These institutions originated in ideas that promoted the well being of mankind, revolutionary in their times. But they were spreading and finally realised by individuals convinced of their rightfulness and effectivity. The globalised world of today is unthinkable without international organisations. Of minor influence on the international level – but no less important – are movements, parties or NGOs that originate in civil society and express legal protest against what their adherents perceive as pressing issues for mankind: the peaceful factions of the international anti-globalisation movement, the ecologist movement and organisations that monitor violations of international law conventions, such as *médecins sans frontiers* and *amnesty international*. Academia is becoming more and more involved with business, and the worlds of theory and practice are merging.

In 19th century Europe, disciplined by Metternich's restoration, there were no forums for discussion let alone institutions that would care about the living conditions of some national group settling in the North of Hungary. Nor did that group have the possibility to appeal to an international court of justice; it could defend its interests and rights only by addressing the Hungarian diet and the emperor in Vienna. Whereas the ideas of Enlightenment and Romantic philosophy were taught, to some extent, at German universities, political practice grew out of the group's distinct political circumstances. One could say that the beginnings of Slovak national politics emerged as a reaction against cultural discrimination. Or to put it in other words: while international and internationalised concepts such as 'human rights', 'civil society' and 'protection of minorities' were yet non-existent, their semantic pendants on the level of nation building were 'national autonomy', 'rights of the non-Magyar citizens' and 'protection of cultural rights'. Moreover, the significance of the term 'autonomy' was shifting according to the claims the national movement made in its efforts to maintain Slovak identity. For Ľudovít Štúr and his adherents, who followed Herder's romantic understanding of individuality, autonomy primarily meant the right to use their language in schools and church administration – not the territorial autonomy of the *okolie* the movement demanded for in 1861. Francisci considered the language issue as the beginnings of his patriotic activities that should last all his life.

In his memoirs, he referred to two events of 1836 that would significantly influence the direction of his personal development. The night his father fell seriously ill with cholera, the family called the physician, who could do nothing more than to suggest a hot bath. The physician Marianček asked the fourteen-year-old teenager whether he knew Latin. Francisci replied yes, upon which the good doctor taught him a Latin proverb that he would only later begin to understand to the fullest: "Homo sum; nil humani alienum a me esse puto – I am a human being; nothing human can be strange to me."[105] The next morning his mother told him that his father had died. The second memorable event happened a couple of days later. After the funeral of his father, young Francisci looked through his collection of books; the elder Francisci had had books delivered on a regular basis from Prague. Janko found a booklet, whose pages were dry and yellow from age; it bore the title *Česko-slovenská grammatika od Šramku* (*Czecho-Slovak grammar by Šramek*)[106]. The student was very astonished to learn of the existence of a Slovak grammar.

> "I was studying, from the age of six, the grammars of Latin, Hungarian and German and had also started to study the Greek and Hebrew grammars, as they were taught in the higher classes. But I had never heard about a Slovak grammar before and had not the slightest idea that it really existed. Yet look, here, I see a printed Slovak grammar right in front of my eyes! ... That was the awakening of the Slovak in me."[107]

---

[105]   Ján Francisci, "Vlastný životopis," in *Vlastný životopis. Črty z doby moysesovskej* (Bratislava: Slovenské vydavateľstvo krásnej literatúry, 1956), 37-265; 62-63.

[106]   The author of the grammar was the linguist Adolf Joseph Šramek (also Schramek) (1747-1803).

[107]   Francisci, "životopis", 63.

One short dialogue in *Janko Podhorský*[108], one of his most famous novels playing in 16th century Hungary ruled by Jan Zápolya (1487-1540), seems to predict the fate of the nation. Janko Podhorský, the seventeenish son of a peasant family living in the Tatra Mountains, is called to war against the invading Ottomans. Jankos' grandfather, who reminds them of their duties to god, their families and their country, sends off Janko, his brothers and some ten young men of the village. After a couple of fortifying toasts they finally leave to join the main camp. On their way, Janko reminisces his life in the familiar Tatra region and admits his fear of dying. He encourages himself by thinking of the skies above the mountains.

> "Janko: 'In free flight, like these eagles, we shall fly down to the Turkish clouds to dispel and chase them from our clear skies.'
>
> 'May the lord help us.' Černianský replied. 'But, if I am right, a nice piece of work will await us down there, because the clouds carry something that is undistinguishable from them, that drew them up here from the distant lower planes and is still drawing them up higher and higher.'
>
> 'But that's the curse of our pitiable country,' Dolinský cried out cleverly, 'that we have a traitor sitting in our lap, who just wants us to perish. It looks as if he intended our good ... but does he really want to? I'd like to see the man, who could convince me of it. He wants to elevate himself at the expense of our death and nothing else. Alas, we know that very well. – And it was him, who brought that Turkish beast down on us and, still, everywhere he gets more help than we do. And that is why we should – our people shall bless us and the lord shall help us – extricate us from him and support the emperor ...'

Janko Ladanský carried on with the political discussion in this way:

> 'It seems that emperor Ferdinand has an agreement with our vice-king Zápolya. That is why he thinks he can do whatever he likes. And remember, if he has a bastard, he will also want to push us to elect that one as our king. ... Oh, he has nice plans. But he doesn't trust the emperor either. He feels his own weakness, that is why he called the Turk to help...'
>
> 'Here and there people say,' Janko said, 'that he supports the new reformed confession for which our princes are going to Germany to get instruction in. But I don't believe him. We have seen what he did with the friends of the new confession in Transylvania, how he tortured them, seized all their property and chased them out of the country. Who once treated us like this, we should never trust again, not even now, when he makes promises and treats us well. We are happy not to trust him and see his vileness. And we are convinced that, should it ever come to that, we shall defend our holy confession against whatever enemy, as fiercely as we defend our country against Zápolya and the Turk.

---

[108]   First published in the almanach *Nitra II*, 1844; Ján Francisci, "Janko Podrimavský," in *Iskry zo zaviatej pahreby* (Bratislava: Tatran, 1977), 67-103.

Because, believe me, nobody but us, neither the emperor nor the vice-king will help us in this matter. Only in ourselves and amongst our kin, will we find support.'"[109]

Continuous loyalty without reward, unrequited faithfulness, obedience to the lord, the authorities and one's family, a deep familiarity with the customs of the countryside – these characteristics Francisci defined as features of Slovak identity. The quoted dialogue reads almost as a desperate prediction of the future: the Slovaks, however loyally they fulfil their duties, won't be rewarded. But they cannot but oblige to the emperor and the regional governor, who use them for their various plans and interests. Although they know that their loyalty will bring disappointment, that they are being sacrificed once more to higher politics, they have to oblige, since only through obligation and sacrifice will their world remain. This is pure romanticism, art placed into a historical context; it is not a political programme nor idea. Isaiah Berlin illustrates the romantic mind in his ever-sensible, insightful and precise wording:

"Suffering was nobler than pleasure, failure was preferable to worldly success ... martyrdom was sacred no matter in what cause ... Independence, defiance by individuals and groups and nations, pursuit of goals not because they are universal but because they are mine, or those of my people, my culture."[110]

In October 1848, the revolutionary government imprisoned Francisci, Bakuliny and Daxner in the south-eastern town Plešivec and sentenced them to death. Francisci composed a melancholic poem that became the symbol of the national struggle during the revolution. The poem coined the expression *traja sokolja* (the three falcons) that he, Daxner and Bakuliný would come to be referred to.

The three Falcons[111]

Hey three falcons! Are you grieving for the world?
Not for the world, but for flying in free skies.

Hey three falcons! Are you grieving for your life?

---

[109]   Francisci, "Janko Podrimavský," 73-74.
[110]   Isaiah Berlin, "The Apotheosis of the Romantic Will. The Revolt against the Myth of an Ideal World," in *The Proper Study of Mankind. An Anthology of Essays* (London: Pimlico, 1998), 560.
[111]   Francisci, *Iskry...*, 64; translation by JB. I would like to thank Adam Bžoch and Markus Giger for their suggestions and help with this translation.

Only that it won't end in thunder and lightning.

Hey three falcons! Are you not frightened of death?
We aren't, we aren't, but we do feel disgust.

Better it would be, and more beautiful, to die
fighting for freedom; yet, it was not meant to be.

Hey three falcons! How deep is your grave?
It is not as deep as it is high.

Hey three falcons! Who will be crying for you?
The tidal wave that will be swelling shall be our tears.

Hey three falcons! Who will be singing for you?
A storm shall howl and dispel the grief.

Hey three falcons! Who will bury you?
The crows and the wind that scatter our ashes.

Hey three falcons! Who will revenge you?
Memories – and the lord, who knows of our fate.

According to Francisci, the poem's emotionality owned much to Daxner, who added the lines referring to their graves, the gallows, respectively, as being high[112]. But their fate should take a different direction.

Pardoned and freed by the troops of count Windischgrätz, Francisci joined the Slovak volunteers. The Magyar authorities arrested him because of his involvement with the *žiadosti*, the revolutionary programme the movement had issued in May 1848. According to his biographer Julius Botto, Francisci had held the position of an administrative assistant to the vice-governor Gustav Zay, who knew about the

---

[112] Francisci, "životopis", 175.

meeting in Liptovský Sv. Mikuláš[113]. The participation turned out to be a crucial step for Francisci, as he saw the possibility to actively pursue national politics. He left language and romantic literature and started recruiting volunteers. We could hence say that the meeting at Sv. Mikuláš, which was born in the *Zeitgeist* of liberalism and nationalism, two inseparable currents of political thought of the 1848 revolution, presented a first opportunity for political activity. Everything seemed possible in these days and the revolutionary enthusiasm extended to the elder leaders Štúr, Hodža and Hurban. They now wanted to unite the *župy* creating a revolutionary institution, which would be the legitimate representative of the nation. In its outlook, this idea was essentially a democratic one in terms of information distribution, participation and discussion; yet, the decisions were clearly influenced to a great extent by the *trojka* Štúr, Hodža and Hurban and their younger adherents. Although the *žiadosti* had no direct result, the declaration was the first open expression of Slovak nationhood that had to be understood in political terms. Daxner and Francisci organised the meeting. Rapant's always objective, dry and in some passages refreshingly sarcastic description gives us a good impression of the atmosphere:

"All the leading persons of Slovakia participated in the meeting. The better part arrived a day earlier (9.V.). The inhabitants of Mikuláš, however, refused to house them and so the majority, some 20 persons, went to the parish of the close by Trnovec, where the evangelical pastor Lehocký provided lodging. The discussion about the petition, whose final version was to be adopted the next day, started already while they were having dinner. Most of the delegates were armed; they ended up doing some military exercise under the instruction of Hurban, who wore a sword. Behind the parish, some shooting took place that angered the locals. After dinner, they sang various Slavic songs in Slovak, Polish, Serbian and Czech; the biggest attention was paid to the song of Branko Abaffy from the Banat that called for a devastating attack on Buda and the Magyars."[114]

---

[113] Juliuš Botto, *Jan Francisci. Nakres životopisný* (Matica Slovenská: Rimavská Sobota, 1922), 18. Botto writes that Francisci himself decided to leave his position to work for the nation. Francisci writes in his memoirs that he found himself practically in front of closed doors after his return. Zay had dismissed him *in absentia*, most probably for his participation in the national gathering; Francisci, "životopis", 159. We think that Francisci's version is closer to the truth. On Botto and the role of myths in Slovak historiography see Kováč, "Philosophie und Mythologisierung der slowakischen Geschichte", *Österreichische Osthefte 35*, no. 4 (1993): 517-536.

[114] Daniel Rapant, *Dejiny slovenského povstania r. 1848-49. Diel prvý slovenská jar 1848* (Turčiansky Sv. Martin: Matica Slovenská, 1937), 295. Leopold 'Branko' Branislav Abaffy

Francisci wrote the protocol of the gathering. The debates about the single points of the petition dragged on, but the delegates finally accepted the points. Hurban closed the issue with the remark, if their demands would be fulfilled by honest civil servants, the Slovaks could fearlessly join hands with the Magyars again and, as they used to do in the past, shed their blood together now for the revolution, upon which Abaffy replied that this would hardly be possible, since a Croatian rebellion against the Magyars would imply that the Slovaks fight their Slavic brothers[115].

The meeting's democratic spirit that bordered on painful pluralism gave way to other controversial issues. Some delegates quarrelled about the alleged cowardness of the *Narodné Noviny (National News)*, which, they believed, should report about issues of national interest in a more courageous fashion. Štúr, the founder and editor, flat out refused. His and his co-workers' financial means were very limited, he replied, so they had to stick to careful wording in order to avoid the fines they couldn't afford to pay. Some discussed the idea of a Slovak ministry, which others rejected arguing that the Magyars would never allow an independent Slovak political institution within Hungary's administration. Others thought about founding a *l'udová škola*, a national school in the sense of *Volksschule*, providing education for adults.

A fiery dispute arose about the way the declaration should be made public. Hurban suggested positioning the National Guards – probably no more than five to six delegates with a co-assignment, bearing out-dated arms – in front of the town council, whip in the local population and the inhabitants of the neighbouring villages and have the declaration proclaimed on the main square. Hodža opposed, arguing that the majority of the people would lack the intellectual maturity to understand the contents of the *žiadosti*[116]. This was neither a new opinion nor a statement never heard before; more than once, Štúr had criticised the educational backwardness and intellectual passivity of the population[117]. Hurban exploded, threw his pen on the

---

(1827-1883) was a Slovak playwright and author. After the revolution he studied theology and became an evangelical pastor.

[115]   Rapant, *Dejiny* ..., 297.

[116]   Rapant, *Dejiny*..., 297.

[117]   Štúr in 1846: "To the largest extent we have to blame ourselves: our inadequacy, our one-sidedness, our laziness, our passivity ... Our families want their sons to be like they are ... to occupy themselves in the same fashion as they once did." "Dôležitost volenia rozličneho stavu pre nas (1846)," in *Dielo v piatich*..., vol. I, 1954, 191–202; 196.

table and shouted that Hodža would not give all that was in his powers for the nation's good. Hurban's people in Nitra were united in their support of him and the national cause. Hodža replied dryly that he did everything he could, but it wasn't his fault that they didn't reach their goal. Hurban had an easier stand in Nitra anyway, where he didn't have to deal with a band of aristocratic Magyar-lovers[118]. He wanted the declaration read in the town of Kasín, in front of a few people. Many delegates preferred Hurban's suggestion, whereupon Hodža left the room. He came back for the voting only after Štúr persuaded him to join the debate again. After further discussions, however, most of the delegates chose Hodža's suggestion, and it was decided that the declaration would be proclaimed in the local Andras baths in front of the guards and any who just happened to be there. After further instructions about collecting signatures, the delegates left for a banquet. Hodža led them through the main street to the pub that was right next to the governor's building. No locals joined the delegates, who wore flags and cockades in white and red. The Vice-Governor Edmund Szentivány, informed about earlier events by complaints from the locals, received the news immediately and, accompanied by a couple of nobles, drove to town, right into the very nest of Panslavism, as he wrote later in his report[119]. Pastor Lehocký had to answer all his questions about these strangers causing trouble and wearing oddly coloured cockades. Hodža instructed the pastor to answer that they had gathered to debate about a petition to the emperor, the imperial assembly and the ministries.

The Slovaks were indeed in an almost hopeless situation, burdened with goals and considerations that mutually excluded each other: the *žiadosti* had to take into account the solidarity with the fellow Slavs; yet, the Poles supported the Magyar liberals, the Serbs were flirting with the revolution yet kept to their neutrality, while the Croats opposed the Magyars. The Slovaks shared the liberal goals of abolition of serfdom and the general anti-aristocratic spirit with the Magyars, but they had to find points of negotiation as a Slovak independent nation state was an utterly unrealistic idea, not only because the majority of the population lacked the educational level

---

[118] 'Maďarónské pany' is a contemptuous expression for Slovak aristocrats, who curry favour with the Magyars; Rapant, *Dejiny...*, 298.
[119] Rapant, *Dejiny...*, 298-299.

required for independence. Revolutionary goals that would benefit all mankind and the pursuit of national goals became enmeshed.

To conclude this section, the concept of 'autonomy' applies to the Mikuláš demands as regards the liberal idea of equality that can be realised only by equal hence democratic representation: the equality of Hungary's nationalities with proportional representation in the Hungarian parliament as well as autonomous diets on the district level for every nationality. The national demands focussed on the recognition of Slovak as the language of administration in the Slovak counties. The Slovaks understood the autonomy of their regional diet as guarantee for independent decision-making on issues such as schools, education, and church service. The goal was to ban Magyarisation from the inner issues of the nation, not to contest Magyar dominance in Hungary. Autonomy was therefore understood in a positive, constructive fashion clearly limited to cultural rights – and not as territorial autonomy, which would have called forth the federalisation of the kingdom. There was no mention of a territorial re-construction of the kingdom in the *žiadosti.* From the perspective of the Magyars, however, the very concept 'autonomy' rang alarm bells; wrongfully identifying the Slovak claims for the very liberal values they demanded from Vienna with their own wishes for sovereignty, they interpreted 'autonomy' in the sense of territorial autonomy – which they were not. Yet, the Magyar elite predicted correctly that autonomous diets *per se* would at first have a decentralising effect and could become the beginning of demands for territorial autonomy, which run counter their general plan of hegemony in the kingdom. They wanted to pro-actively secure their hegemony and that included, deliberately or not, identifying the Slovak claims as the literal pick of the iceberg: the pick were the cultural rights, the iceberg was one of the most frightening concepts in Central European history at that time: the ghost of Panslavism. The numerical majority of the Slavs in the Danubian monarchy and their growing self-awareness raised considerable fears of the governing Austrian and Magyar elites that mighty Russia would in some way support her oppressed Slavic brothers in Central Europe.

Francisci's political goal in 1848 was identical to that of the national movement: he wholeheartedly supported the Mikuláš claims. In his memoirs of 1892, the seventy year old patriot defended the *žiadosti*:

"Since then [the revolution, add. JB], people often and repeatedly asked one question: Was it a rightful decision of the Slovaks to voluntarily take up arms for the emperor and the dynasty? Or should they have rather supported the Magyars against the emperor and the dynasty? ... I hold that the Slovaks had no choice. First: the Slovaks agreed with all Slavic branches [kmeňmi] in Austria-Hungary about supporting the emperor and, also, that such agreement had to continue. True, the Poles did not keep their word and left to support the Magyars. Second: the quiet, loyal and legal steps the Slovaks had chosen in the past to defend themselves against the arbitrariness and violence of the Magyars had not only been completely useless, but the Magyars persecuted the patriots, who were trying to protect the nation, with imprisonment and the gallows, whereupon the Slovaks had no other choice than to take up arms to protect the nation and defend their own lives. Third: The Slovaks could expect no benevolence from the Magyars whatever the constellation or consequences of the fight, given the hitherto experiences and the direction regional politics had taken. In earlier times as much as today, the Magyars are carrying on the policy of magyarisation, declaring it as vital national interest. Fourth: the Slovaks, had they been real or enforced supporters of the Magyars, would not have achieved their goals; neither the abolition of the Habsburg or any other dynasty, nor the lamenting about the Republic would have led to success, be it to the benefit of the Magyars, the Slovak nation, the Hungarian country or the Hungarian state. Also, because, very simply put, there was a decisive opponent of the revolution, the noble and powerful defender of legitimacy, Czar Nikolai I, who not only rejected the Hungarian crown offered to him, but would have never accepted those goals to be realised."[120]

So far Francisci's assessment of the events of 1848. The fact that he accepted a distinguished position in the Hungarian administration following the crushed revolution, bears, in my opinion, witness to the difficult economic situation the Slovaks faced – and not to a weakness of his character. In what way was he involved with the memorandum?

I. 1. 2.   The *Pešťbudínske vedomosti* and the memorandum of 1861

Francisci described the rewards[121] some of the Slovak volunteers received from the emperor. At the time of the dissolution of the troops, officers not subject to an imperial pension received a three months final salary, while the common soldiers received a month's final salary. The troops were dismissed with a festive ceremony followed by a festive lunch and grateful words by the emperor. Hodža was the only officer to be rewarded with the cross of honour, which he accepted. He and Hurban were re-habilitated and returned to their parishes in Mikuláš and Hlboko,

---

[120]   Francisci, "životopis", 221-222.
[121]   Francisci, "životopis", 229.

respectively. Štúr was offered a position at the legal court in Trenčín, which he rejected, succumbing to a desperate depression in the years to follow. He moved to Modra, where he supported the family of his deceased brother Karol and wrote his famous book *Das Slawenthum und die Welt der Zukunft* (*Slavdom and the world of the future*)[122], a history of the Central European Slavs from a Panslavist perspective. All three were put under police surveillance. After their dismissal, Francisci, Daxner and Bakuliný went back to their native Gemer diocese in the Banská Bystrica county, where Francisci hoped to find a position. He took on several temporary employments and got married, until he applied in 1853 for the position of secretary in the political administration of Upper Hungary.

> "... at the beginning of 1853, applications were invited to fill vacancies in all political institutions in the country. It was the first time I had applied for a position in the civil service. ... According ... to the decree of 7 July 1853, number 11.753/11.106G, issued by the Imperial Royal Governor of the region, Archduke Albrecht, with the highest accolade from his Imperial Royal Excellency of 21 June 1853, I was appointed Imperial Royal District Commissar, with an annual salary of one thousand two hundred ducats, and sent to the Comitatus of Velké Varadi to begin my service in Debrecen."[123]

Francisci served six years in Debrecen in Eastern Hungary, before he was sent in 1859 as council of the administration of the *comitatus* to the capital Velké Varadi and from there to Buda in 1861. The years from 1853 to 1861 are not dealt with in his memoirs, but a closer look at his letters reveals that he was more than ever committed to the national cause. In the few letters he sent out he corresponded with acquaintances and friends, made new contacts to promote the national cause, took care of advertising for journals and publications in Slovak and wrote bills. He even went into the trouble to collect money to pay for some debt Štúr had left behind. One has the strong impression that he was anxiously striving for the professional behaviour of the *narodovci,* thus the impeccable reputation of the movement. His tone was always polite, yet determined, and he spoke frankly and stuck with the issues. Whenever he met disagreement, he expressed his concerns in a explanatory fashion leaving room for the other's viewpoint and the possibility of a compromise. These features of his character would have made him an excellent diplomat.

---

[122]   Ľudovít Štúr, *Das Slawenthum und die Welt der Zukunft* (Bratislava: Šafaříková společnost, 1931). Adam Bžoch published the first complete version in Slovak: *Slovanstvo a Svět Budúcnosti* (Bratislava: Slovenský Institut Mezinárodnich Studii, 1993).

[123]   Francisci, "životopis", 260.

In the period of time from 1851 until February of 1861, there are only six letters, whereas his correspondence from February 1861 until July 1902 consists of two hundred and ninety seven letters[124]. The years under the neo-absolutist system, with its rigorous censorship, correspond with Francisci's sparse yet effective correspondence. The October diploma loosened the tight reins allowing for political opinions to be expressed more freely. For the Slovaks, so Francisci thought, the time was ripe to found a journal that would give the leading intellectuals a forum to debate about national politics and the national public to participate in these debates. He was the editor in chief of the *Pešťbudínske vedomosti* that, according to the historian František Bokeš, also set out to provide the Slovak nobility with the opportunity to voice their concerns[125]. Daxner, Ján Mallý-Dusarov and Mikuláš Štefan Ferienčík had a say about the publication programme, which they understood as pluralist, multi-faceted and working toward the benefit and prosperity of the national development[126]. The newspaper opposed centralism and the programme's main political orientation was threefolded: first, civil rights, in particular the equality of citizens in all its facets; second, the literary needs of the Slovak nation and third, the traditional importance of Slavic solidarity dealing with issues concerning the Slavic brother nations. Francisci received an editor's licence for the *Pešťbudínske vedomosti* without any problems

---

[124] Michal Eliáš, ed., *Listy Jána Francisciho 2 (1851-1902)* (Martin: Matica Slovenská, 2004).

[125] František Bokeš, "Slovenské národné hnutie a memorandum," in *Memorandum v slovenskej literature* (Bratislava: Slovenské vydavateľstvo krásnej literatúry, 1961), 7-63; 21.

[126] Bokeš, 21. Mallý-Dusarov (1829-1902) was a Slovak politician, Catholic priest and author of *Die Wahre Rechts-Kontinuität in der Ungarischen Frage* (1864; The true continuity of laws in the Hungarian question) and *Katolícky kostol je skutočne dom boží* (1889; The Catholic Church is the true House of God). After his graduation in Vienna in 1852, Dusarov served as priest in Banská Štiavnica and was appointed prefect of the Terezianum in Vienna in 1859. His clerical position of a canon led him to the dioceses in Bratislava in 1885 and Esztergom (Gran, Ostřihom) in 1888. He was an early contributor to the *Pešťbudínské vědomosti*, one of the first members of the *Slovenská nová škola* (Slovak New School) in literature and supported the programme of the National Party. Ferienčík (1825-1881) was a Slovak poet, playwright, editor and translator. He served in the volunteer army in 1848 to 1849, studied philosophy and theology in Levoča and law in Prešov. From 1870 he worked for the *Matica* in Martin. He was not a leading intellectual of the national movement, but became known for his editorial work in several newspapers. He introduced the feuilleton as a literary expression, in which he regularly commented on international politics.

and on 21 February 1861 he wrote to Pavol Dobšinský[127], asking him to advertise the new journal. The first issue of *his political newspaper* would be published between 15 and 19 March and henceforth appear twice weekly. Pavol should also spread the word that the programme would be published in a couple of days, so that the *narodovci* and the public could inform themselves about the contents of the upcoming issues[128]. Francisci exerted exact control about the newspaper's contents and finances. Rather impatiently, he wrote to his *braček Paľko* (little brother Pauli) only two months after the launch of the *vedomosti*, complaining about the lack of subscribers:

> "It is indeed ridiculous that our people are even afraid to subscribe to a Slovak newspaper. Had they so acted during the last ten years, when they couldn't move, for which there was no need anyway as our national politics passively abided to the situation, I wouldn't be wondering. But now, when one should only be waiting for the immediate consequences of the most powerful and widespread activities to show, now, when one must not miss the moment, such behaviour is beyond my comprehension. Are the Slovaks already so mortified that they lack the ability to understand when and how they have to work for their national life? Three millions – and so much cowardy! The Croats are expressing their closeness for us in newspapers, national meetings, at the diet and everywhere; the Serbs, Romanians and Ruthenians are identifying their interests with ours and are openly declaring their *inextricable solidarity* with us in front of the world – and we? Lord, forgive us our sins!"[129]

Francisci's angry remarks about the passivity of the population would not keep him from his continuous efforts. After having let off some steam, he participated in the meetings, preparing the national gathering in Turčianský Sv. Martin, which he would chair. Roughly two hundred persons from all parts of Slovakia came to Martin; most of the registered members were townspeople, representatives of the clergy, lower nobility and intellectuals[130]. Daxner, who had written the draft, was also responsible for the final version. The negotiations and discussions about the *okolie*, the Slovak county, soon divided the delegates into two groups: the first believed that the solution to the problem of how to establish the equality of the Slovaks and, of course, all nations in the kingdom, depended on the recognition of a Slovak county, a clearly

---

[127]   Dobšinský (1828-1885) was a close friend of Francisci and worked as folklorist, editor and poet.
[128]   Eliáš, 41; italics by JB.
[129]   Eliáš, 41; italics by JB.
[130]   Bokeš, 31.

deliniated space, in which the Slovaks as the dominant minority were granted the autonomy of their language and culture[131]. The majority of the delegates and the adherents of Francisci and Daxner favoured the *okolie*. The second group, among them Ján Palarík[132], preferred the exact opposite: To them, the *okolie* was not only a maximalistic claim that would anger the Magyars, but also an unnecessary one, since they believed that the recognition of language and cultural rights should be separated from political claims. The delegates finally adopted the demand for the *okolie*, yet the debate carried on for years and led to the foundation of the *nova škola slovenská (new Slovak school)*, a group within the movement that opted for cooperation with the Magyars.

Francisci stressed in his article *The Northern Slavs in Hungary, i.e. the Slovaks and Ruthenians and the regional Hungarian diet*[133] the importance of a co-operation of Ruthenians and Slovaks, who shared the Upper Hungarian region. They should, *with respect to the existing borders of the župy within the kingdom and the legal institutions of the region,* demand for a re-organisation of the borders of towns and villages according to the ethnic group that formed the majority. The areas, where the Slovaks settled, should be declared Slovak by re-drawing the borderlines of the major towns [hranice stolíc podľa národopisnej čiary sa vnovo porobili], the Ruthenian areas Ruthenian in analogy[134]. The language of administration in these newly designed areas would be Slovak, and Russian, Ukrainian respectively. In areas with a mixed population, which always was and is the *litmus test* of the democratic and minority-friendly attitude of a nation or nationality, both national groups should form one community and agree on a language of administration, which could be either Slovak or Russian. Francisci further addressed the electability to positions in administration and church institutions; only citizens of the nationality dominating the area should have access to these positions, to exclude the dominance of other nationalities in the local administration and, of course, to limit Magyar influence. He also suggested the building of a national parliament or diet [sbor alebo snem

---

[131]   Bokeš, 34.

[132]   For Palarík's arguments against the *okolie* see chapter II.

[133]   Francisci, "Severoslovania v Uhrách, t.j. Slováci a Rusíni, a krajinský snem uhorský," in *Memorandum v slovenskej literature* (Bratislava: Slovenské vydavateľstvo krásnej literatúry, 1961), 171-174; 171.

[134]   Francisci, "Severoslovania...", 171.

národný], which should be strictly non-political[135]. Such an institution would provide a forum for the nationalities to meet and discuss economic problems, church matters and educational issues. Also, the other minorities in Upper Hungary, the Germans in the Zips, the Hajduks, Jazygs, Kumans and the Saxons in Transylvania should be integrated into this democratic order that would grant the cultural and national autonomy of the Upper Hungarian population.

It seems, indeed, rather naïve of Francisci to insist on the a-political feature of such a parliament; equally naïve was his belief that the population in the mixed areas would, without any legal or constitutional bindings, get along so well as to agree upon the language of administration and the persons eligible to the administrative and church positions. Yet this naïvité was a result, or perhaps a relict of his romanticist thought that bureaucratic institutions could never express the spirit of the nation, the belief that his tolerance equalled the tolerance of the other nationalities. We think that he was either not aware of how immensely political his suggestions would sound to the Magyars, or then, deliberately declared the demands as a-political in order to let the suggestions sink into the minds of his readers. His article, however, is testament to his pragmatism and his willingness to establish equal treatment on the basic principle of a new internal order that originated in the very idea of equality of nations. In modern words, Francisci had written a draft, which could be called a blue-print for a minority policy that respected the multiethnic composition of the population.

> "Already since ancient times, there exists in our Hungarian legislation one acknowledged principle: *to protect the autonomy of a minority in regard to its personal interests*, so that it can defend and secure itself against the pressure of the majority."[136]

I. 2.   Political legitimating

I. 2. 1.   Pragmatism

We described Francisci above as talented pragmatician gifted with psychological skills that would have made him an excellent diplomat. These skills originated in his focus on reality, on what could be pragmatically achieved; they did not make him a

---

[135]   Francisci, "Severoslovania...", 173.
[136]   Francisci, "Severoslovania...", 173.

theoretician of the calibre of a Štúr or a Palacký. That is the reason for the shortness of this chapter.

Francisci did not analyse Hegelian thought and its importance for the nation, nor was he interested in publishing treatises about revolutionary theories or human rights. His national identity was language-based and his close relation with Štúr makes it very likely that he was influenced by the thought of the father of the Slovak language. But nowhere, not even in his memoirs, did he refer to Herder, Kollár or Hegel. A closer look at his articles published in his *Pešťbudínske vedomosti* confirm his matter-of-factness, as well as a lack of theoretical considerations. One of his biographers attested Francisci to be, indirectly, influenced by Rousseau and Hegel[137]; yet, we have not found any evidence in the selected texts, let alone quotes of the two philosophers or references to others. What we can say for certain is that Francisci received, considering the educational institutions in Upper Hungary at the time of his formation, a solid education in classics, law and theology that enabled him not only to correspond in Hungarian, Russian and Latin, but also to occupy high positions in the Hungarian administration. He certainly adhered to Kollár's reception of Herder, that is the romantic concept of *Slavic solidarity*. The *Zeitgeist* of 1848 that held high the Enlightenment's rationalism, the idea of the equality and freedom of all nations and individuals must have enforced him in his engagement. The *distinct Štúrovian blend* of romanticist pluralism, the claim for freedom and equality and Protestantism did not pose a contradiction. This peculiar combination of ideas could unfold owing to the political conditions of Hungary, since the Magyar reform period as the revivalist movement of Magyar nationhood and the Slovak awakening developed side by side in the early 19th century. In Francisci's eyes, theorising about Rousseau's concept of man's original goodness and freedom that is being corrupted by society, would have simply meant to egoistically endulge in theory while others went into great efforts. In the years after the *Ausgleich*, when it became quite clear that none of the Slovak demands were even close to fulfilment, on the contrary, when the nation had to face an increasingly oppressive Magyarisation, he did not despair. His wish to anchor the Slovak language deep into the minds of the population seems almost obsessive, yet makes perfect sense, given his definition of identity as language-based.

---

[137] Miroslav Pius, *Ján Francisci- Rimavský a vrcholná fáza slovenského národného obrodenia* (Bratislava: Národné osvetové centrum, 1997), 36-37.

He never ceased to keeping up the contacts to his colleagues, publishing and advertising. With the closing of the *Matica slovenská* he dealt as with previous political disappointments: after some anger and sadness expressed in his letters to friends he went back to work. It was most probably his stable psychological disposition that distinguished him from the sensitive and depressive Štúr, who was a great theoretician, but lacked the psychological resilience required for mastering hopeless situations.

Francisci did not refer to Hegel when explaining to Vladimir Ivanovič Lamanskii[138] the importance of a continuous Russian support of the Slovak cause; neither did he venture into the details of public international law to legitimate the national claims. His belief in the evangelical faith, but much more the pressing and unnerving every day issues of collecting money, writing bills, distributing news etc. prevented him from developing enthusiasm about socialist ideas. Constitutional questions were no issues to him, as it was, from his viewpoint, futile to theoretise about a situation that was far from being realisable. We can, however, say for sure that he was convinced of the rightfulness of *rational natural law*[139]. Natural law provided the nationalities in 19th century Central Europe with a powerful moral weapon: practically all demands a group could claim for – that is the entire 'catalogue' reaching from language rights, territorial autonomy, local self-government to sovereign independence – could be legitimised with natural law that, at the end of the day, derived its moral power from a transcendent realm inaccessible to the human mind. This realm was the sphere of the creation of mankind, which a Catholic bishop, a Lutheran pastor, a Muslim imam and a Jewish rabbi alike believed to be the lord. For an atheist, this realm was nature revealing itself in the advancements natural sciences research was achieving. Naturally, our description of this range of interpretation presents in itself a consequence of liberal thought; we

---

[138] Lamanskii (1833-1914) was a Russian professor for Slavic languages and literature at the university of St. Peterburg. He was a student of the famous philologist and Slavist Izmail Ivanovič Sreznevskii (1812-1880). He was a member of the Slavic Committee and co-founder of the Slavic literary fond that supported various individuals and groups in Central Europe and the Balkans with financial means. Lamanskii translated Štúr's *Slawenthum* into Russian and was involved with organising the congress of the Slavs of 1867 in Moscow; he published widely about literature and linguistics;
http://mirimen.com/co_beo/Lamanskij-Vladimir-Ivanovich-2009.html; accessed 5 June 2008.

[139] See our description of rational natural law in the introduction, X.6.

think, however, that although atheism could not be expressed freely in 19th century, it nevertheless existed. Natural law had the advantage that it could be used as a terrifyingly convincing moral argument by the most sincere Christian as well as the most cynic atheist. To use a metaphor: Natural law became the slingshot of the oppressed Davidian nationalities, who fought a hopeless battle against the positive law of the Goliaths, the ruling Austrians and Magyars. Positive law, in its expression of historic state rights, was being increasingly considered the law of the oppressor. In 1885, Francisci described the enforced Magyarisation that unfolded under the Tisza government in a letter to Lamanskii, asking him for financial support. Let us conclude this chapter in his own words:

> " The goal is clear: above all, not to allow any manifestation of our existence as nation, then to extinguish the nation's identity; to hinder the rising of a next generation of the intellectual elite and, lastly, to turn the Slovak nation into a tame mass of individuals, which is stupid; unconscious; incapable of thinking independently about national issues and even more so about human values; capable only of providing funds and shedding blood; against themselves and against their leaders; against their benefactors and – God forbid – future saviours. ... In this sad and dangerous situation, we are struggling stubbornly against this brutally organised and overwhelming power with the means we have at our disposal: the living word, the printed word – journals and brochures; the care of the intellectuals; travels to, exchange with, recognition and mutual support of the other equally oppressed nations, in particular the Ruthenians, Serbs and Romanians. And we are fighting the persecution that is unjustified, biased and financially unfair; violates citizens' rights [občianske práva sužujúcimi]; humiliates the people's feelings; countermines the successes in professional lives and economic progress; punishment and incarceration that destroy careers in all parts of public life."[140]

---

[140] Eliáš, 303, 304. Francisci's letter was signed, besides others, by Pavol Mudroň (1835-1914), a lawyer, *narodovec* and co-founder of the *Tatra banka*, the first Slovak bank.

Ján Francisci - life in brief

(Pseudonym: Rimavský, Slavoľub, Vratislav)

1 June 1822	Born in Hnúšta, district of Banská Bystrica. After primary education, he left for the Lutheran lyceum in Prešporok (Bratislava, Pressburg, Pozsony) and became involved with the romanticist-nationalist student circle inspired and led by Ľudovít Štúr (1815-1856).
1841	Beginning of his wide-ranging publishing activities. His translations, poetry and novels were published in the journals *Tatranka* and *Nitra*.
1844	Twenty-eight students left the lyceum in protest against Štúr's dismissal from his teaching position. Together with eleven others, Francisci left for the lyceum in Levoča. The event became known as "the exodus of the Štúrovci to Levoča". He was elected chairman of the group *Jednota* (*union*).
1844-46	Publication of his novel *Janko Podhorsky*, a modernised version of a popular Slovak fairy-tale from the 16th century.
1845	Publication of his collection of Slovak fairy-tales, *Slovenskej povesti*, in Levoča.
1847	Worked as lawyer in Prešov and served as assistant to the *podžupan* (vice-governor) Fay of the Gemer diocese.
1848	On 15 May, he participated in the national gathering at Liptovský Sv. Mikuláš and was appointed captain of the newly founded National Guards. He, Štefan Marko Daxner (1822-1892) and Michal Bakuliný (1819-1892), known as military leaders and "the three falcons" (*traja sokolia*), were supposed to agitate among the South Slavs in order to unite the Serbs and Croats against the Magyars. On 3 November, he was caught by the Magyar authorities and sentenced to death by Lajos Kossuth, but was later pardoned and given a three-year prison sentence. Freed by count Windischgrätz, Francisci joint the Slovak voluntary troops again.

1849	After the Magyar defeat he was appointed secretary of the commissariat of the district Zvolen.
1853	Appointed district secretary of the *comitatus* of Velké Varadi for the town Debrecen, in South-Eastern Hungary.
1859	Vice-chairman of the town Council of Velké Varadi.
1860	Vice-chairman of the town Council in Buda.
1861-1863	In Pest, Francisci founded *Pešťbudínské vedomosti (Budapest News)* and served as chief-editor of this first political newspaper in the Slovak language. Despite his high positions in the Hungarian administration, he kept to his Slovak identity and the national movement. In 1861, he chaired the national assembly in Turčiansky Sv. Martin and was crucially involved in the debate about the future of the nation's political claims, which resulted in the *memorandum of the Slovak nation*. His political and journalistic merits extended to the co-foundation of the national cultural organisation *Matica slovenská* in 1862.
1863	Appointed to the executive council of the Hungarian administration in Debrecen, Eastern Hungary.
1867	After the Austro-Hungarian *Ausgleich* (compromise), he worked in the k.k. financial administration and was active in Slovak cultural organisations, especially in editing journals and promoting literacy and education.
1889	Published his *Iskry ze zaviatéj pahräby* (Sparks of a dying fire) in Turčiansky Sv. Martin.
7 March 1905	Died in Turčiansky Sv. Martin.

Ján Palarík, © SNK

II.   Ján Palarík (1822 - 1870). Liberalism and Constitutionalism[141]

II. 1.   Political goals

II. 1. 1.   With civil rights toward a federation

Palarík's political goal was the spreading and anchoring of liberal ideas that would lead to a federative status of the kingdom's nationalities. Favouring a *Slovak-Magyar co-operation*, he held that the Slovaks should first educate themselves in the theory and practise of liberalism. So prepared, they would be able to join the Magyars in their fight against Vienna. Then, at a later point in time, they could negotiate their status of equality and autonomy demands that he projected as the effective creation of a Hungarian federation. Sharing with the Magyar liberals the goal of the Hungarian constitutional state, he was, however, not aware how important the idea of homogeneity was, even to the moderate liberals. In his article *What can we expect from the Hungarian constitution for our nationality* [narodnosť] *and what, above all, do we need right now?*, he expressed his political goals in one sentence:

> "The constitution allows the freedom of the word, the freedom to spread one's beliefs, the freedom to issue a petition, the freedom to build a federation [spolkovitosti] and if we Slovaks use all this wisely *on our way to lawfulness*, we shall not perish."[142]

Palarík was familiar with the works of Thomas Hobbes (1588-1679) and Charles de Montesquieu (1689-1755)[143]. He did not actively participate in the 1848 Revolution, or in the gathering at Liptovský Sv. Mikuláš but was a most ardent defender of civil rights, and in particular, the right to free speech. To him, the fight for civil rights was the principal condition of patriotism. His various essays and articles dealt with liberal

---

[141] I published parts of this chapter in "Montesquieu in Upper Hungary? Ján Palarík's Slovak constitutionalism and its failure," in *Czech and Slovak Culture in International and Global Context* (Halama Publications: České Budějovice, 2008), 210-214.

[142] Ján Palarík, "Čo máme očakávat od konštitúcie uhorskej pre našu národnosť a čo nám teraz predovšetkým treba?" in *Memorandum v slovenskej literature* (Bratislava: Slovenské vydavateľstvo krásnej literatúry, 1961), 200-203; 201. The article was first published in *Priateľ školy a literatúry II,* (1860): 354-355; italics by JB.

[143] Mikuláš Gasparík, "Ján Palarík – bojovník za prava a reč ľudu," in *Za reč a práva ľudu: kultúrnopolitické články* (Bratislava: Slovenské vydavateľstvo krásnej literatúry, 1956), 7-24; Tibor Pichler, *Národovci a občania: o slovenskom politickom myšlení v 19. Storoči* (Bratislava: Věda, 1998), 77-95.

and democratising issues such as the distribution of church lands to the people, free elections of the clergy and autonomy of the seminaries. The Catholic clergy used to punish his rebellious disobedience and sharp critique with reprimands and once even imprisonment. He wrote in various genres including theological treatises, dramas and comedies to express his patriotic and anti-clerical views with excommunication as the sword of Damocles always hanging over his head. A quite unusual *narodovec*, he was deeply committed to the advancement of the nation's tolerance and freethinking.

Despite being born in the same year as Francisci, Palarík differed from the literary nationalism and romantic enthusiasm of the Štúr generation and their followers. Unlike the "immortal" Kollár, he stressed that *Slavonic reciprocity* had political aspects one should not deny. *Reciprocity* was of course a literary and cultural movement, but the fact that the Slavs in Central Europe and the Balkans lived under foreign rule, was turning the idea and movement into an increasingly political issue, which the congress of the Slavs of 1848 had demonstrated[144]. The adherents of *reciprocity*, the most prominent members were Kollár himself and Štúr, kept denying the movement's political aspects; this had led to Europe's fear of an alleged political Panslavism[145]. Russia, with her military might and absolutist system was deepening these fears with her verbal support of the Central European and Balkan Slavs. The exception of the all-Slavic *reciprocity* were the Poles non-Slavic Europe identified with as they called for a re-constitution of their sovereign state and were ardent adherents of civil rights. For Palarík, there was a simple way out of the "panic fear" of Panslavism:

> "Treat therefore the Slavs with justice [spravodlnosť] in order to protect the laws of civilisation; allow the Slavs their own national life and freedom and you won't have to fear our panslavism ... Panslavism is not the enemy of other nations and their freedom, but opposes the rule of their regimes that forced themselves on the Slavic nations. The direction of true panslavism is *truly liberal* [čisto liberálny]; as every regime, be it physically or morally imposed, represents an act of violence and subsequent injustice, oppression and enslavement, which have no place in the realm of true freedom!"[146]

His views on *reciprocity* differed from the majority of the national movement and he was rather isolated, owing to his suggestion how to achieve autonomy: it was feasible

---

[144] Palarík, "O vzájemnosti slovanskej. Úvahy politicko-literárne", *Lipa III*, (1864): 277-297; 287.
[145] Palarík, "O vzájemnosti...", 287.
[146] Palarík, "O vzájemnosti...", 297, italics by JB.

only in a co-operation with the Magyars, who had fought Vienna's centralism since their defeat in 1849. Should Hungarian and, with that, Slovak autonomy stand any chance of realisation, so Palarík thought, then Vienna had to be pressed to reforms. His pro-Magyar position provoked sharp criticism and even sharper polemics from the majority of the movement.

The most distinctive feature of his character was most probably his intellectual easiness in opposing any dogma and swimming against any current of thought he believed to be bereft of reason and true humanity, be it the Catholic clergy's vows of obedience or the national movement's demands for the *okolie*. Palarík's position was clear: he was a Slovak nationalist and therefore opposed Magyarisation. Language rights were one issue, but political rights were quite another matter. In his eyes, it was both unrealistic and illegal to pursue a status of autonomy regarding the Magyars as the main obstacle, since they had more political leverage in Vienna anyway. Also, Slovak political demands should be demanded with respect for the constitution, even if the constitution included illegal amendments. Since he conceived of Slovak autonomy as an issue to be negotiated with Buda and not Vienna, he disentangled the autonomy demands from the language and cultural rights – which was unthinkable for the majority of the national movement. All factions involved misunderstood him or wanted to misunderstand him: From the viewpoint of Vienna and the larger part of the Slovak national movement, Palarík supported the virulent Hungarian secession, thus was a potential traitor to both the empire and the Slovak cause. The ruling Magyars saw his engagement in the Slovak national movement as close to treason, since it was directed against Magyarisation. In this situation of loyalties that were polarised along national lines, his liberal constitutionalism did not make him any friends. His ideas and views were diametrically opposed to those of the majority of the national movement.

Palarík's strategy of supporting the Magyars and, at the same time, working to enhance Slovak national individuality was based on his rejection of Austria's conservative centralism. In his article *Na dorozumenie* (*Explaining my point of view*) he delivered an analysis of the consequences of the October diploma:

"My contribution, shared by many patriots and fellow citizens, suggested abstaining from any decision as long as the parliament and the king disagree over Hungary's rights in the Austrian Empire. Any decision would only give rise to new controversies and escalate the already tense relations between Slovaks and Hungarians. I wished that in these important

times the entire Hungarian kingdom would unanimously call for the historical state rights
of the Crown of St. Stephen thereby opposing the centralist German government. I had the
hope that the direct support of our common Hungarian fatherland would indirectly lead to a
strengthening of the *Czech and Polish federalists in the Imperial parliament* to such extent
that would allow them to win the majority of votes against the German *centralists.*" [147]

Palarík assessed the idea of the *okolie* in his ever-critical fashion:

"I am, however, firmly convinced that the idea of the autonomous district is comparable to
the picture of a baby in the womb of an immature mother, who is dying in premature and
painful labor. I did not fight the call for the district because of considerations about the
territorial and political integrity of Hungary that a separation would threaten. Since all
regions and lands of Hungary are subject to the Imperial constitution and the government in
Buda, our debates on national rights should therefore not focus on negotiations about
territorial divisions. My severe doubts are further based on my reflections that the call for
an autonomous district would not only destroy the much needed political harmony and
unanimity of the nationalities in this region, but would also be a contradiction of our
common goals of liberty and nationhood, which would be to the benefit of the German
centralists."[148]

The Slovaks shared with the Magyars the goals of liberty and nationhood, which
demanded unity against Vienna, as the empire's centre was primarily committed to
its own maintenance. A united Slovak support of Hungary's claims for autonomy
would bring results in due time –supporting Vienna most certainly would not. In his
efforts to convince the majority of the national movement, Palarík was prepared to
accept the *status quo*. The only option he saw was to postpone the claim for the
okolie:

"Therefore, it cannot be a matter of indifference to the Slovak people, whether the
Hungarian or the centralist-German party wins [in the parliament, add. JB]. The Slovak
nation should not hold to a neutral stand, but join the Hungarians, although they, for the
time being, might refuse the establishment of the "Slovak county". Yet, if the "county" is
really the goal of our national aspirations, then the constitutional way backed by the explicit
solidarity of all oppressed nations is the swiftest way to achieve it. This possibility does not
exist in the centralist-German system."[149]

The *okolie* and the Slovak cultural rights should be addressed separately, under usage
of all possible legal means in the local and regional diets. For Palarík, this was less a

---

[147] Palarík, "Na dorozumenie," in *Za reč...*, 76-83; published first in: *Priateľ školy a literatúry III*,
        č. 35, 1861. All English quotes in this chapter refer to my translation in *Preparing liberty*, 115-
        123, 116-117.
[148] Baer, *Preparing Liberty*, 117.
[149] Baer, *Preparing Liberty*, 120.

struggle on two fronts than a question of applying moderation and focussing on the right solution. Radical claims were not feasible, and the Slovaks would gain nothing by trying to threaten the Magyars with loyalty to Vienna. On the contrary: standing against their only ally powerful enough to urge Vienna to reforms, the Slovaks would only bereave themselves of the single chance to have a future say in the kingdom. Palarík had learnt the lesson of 1848:

> "The Slovaks know very well that if Hungary loses, so do they and everybody will have to live under centralist German rule. But what does it count! The leaders of the Slovak nation look farther than their nose! In Austria's centralisation they see the salvation of the Slovak nation. Already in 1850, they had fought against the federalists in favour of the centralisation, particularly against *Havlíček* in the *Vienna daily (Viedensky denník)* and minor brochures. They supported Vienna's centralist system by, at least indirectly, fighting for 'the patent' and now they expect it to be a guarantee for the 'Slovak county'!"[150]

He failed, however, to have learnt from the political rationale of the Magyar state theory and its unfortunate prospects for the nationalities. Correct in his assessment that the Magyars presented the most significant challenge to the empire, he overestimated their willingness to negotiations with the nationalities. We think that Palarík, due to his philosophical training and personal acquaintances with Hungarian liberals, failed to see the importance of the ideological goal of a homogeneous Hungarian state.

> "These reflections given, I had to return the attack by the *Hungarian Country* that was not only directed against my liberal views, but also based on the failure to properly understand my political functions. My intention was to protect myself, not to hurt anybody, let alone to compromise the national cause I have dedicated my life to. So far, only the Slovak public knows that my national activities have taken a political course that is different from the gentlemen *Hodža, Hurban, Dobrianskij, Francisci,* and others, albeit I respect their merits. I appreciate their viewpoints too, but in regard of the current political constellation I have nothing in common with them, for their opinions are the very opposite of mine."[151]

Insisting on backing the constitution, he defended his right to have a different opinion in national affairs:

> "My point stands in direct opposition to the *national leaders,* but nobody has the right to question my love and devotion for the nation. Nobody should call me 'traitor' and 'maďarón' as long as my acts speak for me."[152]

---

[150]   Baer, *Preparing Liberty,* 122.
[151]   Baer, *Preparing Liberty,* 120-121.
[152]   Baer, *Preparing Liberty,* 123.

In 1868, two years before his untimely death and one year after the *Ausgleich*, Palarík still believed that a federation in the kingdom, the recognition of the Slovaks as the state-constituent nationality and hence the *okolie* was possible. But 1868 was also the year of the adoption of the nationality laws. Now even more than ever, so Palarík must have thought, the nation should co-operate with the Magyars to achieve their goals – which had ceased to be common ones as the Magyars had achieved their autonomy with the *Ausgleich* and started to build their state to their liking, which did not include negotiations with the nationalities. Palarík, however, ignored this crucial fact, clinging desperately, so it seems to us, to his goal of a Hungarian federation. In his article *Nová škola*[153], he even spoke of Palacký's draft federation of 1848 as still being a political option in the years 1861 to 1865, reproaching the members of the *stará škola* their support of minister Schmerling! As a prominent member of the *nová škola slovenská*, a minority within the movement that favoured co-operation with the Magyars, he defended their viewpoints against the polemics of the *stará škola* in their new organ *Slovenské Noviny*. Stressing the importance of free speech and pluralism, he rejected the offensive label of "he who serves two masters and wears two colours" the *Pešťbudínské vedomosti* had recently called their group[154]. Since the memorandum of 1861, they and Palarík were convinced that the political direction of the *stará škola,* which supported the Austrian empire in the hope that this loyalty would bring them autonomy, was wrong. The recent polemics against them only demonstrated that the members of the *stará škola* lacked political realism as they refused to politically engage here at home – *tu doma*[155]. Focussing on the impossible, the *okolie*, they kept signalling Vienna their loyalty, ignoring the fact that she was not at all thinking of providing the Slovak nation – nor any other save for the Magyars – with a status of equality. The adherents of the *nová škola*, by contrast, had already given up their belief and trust in Vienna in the era of Bach's neo-Absolutism. Austria

---

[153]   Ján N. J. Bobula founded the *Slovenské Noviny* in 1868. The newspaper of the *stará škola* was the *Pešťbudínské vedomosti* Francisci had founded. Very informative on the *nová škola slovenská* is Luboš Kacírek, *Nová škola slovenská a jej snahy o modernizáciu slovenskej spoločnosti* (Bratislava: SAV, 2007). An excellent analysis provides Bohus Kostický, *Nová škola slovenská* (Bratislava: SAV, 1959). Recommendable is further Belo Polla, ed. *Matica slovenska a narodnostna otazka* (Martin: Matica slovenská, 1997). I thank Roman Holec for these suggestions.

[154]   Palarík, "Nová škola," *Slovenské Noviny I*, č. 36, 24. 3. 1868, 1.

[155]   Palarík, "Nová škola", 1.

was simply not interested in the equality of her nations, as her main goal was to maintain her centralistically governed empire controlled by the German nation[156]. The only successful nation were the Magyars, who had achieved their demands:

"The dualistic system of 1867, constructed by Austria, confirmed us once more in our views ... already in 1861 we had recommended the nation to adopt the viewpoint of the Hungarian state ... and stop being strung along by Austrian-German ministers, who used the Slovaks as pure instrument for their non-Slavic goals ... to work with united forces and legal means here at home; not to expect redemption from unreliable allies and helpers in Vienna..."[157]

The members of the *stará škola* should cease to behave more Austrian than the Austrians themselves, since it was utter nonsense to believe that Austria would reverse the dualistic system by establishing the *okolie*. The Slovaks would achieve equality and liberty only if the nation was united in their struggle here at home in the Hungarian state.

"We want the equality of nations and a federation of the Hungarian nations ..."[158]

Palarík concluded his article stressing that the only difference between the two schools were their views about the *okolie*; the nation would, however, benefit much more if the two groups joined forces and focussed on what laid within their political grasp. They should engage here and now to secure the usage of the Slovak language in the municipal legislation and administration, as well as those in primary and higher education. These issues were as important as the self-government [samospráva] in the administration and the education of the youth[159]. Once these basic goals were achieved, they could then start to fight for the equality status. But if they failed to reach these fundamental demands, any engagement for the *okolie*, be it in Vienna or Budapest, would be futile. It would further befit the Slovaks to exercise a basic and general tolerance toward different opinions. As important as their national cause was, the existing lack of pluralism was a serious flaw. Addressing the *stará škola*, he ended with an expression that was so typical for his liberalism:

---

[156] In analogy to the usage 'Hungary' for the political building and 'Magyar' for the ethnos, Palarík used 'German' for the Austrian nation and referred to 'Austria' in a political-constitutional-ideological meaning.

[157] Palarík, "Nová škola", 1.

[158] Palarík, "Nová škola", 1.

[159] Palarík, "Nová škola", 2.

"But, please, don't immediately dismiss any differing views as treason of the nation, stop acting as if you were the pope's nation and every word of yours dogma. We believe in dogmata only in religious affairs, in the realm of politics, however, we want to have freedom of thought and opinion."[160]

II. 2.   Political legitimating

II. 2. 1.   Montesquieu or the spirit of *The spirit of the laws*

"O you dear Austrian dualism! How terribly astonished would the immortal Montesquieu in heaven be, who said: if a state throws away the fundamental sense of it's being, its status shall worsen. What other fundamental sense of a state is there than the law of its unity, the sense of its appearance?"[161]

In his last newspaper articles in the years 1868 and 1869, Palárik critisised the *Ausgleich* and its consequences for Hungary. One cannot help but be astonished by these unexpected statements, since he had in the past repeatedly spoken out for a Hungarian federation, whose creation would have been easier within the constitutional framework of dualism, without the Austrians mingling into Hungarian affairs, to put it bluntly. One wonders whether Palárik, who time and again condemned Austrian centralism, changed his views to the exact opposite claiming for the unity of the Austrian empire? What was wrong with dualism?

Since his early years as a Catholic priest, when he had criticised the clergy's abuse of power and engaged for a church that should be closer to the word of the lord, Palárik's thought did not undergo any significant changes, nor did he change his views in his last two years. Since the national meeting in Martin, however, his publications focussed exclusively on politics. 1861 was a key year for his political thought and writing – and with that his conviction that only constitutionalism and liberalism would present a solution for Hungary. It seems that he resigned in 1869 when he went into some lengths to condemn the national egoism of the Magyars[162]. But what exactly did he understand under constitutionalism? This is one of the most interesting questions in Palárik's thought.

---

[160]   Palárik, "Nová škola", 2.
[161]   Palárik, "Účel Austrije pod centralismom a dualismom," *Slovenské Noviny I*, č. 42, 7. 4. 1868, 2.
[162]   Palárik, "Národnie sobectvo zkáza národa," *Slovenské Noviny II*, č. 54, 20. 5. 1869, 1.

Before we try to delve into the depths of his thought, let us now make a brief excursion into the political thought of Charles de Montesquieu (1689-1755). This will allow us to assess Palarík's reception of the French philosopher more precisely.

Charles de Montesquieu published *The Spirit of the Laws* in 1748. The nature of man depends on external factors such as climate and geographical particularities that create and shape a social group's religion, customs, *mores* (customs, *Sitten*) and, most importantly, a body of laws. According to Montesquieu, the first law of nature is peace, since man alone feels his own weakness, which makes him flee others; the second is self-preservation or seeking nourishment; the third procreational pleasure, and the fourth the desire to live in society[163]. This fourth desire leads man to join his fellow men – and here begins the state of law (*Gesellschaftszustand*) that philosophers before him, mainly Thomas Hobbes and John Locke, conceived of as the decisive break with the state of nature (*Naturzustand*) required for the beginnings of society, justice and public morals. Montesquieu was not as clear about this important transition from the state of nature to the state of law. He immediately went into defining the political institutes and institutions that would make societal life feasible, adding an inter-national element. In his view, individuals live in different groups, read societies. Feeling their united strength, they seek to protect their group against other groups by establishing laws. These positive laws – as laws set by men – are embodied in the Right of Nations or international law. Montesquieu further distinguished *political rights* from *civil rights*: the first are laws that define the relationship of the governed and the governing, while the latter concern the laws that regulate the relationships of the citizens themselves[164]. Drawing on these positive laws, which derive from human reason, Montesquieu then distinguished between governments and their inherent principles:

> "... virtue, in a republic, is the love of one's country, that is, the love of equality. It is not a moral, nor a Christian, but a political virtue; and it is the spring which sets the republican government in motion, as honour is the spring which gives motion to monarchy."[165]

---

163 Montesquieu, *The Spirit of the Laws* (Cambridge: Cambridge University Press, 1989), book 1, chapt. 2, 6-7.
164 Montesquieu, book 1, chapt. 3, 7.
165 Montesquieu, Author's foreword, xliii.

Every government is based on a principle or a motivating force, or, to express it in modern terms, the socio-cultural disposition of the individuals. Three principal government types deriving from the nature of man determine political rule:

> "...republican government is that in which the people as a body, or only a part of the people, have sovereign power; monarchical government is that in which one alone governs, but by fixed and established laws; whereas, in despotic government, one alone, without law and without rule, draws everything along by his will and his caprices."[166]

A republic (Montesquieu used the terms "republic" and "democracy" interchangeably) is based on the principle of *virtue* (*vertu politique, l'amour de l'égalité, des lois et de la patrie*); an aristocracy on *honour* (*l'honneur*) and a despotic regime on *fear (la crainte)*. Disregarding the despotic regime as a form of government to be found in non-European states such as China, Japan, Muscovy, in short, as befitting to Asian rule, Montesquieu further elaborated on positive laws, which he separated into *legislative, executive and judiciary powers*. His examination of the relationship of the three powers in a republic made him a principal political philosopher of modern democracy:

> "When legislative power is united with executive power in a single person or in a single body of the magistracy, there is no liberty, because one can fear that the same monarch or senate that makes tyrannical laws will execute them tyrannically. Nor is there liberty if the power of judging is not separate from legislative power and from executive power. If it were joined to legislative power, the power over the life and liberty of the citizens would be arbitrary, for the judge would be the legislator. If it were joined to executive power, the judge could have the force of an oppressor. All would be lost if the same man or the same body of principal men, either of nobles, or of the people, exercised these three powers: that of making the laws, that of executing public resolutions, and that of judging the crimes or the disputes of individuals."[167]

According to Montesquieu, the best form of government is not necessarily a republic. The separation of powers can be established in a monarchy, where a prince and nobles rule according to the principle of honour. Most kingdoms in his time, so Montesquieu observed, were moderate, with the prince exerting legislative and executive power. A monarchical constitution, however, can delegate a part of the discussion about new laws to the assemblies of the nobles and the people, who each have their chosen representatives.

---

[166]   Montesquieu, book 2, chapt. 1, 10.
[167]   Montesquieu, book 11, chapt. 6, 157.

So far our brief excursion to Montesquieu's thought. Now, in what issues did Palarík take up Montesquieu's ideas? What form of governmental power, what type of constitution did he prefer? Did he opt for a republican or a monarchical constitution?

Palarík often referred to his "immortal Montesquieu" – the highest accolade he gave – in his articles on national politics, which he understood as Slovak-Hungarian politics. Yet, he abstained from detailed statements about what a future Hungarian constitution should entail. He did not comment on the separation of powers nor on any of the three constitutional types. We have not found any clear description nor suggestions regarding constitutional design save for his comments on the draft law on the rights of the nationalities of 1861[168]. In this article, he listed a Slovak translation of selected points of the Hungarian draft bill he considered important and followed with his critique point for point. The draft was divided into sections A to D: A determined the rights of the citizens of the Hungarian nationalities and the corporations; B entailed different points of the legislation; C included issues on the level of the state, while D contained stipulations about the Hungarian diet. It is very interesting to read Palarík's critique of the single points, as his argumentation here was almost identical to the traditional ones of the national movement: he wholeheartedly – in some points in a sarcastic tone – defended the language and cultural rights of the nationalities. He protested first against the definition of the concept 'nation': The draft bill, so Palarík, conceived of the Hungarian populace as a political nation[169]. This political nation consisted of Magyars, Slovaks, Romanians, Serbs, Ruthenians and Germans. The citizens were granted *civil liberties* [občanská sloboda] meaning civil rights that extended to individuals, but the *national liberties* [národná sloboda] that should determine collective or group rights were missing. According to the draft law, the national groups had no right to engage for collective interests, needs and opinions, in brief, for any actions constituting them as a group; it was therefore necessary to establish a constitutionally granted "permanent national commission" [permanentný výbor národní, zákonom potvrdený], which would deal

---

[168] Palarík, "Návrh zákona o rovnoprávnosti národov v Uhrach, od vätšiny výboru snemového vypracovaný," *Priateľ školy a literatury III*, č. 35, (1861): 269-272.

[169] Palarík, "Návrh zákona…", 271.

with their matters[170]. Otherwise, the claims of the groups would be met only on paper and according to the whim of the administrator in charge. On section A he sharply commented that the deliberate lack of clarity of formulation would only benefit the Magyars. The unclear wording of what the language of communication was left much room for different interpretations, which, in turn, would leave the final decision in any case to those in power. The draft bill stipulated, among other points, that

> "1. Every citizen has, under the guarantee of the constitution, the right to use his mother tongue when addressing the state administration.
>
> 2. The administrative bodies have the duty to accept only documents that are written in the language of communication of the community or the language in use in the region.
>
> (3. ...)
>
> 4. The language of the administration of a community determines the assembly of the community; it also includes that upon claims by the minorities their languages have to be used in the dealings with the administrative bodies."[171]

Palárik pointed his finger, or rather his acrimonious pen, on the very concepts that caused the lack of clarity: 'individual' [jednotlivec], 'community' [obec] and 'minority' [menšina, minorita]:

> "1. Will a Magyar-loving individual [jednotlivec maďaronský], who is a Slovak by birth and somewhere learnt to speak Hungarian, have the right to bother the Slovak community with his Hungarian letters? Will the community's administrative bodies have to learn Hungarian because of one individual?
>
> 2. Without any doubt, one has to understand this stipulation in the sense that the administration has to accept Slovak letters that are being sent from a Slovak community, and that letters in the Slovak language have to address only Slovak-speaking towns. But what about a mixed town such as, for example, Pest that has, amongst other nationalities, a large number of Slovak inhabitants? Can a Slovak in a town with mixed population, where the administrative language is not Slovak, address the authorities with a Slovak letter?
>
> (3. ...)
>
> 4. The term 'minority' must not be understood as just a couple of magyarloving individuals, but as the majority of the inhabitants of a mixed community [vätši počet obyvateľov miešanej obce]."[172]

Section D of the draft bill contained stipulations regarding the Hungarian diet; the assembly's sessions and negotiations were to be held strictly in Hungarian. Palárik

---

[170]   Palárik, "Návrh zákona...", 271.
[171]   Palárik, "Návrh zákona...", 270.
[172]   Palárik, "Návrh zákona...", 271.

did not argue this point, on the contrary, he deemed it necessary, in an unusually swift manner, to comment – or rather brush over – the point, saying that the diet should restrict the languages of the kingdom[173]. The diet should use its institutional legitimacy to prevent further languages to rise, whose speakers would claim for the status of language of communication on the highest political level. Here, we can see a fascinating point in his argumentation that we interpret as a sign of his political pragmatism rather than intellectual elitism: Close to Palacký's argumentation in *Idea státu Rakouského* (*The idea of the Austrian state*)[174], Palarík was well aware that the multi-lingual composition of the Hungarian populace would unleash a wave of claims for the usage of the nationalities' languages in the diet, once the law on the equality of nations was adopted. A diet where five to six languages enjoyed equal status would simply not function. In establishing of a future federation and its constitution, Palarík favoured Hungarian as the only language of communication in the diet. This was as much a pragmatic as an elitist argument as it involved the educational level of the future delegates: for now, it excluded peasants and workers, who spoke only their vernacular. Individuals with a university degree and / or of noble descent would speak Hungarian as the political language used in the national assembly and the administrative institutions in the kingdom's capital. This involved the thin strata of the higher bourgeoisie and the nobility, but excluded the majority of the nationalities' populace living in the countryside.

We therefore tend to interpret Palarík's choice of constitution as of *transitional character*: The moment a Hungarian federation came into being, the nationalities' elites would be motivated by the principle of honour, due to their social ranking, and, at the same time, by that of equality, due to their political goals. Yet, honour and equality cannot be embodied in one constitution, according to Montesquieu. We therefore think that Palarík imagined an aristocratic constitution that would establish the equality of the nationalities as a first step. Once the federation was in power and working and the equality of educational institutions of the nationalities granted, the lower bourgeoisie, peasants and workers would be enjoying education toward political participation – besides the unrestraint usage of their mother tongue in their regional and local institutions. Then, in this second phase, the time would have come

---

[173] Palarík, "Návrh zákona...", 272.
[174] Baer, *Preparing liberty*, 93-111; 108-109.

to establish a Hungarian republican constitution, whose basic principle was the virtue of her citizens, embodied in the love of equality. These are but interpretations we have drawn from Palarík's statements, yet his critique of the clergy's abuse of power and his demands for civil rights point, in our opinion, to a republican constitution, which would be the last phase of the constitutional process. The way toward a Hungarian republican constitution would be long and stony, but it would be the only option they had – here at home. Furthermore, the constitutional process or, rather, the development of a constitutional process that included all nationalities, would represent the only legitimate way to establish governmental rule based on the will of the people. We think that Palarík saw the true equality of the national groups in Hungary as the first step toward the final goal of equality among all citizens; the first was a necessary phase to be overcome before the latter could begin. In other words: The constitutional process starting with the establishment of the federation was *a transition from an aristocratic to a republican constitution*. Naturally, we cannot claim that Palarík had the final goal of a Hungarian multi-ethnic democracy in mind; we do not think that he anticipated the future to such an extent. Yet, we can deduce from his statements, that such a republic would present the final outcome of the constitutional process he so desperately wanted to initiate.

Most fascinating in his thought is further the dichotomy of the concepts 'nation' in the sense of 'ethnic group' or 'nationality' and 'political nation': *Palarík adhered to both Montesquieu and Herder creating a philosophical contradiction.* This contradiction or dichotomy mirrored the relation of positive law versus natural law or the mutually excluding standpoints of the Magyars and Slovaks regarding autonomy. His allegiance was two-fold: first, as a citizen of the Hungarian state, which meant positive laws extended to the political nation and, second, as a Slovak, which meant to defend the natural law of equality of nations. This dichotomy would not have evolved if the Magyars had kept strictly to their state theory and granted the nationalities their cultural and language rights – which they could not, since the positive law of the Hungarian state theory had enmeshed with the liberal values of the revolution that were setting forth political homogeneity the Magyars understood also in ethno-national terms. The nationalities, on the other hand, could not accept that they were being reduced to mere political citizens with no guarantee of the collective rights that they considered the basis of their identity. The arguments of positive law were increasingly realised by measures that infringed on natural law, causing a climate that both the Magyar and the nationalities' elites could no longer de-escalate.

His article *For our unanimity, Hungarian compatriots!*[175] illustrates the high hopes he held for the negotiations on the February patent in 1861; this article appeared before the draft law on the nationalities he had criticised so sharply that year. Palarík's loyalty to Hungary was unquestioned, when he called his fellow citizens to unanimously stand behind "our common mother, our dear Hungarian country"[176]. He referred to the revolution as a "bloody war" and the Bach years as "the shared yoke" they had brought on themselves as a consequence of their disunity; they would all live better under the "motherly care of the constitutional rights and liberties" than under "the iron arms of administrative arbitrariness of a foreign stepmother"[177]. The common goal of the Hungarian citizens would now be to achieve the "guarantee of the integrity and independence of the Hungarian constitution" [garancie, t.j. ubezpečenia celosti, nerozlučnosti a samostatnosti konštitucionalnej našej vlasti uhorskej][178]. The "great work of the political rebirth" [veliké dielo politického znovuzrodenia] of their country would happen only if all nationalities, the Magyars, Slovaks, Croats, Serbs and Romanians could work together like the children of one mother[179]. Under the rule of the Saint Steven, Slovaks and Magyars had founded the state; therefore, they were the eldest brothers and allies of the Magyars, in good and bad times. For eight hundred years, they had shared a common land and a history full of victories and pains and now had the common goal of establishing the constitutional and national liberties under the egis of the crown of Saint Steven. Palarík concluded his article with a quote of baron Jozef Eötvös, to whom he referred as "our famous patriot and former minister of enlightenment, who showed us how to deal with the just and decent demands and needs of the various Hungarian nationalities."[180] His loyalty to Hungary, his constitutionalism and life-long engagement for liberal values would eventually experience a political blow, against which he reacted with the pen, but from which he would never fully recover.

---

[175]   Palarík, "Buďme svorní, krajania uhorskí!" *Priateľ ľudu I*, č. 1 (1861): 2-3.
[176]   Palarík, "Buďme svorní...", 2.
[177]   Palarík, "Buďme svorní...", 2.
[178]   Palarík, "Buďme svorní...", 2.
[179]   Palarík, "Buďme svorní...", 2.
[180]   Palarík, "Buďme svorní...", 2.

II. 2. 2.   Critique of the *Ausgleich*

Palárik must have sensed the dichotomy in his thought and, after the *Ausgleich*, he seemed to have found a way out of his intellectual *cul de sac of Montesquieu's constitutionalism and Herder's national individualism.* In one of his last articles, rhetorically brilliant, but politically already slightly unrealistic, he condemned the dualistic system. He was not alone, but not with a majority either: Hungarian radical liberals were very critical of the compromise, as they believed that the *Ausgleich* had actually cemented their relationship with Vienna – which it did. They wanted what Kossuth had projected and Vienna would never offer: the status of a sovereign Hungarian state with no ties whatsoever to Austria. Vienna was only willing to enter a compromise, which the moderate Magyar elite accepted. Palárik and the Magyar leftists now shared a new concept: the 'pure personal union' [čistá personálna unija]. 'Pure personal union' referred to a sovereign Hungarian state, whose ties to Austria would be reduced to the absolute minimum, a constitutional relict, so to speak, of their past common history: the personal union of the Austrian emperor being the Hungarian king. 'Pure personal union' became a key phrase in Palárik's last longer article titled *The goal of Austria under Centralism and Dualism*[181].

> "Montesquieu expressed in his world famous œuvre 'L'esprit des loix' this axiom: 'a state can change only in two ways: either his order [sriadenie] or constitution [ústava] enhances or it worsens. If it protects the fundamental conditions of its existence, it will advance, if it looses them, its constitution shall deteriorate.' I would add to this: if it disposed of its fundamental mistakes that are the main reason for its failure, it would advance, if it kept them, its order would decline."[182]

He applied Montesquieu's thought to the dualistic system, which he called "that deceiving achievement of Beust and Deák" [tohoto osúdneho diela Beust-Deákovho]; did the Austrian state improve with the *Ausgleich* or did it deteriorate?[183] For Palárik,

---

[181]   Palárik, "Účel Austrije pod centralismom a dualismom," *Slovenské Noviny I*, č. 39, 7. 4. 1868, 1.

[182]   Palárik, "Účel Austrije...," č. 38, 28. 3. 1868, 1.

[183]   Palárik, "Účel Austrije ...", 28. 3. 1868, 1. Friedrich Ferdinand duke of Beust (1809-1886) was the principal architect of the *Ausgleich* for the Austrians and an adversary to Bismarck's plans to create a German Empire without Austria. In 1867, the *Kaiser* appointed him foreign minister and then Imperial chancellor. Incapable of preventing Austria's extrication from the German *Reich*, Beust was dismissed in 1871 and appointed Austrian ambassador to Great Britain and France. He retired in 1882.

the answer was easy: Austria was worse off after the *Ausgleich* than before, because Beust's "hot German heart" [teplé nemecké srdce] had introduced to Austrian politics the danger of German cultural dominance. The *Ausgleich* only encouraged the Germanisation and German centralisation that deepened Austria's hitherto political mistakes – without a real understanding of the empire's constitutional traditions. Mocking Beust, who himself had apparently coined the saying of the "hot German heart" when appointed Austro-Hungarian foreign minister, Palarík stated in a sarcastic tone that a Prussian like Beust could not understand the *finesses* of Austrian politics:

> "Could he be capable of regenerating, on the basis of the historic rights of Austria's various countries, the commensurate federalism and equality of rights of the nations, which is the only possible, just and successful order in Austria that is in the common interest of the throne, the countries and the nations that constitute the Austrian empire?"[184]

Apart from the fact that the majority of the Magyar elite welcomed the compromise, which he certainly was aware of, Palarík continued with his, in modern terms, bashing of Beust. The German, who had a secret goal [tajný cieľ], had successfully and slyly convinced the naïve Deák that the *Ausgleich* benefitted both nations[185]. But Hungary actually lost more than she had gained. Palarík summed up this loss in four points. Firstly, Hungary did not have her own foreign ministry. Theoretically, Austria and Hungary shared the ministry of foreign affairs, where both states had equal say, but Austria *de facto* dominated foreign policy as the minister appointed was a German and the ministry located in Vienna. Secondly, Hungary did not have her own army. She participated in the Austro-Hungarian army that was in theory common, but, again, *de facto* dominated by the Austrians, who held the highest command. Thirdly, Hungary had to pay for the common ministries where she had no real say and fourthly, she had accepted to pay for a certain *quota* of Austria's debts, so that the neighbour could survive. In theory, Palarík continued, both states were surely equal and independent, but Vienna had the institutional and financial power of both states at her disposal. Hungary did not even have her own army to control her territory. Practically, Austria was building a German state with the help of the Hungarians and her main goal was to dominate the empire with the means that were

---

[184]   Palarík, "Účel Austrije ... ", 28. 3. 1868, 1.
[185]   Palarík, "Účel Austrije ... ", 28. 3. 1868, 1.

her fundamental mistakes mentioned above: cultural Germanisation and political centralisation. Palarík went to some lengths, quoting Hungarian newspapers and politicians critical of the *Ausgleich*. Dualism had encouraged the Austrians to centralise the empire; the nationalities living in the Austrian part had lost all hope of gaining equality and liberty. The historic rights of the Bohemian crown, Galicia, the Ruthenians, Poles and Slovenians were being ignored by Viennas's centralised rule. The dualistic system was established to "directly" [bezprostredne] subjugate the Magyars under Vienna's goals and "indirectly" [prostredne] the Slavs[186]. Hungary, unfortunately, was not willing to concede equality and autonomy to her nationalities, which were the fundamental rights of every nation. She would have to do just one thing to ascertain the loyalty of her nationalities, which would allow her to pursue her principal goal of sovereignty:

> "Give us Hungarian Slavs and Romanians what rightly belongs to us according to *natural law and the historic state rights*; declare the difficult but divine word of justice; ... guarantee all Hungarian nationalities equality with the Magyars ... put the brave Croats on their feet by acknowledging their 'triune kingdom' that belongs to the crown of Saint Steven: and we shall all then, as free and equal brothers, united in our love and loyalty to our Hungarian state, stand like solid stones of a castle wall – and the pure personal union becomes through that single act – a fait accompli."[187]

A "dualistic system in perfection" [dualism dokonálý] would then arise: both parts would each become federative states connected only by the sublime personality of the emperor, who governed in pure personal union, and their common interests[188]. The equality of all nationalities was the only option Hungary had; it was up to her to decide whether she would advance toward sovereignty or take a step back to absolutism. To strengthen his point, Palarík mentioned the historic state rights argument that did not apply to the Slovaks, as Slovakia had never been a crown land; we think that he deliberately used the state rights to stress Slovak equality with the Croats and the Romanians. He continued stating that the dualistic system had even aggravated the empire's internal order: in Palarík's view, the *Ausgleich* would become a financial burden both states could not effectively carry. Under centralism, the integrity of the Austrian state was at least existent, while dualism had made it a

---

[186]   Palarík, "Účel Austrije ... ", 31. 3. 1868, 1.
[187]   Palarík, "Účel Austrije ... ", 31. 3. 1868, 1; italics by JB.
[188]   Palarík, "Účel Austrije ... ", 31. 3. 1868, 1.

"state-cripple" that lacked legs to stand on and shoulders to defend itself[189]. The monstrum that emerged from dualism was neither one state nor two, but something in between. He concluded his article imploring his readers as well as the government:

> "Keep thinking and considering the matter as you wish: without complete equality of the nationalities, without a federative order in Hungary and the entire monarchy there will be no salvation! Otherwise we shall go back – to absolutism. And then what?"[190]

II. 2. 3. The rejection of natural law

Palarík seemed to have resigned only in the year before he died. In his last article *National selfishness damages the nation*[191], he made the comparison between the nation and the individual, which was a characteristic theorem of natural law theory. A selfish individual did not know what the love of the next meant; a nation, possessed by egoism, did not understand other nations' wishes for equality. He, who would not have feelings and a heart for foreigners, would end up lacking these for himself. A nation would perish if it did not extend to others the same rights its citizens were enjoying. The origins of hatred, laziness, injustice and finally disintegration lay in a nation's obsession with itself, as the history of ancient Rome and Sparta had demonstrated. The empires of the Mongols, Avars and Huns had perished for the same reasons[192]. The latest events regarding the election of the papal delegate of Hungary, so Palarík, showed clearly that the Magyars' national egoism would finally bring them down. He ended his brief article on a sad note:

> "In our days, nobody should try to reactivate national selfishness, not even driven by love for one's nation; it would only lighten the way toward one's grave."[193]

If Palarík fought until his last months for the equality of Hungary's nationalities, he did so in a philosophically fascinating way: His rejection of natural law from the area of politics was based on his admiration for Montesquieu's constitutionalism and his adherence to liberal values. A minor factor for his allegiance to the Hungarian state theory might have been his confession: as a Catholic, he did not experience Magyarisation in his own parishes, as the liturgical language of the Catholics was

---

[189] Palarík, "Účel Austrije ... ", 7. 4. 1868, 1.
[190] Palarík, "Účel Austrije ... ", 7. 4. 1868, 1.
[191] Palarík, "Národnie sobectvo zkáza národa," *Slovenské Noviny II*, č. 54, 20. 5. 1869, 1.
[192] Palarík, "Národnie sobectvo... ", 1.
[193] Palarík, "Národnie sobectvo... ", 1.

Latin, which was not subject to assimilation. One might assume that he was simply unaware of the specific discriminations the Protestants were enduring in their church affairs. However, he strictly separated language and cultural rights from political rights, assigning his modest acceptance of natural law to the former, while he conceived of the latter as an issue of positive law. To him, Slovak identity was a natural thing the lord had extended to all nations. Therefore, all nations should be equal in the expression of their true self. He certainly considered Herder's romanticist pluralism as a right, *but not as a political right*. He accepted natural law as the theory that justified the existence of various nations and their equality in front of the lord, or the highest being, or a metaphysical horizon. But, and this is the point where he most differed from the members of the *stará škola*, it was not legitimate to use natural law to claim for political rights. He considered politics as the realm of positive law, the law made and agreed upon by men. On earth, men should decide about their rights and the way their political order and their institutions should be established. If natural law should grant cultural and language rights, positive law, at its best a federative constitution, should acknowledge civil rights.

In Palarík's mind, which was diametrically opposed to the thought of the *stará škola,* natural law became an instrument to demand equality only because of a misinterpretation of the basic concept of equality. In its original meaning, equality was understood as the equality of men because of their common gift of reason. Reason made men and therefore nations equal in front of nature or the lord or a metaphysical horizon. To deliberately merge natural law with positive law, to interpret natural equality with political equality was, to say the least, premature. In keeping to the *divide between natural and positive law*, he was old-fashioned and elitist; his unusual views, however, made him one of Slovakia's most daring and courageous thinkers. Political rights belonged to the realm of positive law; they had to be negotiated and agreed upon, hopefully by representatives that were well-educated and morally superior, or so he must have thought. Natural law played an immensely important role in his nation's awakening and identity, but these were cultural and educational matters, which had nothing to do with political order or political rights. But he failed to acknowledge one crucial fact: *cultural and language rights that could not be enjoyed would turn into political demands*. The right to use one's language openly was an empty right that existed only on paper, if the language *de facto* could not be lived, spoken, expressed. Such a right was nothing, neither guarantee nor acknowledgment. The fact that Palarík did not share this point with the national movement must have provoked the almost hateful comments about his treason of the nation.

In his strict separation of natural and political equality, of Herder and Montesquieu, Palarík made a choice that affected him badly. Rather short-sightedly, which, we hold, is unusual for a person of his accomplishment, he supported the Magyar liberals, who in the late 1860s were still influenced by the moderates Deák and Eötvös. He failed to see that the Magyars elites' wish for homogeneity and hegemony affected the nationalities' cultural rights. Yet, the moderate Deák had negotiated the *Ausgleich*, which *de iure* and *de facto* provided the Magyars with the constitutionally granted power to assimilate Hungary's national groups. But Palarík was perhaps not willing or capable to reconsider his views. He joined the Magyar radicals that criticised the compromise – and were not successful.

Palarík's political goals were the autonomy of Hungary, connected to Austria only by the pure personal union, a federation of all nationalities and, for the time being, a monarchical constitution, which would pave the way toward a republic. At the end of the day, we think, he would have spoken out for a Hungarian multi-ethnic democracy, in which all citizens would enjoy civil rights that were not restricted to the individual, but included collective rights. We could say further that he did not push the issue of the *okolie*, as the *Zeitgeist*, and above all, the Slovaks themselves were not ready. How to proceed towards local self-government with citizens that had no idea of liberal values such as pluralism and tolerance? Most probably, he would have fought to diminish the influence of the Catholic Church by appealing to the enlightened nature and liberal spirit of the new Hungarian state. Palarík dreamt of a Hungarian federation and chose constitutionalism as his instrument. In his hopes for a federation granting equal status to all national entities he was very close to Palacký, whose *Austroslavism* promoted loyalty to Vienna against the Magyar liberals in the 1848 revolution.

Ján Palarík – life in brief

27 April 1822   Born in Rakova in the Kysuče region. He studied theology, languages, literature and philosophy at the Catholic seminaries at Esztergom (Gran, Ostřihom), Pressburg and Trnava. Among his favourite philosophers were Charles de Montesquieu, Adam Smith and Thomas Hobbes. Karel Havlíček's thoughts about Russian autocracy, Austrian foreign policy and his anti-clericalism further influenced and prepared him for his involvement in the Slovak national movement.

1847   Appointed as Catholic priest and kaplan in Starý Tekov. He did not actively participate in the 1848 Revolution, but chose the intellectual path to contribute to the liberation of the nation. He was very critical of the Catholic clergy, who exercised faith in a self-supporting fashion, rather than caring for the people.

1850   He founded the religious journals *Cyril and Method* and *Catholic News*.

1851   Because his various essays and articles dealt with issues such as corruption among the clergy, distribution of church lands to the people, free elections of the clergy and autonomy of the seminaries, the church punished him for his insubordination with three weeks' imprisonment at the Franciscan monastery in Esztergom. After a short stay in Banská Štiavnica, he was assigned the German parish in Pest, where he lived until Countess Esterhazy invited him to lead the diocese in Majcichov in 1862. Threatened with ex-communication, Palarík expressed his liberal and anti-clerical views hidden in didactic plays in various genres that were intended to advance the nation's education and awareness of its cultural identity.

1858   Publication of his play *Incognito*.

1860   Publication of his play *Drotár.*

1861   Publication of his memoirs of the Slovak National Assembly in Turčiansky Sv. Martin, *Denník Národnieho slovenského shromaždenia dňa 6. a 7. junia r. 1861.*

1863   Member of the committee that prepared the foundation of the *Matica slovenská.*

1868   His belief in the Hungarian constitution led him to join forces with representatives of what became known in the 1870s as the *Nová škola slovenská* (Slovak New School), a new and short-lived party that demanded the co-operation with the ruling Magyars.

7 December 1870 Died in Majcichov after long suffering from stomach ulcers.

Štefan Marko Daxner, © SNK

III. Štefan Marko Daxner (1822 - 1892). Law and education.

"Before, when absolutism determined the fates of all European nations, only the ruling dynasties and courts had politics: the nations were nothing. When the nations, however, became aware of their identity, their human rights, when they emerged from under the yoke of absolutism to the field of constitutional liberties – from then on also the nations have politics."[194]

If Francisci was a pragmatic organiser and Palárik a rebellious liberal, we could call Daxner the national movement's expert in legal issues and education, in the sense of education policy. He never worked as a teacher, nor did he publish as extensively as Francisci, Palárik, Sasínek, Vajanský and Šrobár did. With the exception of the Slovak gymnasium, his political goals were identical to the ones of the *stará škola*. We shall therefore not repeat the details of the *memorandum* already elaborated upon in the preceding chapters.

Daxner was responsible for the formulation of the *memorandum*, in particular the passages on the *okolie*. His efforts for the legal representation and, later, defence of the movement resulted more than once in his being transferred to regions of the kingdom, where the majority of the population was Magyar. In Košice and Debrecen, his 'Panslavist' activities would either fall on a neutral ground or stop altogether – or so the authorities must have thought. Yet, it seems to me that the more the authorities tried to silence him the more fiercely he fought the injustices of Magyarisation. Shortly before his death, his own church that was caving in to the assimilation peaking under the Tisza government went against him.

Bokeš distinguishes four phases in Daxner's life[195]: First, the *revolutionary – democratic* phase of the young members supporting Štúr's codification, who formulated the Mikuláš demands of 1848 and participated in the revolution. Second, the phase of the *memorandum* and the *Matica* following the end of the Bach absolutism in 1860; they were of crucial importance for the foundation of the Slovak gymnasium in Veľka Revúca. Third, the phase of defending the *rights of the Evangelical church* and the *Slovak gymnasium*, which started after the *Ausgleich* of 1867. In the fourth phase – with Daxner already ill – he concentrated on defending

---

[194] Štefan Marko Daxner, "Politika je obrana záujmov", *Peštbudínske Vedomosti I*, č. 9, 16. 4. 1861, 1.

[195] František Bokeš, "Dnes", in *Štefan Marko Daxner. Život a dielo v dokumentoch* (Osveta: Martin, 1976), 167.

individuals who were in existential difficulties owing to their national engagement. He financially supported the editor and teacher Karol Salva, whom the church had stripped of his functions. The young evangelical pastor and philosopher Daniel Lauček was not allowed to assume his position, although the church authorities had promised him a parish close to Tisovec[196]. Daxner invited him to stay at his farm in the mountains of Tisovec, where Lauček could enjoy the quiet atmosphere to work on his philosophical œuvre *On human consciousness* (*Ľudské povedomie*). How important justice, law and rights were to Daxner and how continuously and persistently he defended them, is evident in this quote:

> "If it was possible that the court publicly declared the innocence of Jean Calas, whom it had unjustly sentenced to death and executed, so I firmly believe that this will also happen to me."[197]

Thanks to Voltaire, the case of Jean Calas, a Huguenot textile worker from Toulouse, became known as the *Calas affair*. The great philosopher unleashed a press campaign revealing the corruption in France's legal system. The affair gained notorious fame all over Europe. In 1761[198] the son of Jean Calas, who had had the intention to convert to Catholicism, was found hanged in his father's textile shop. The judges' anti-Huguenot prejudices influenced the verdict with the biased argument that Jean Calas would rather have had his son killed than let him convert. He was sentenced to death and executed. Voltaire's tireless campaign for religious tolerance and his critique of the corrupt administration led to the establishment of a commission investigating the case. The court rehabilitated Jean Calas posthumously in 1765.

Daxner's reference to the Calas affair seems, at a first superficial sight, somewhat exaggerated; after all, he had not been sentenced to death. He was already retired with a state pension. Yet, the lawyer protested against the essence of the problem Voltaire had pointed his sharp feather on: the *institutional discrimination* of persons that disagree with the state and the church on religious issues, political ideas and, in Daxner's case, national identity. His own church was stabbing the national movement in the back by carrying the assimilation out all too eagerly. Clearly, the

---

[196]   Daniel Záboj Lauček, "1872-1881. Budeme teda trpieť za vec našu", in *Štefan Marko Daxner...*, 138-139.

[197]   *Štefan Marko Daxner...*, 141.

[198]   For an excellent analysis of Voltaire's campaign on behalf of Calas see Roger Pearson, *Voltaire Almighty. A life in pursuit of freedom* (London: Bloomsbury, 2006).

unity of the times of the *memorandum* and the *Matica*, with the churches of both confessions standing behind the national movement, was gone. When the citizens of Klenovec openly protested against the dismissal of Salva, the so-called *riots of Klenovec* (*Klenovské vzbury*) were the straw that broke the camel's back. The church used Daxner's defence of the citizens to strip him of his functions and accused him of having incited the turmoil.

Although human rights and the legal system had made progress thanks to the French and the 1848 revolution, the Hungarian administration was far from being a rule of law state –so Daxner must have thought. The rift between constitutional text, interpretation and reality targeted Slovak individuals and institutions while violating the rights of the kingdom's other nationalities. As long as individuals and institutions enjoyed the protection of the law and civil rights only if they behaved according to the wishes of Budapest, if they renounced not only on all national activities, but also on their individual convictions and thoughts, then the rule of law state as the guiding idea of Hungarian statecraft since 1848 was not existent.

Daxner came from a wealthy upper middle-class family and enjoyed a good education; his lawyer father held a higher administrative position in the *župa*, while also acting as an inspector for the Evangelical church in Tisovec. Certainly, his wealth and university education made it easier for Daxner to support fellow Slovaks in financial difficulties and to offer free legal service. But young Štefan, whom his Slavophile fellow students at the Pressburg lyceum would call 'Marko' because of his physical similarity to the Serbian prince Marko Kraljević (1335 - 1395), showed an unusual psychological stability and physical strength. The following anecdote demonstrates not only Daxner's resilience, but gives us an impression of the atmosphere at the Pressburg lyceum, where most of the Slovak students came in touch with the romanticist idea of Kollár's *Slavic reciprocity* and the early Slovak nationalism promoted by Štúr.

Professor Gabriel Kováč-Martíny, an authoritarian teacher, conducted a rather painful experiment of physics, demonstrating the power of the vacuum. A student was asked to come forward and cover the surface of the machine with his palm. The professor then turned a handle that created the vacuum, sucking the student's hand to the surface. All the students participating were astonished to see that they could not remove their hands. Then came Daxner's turn. He came forward and put his palm on the surface. Kováč-Martíny turned the handle once, and then again, creating a stronger vacuum, until he thought it was enough. Daxner said only: "More." The professor gave the handle another turn; Daxner's moustache did not once tremble, until the professor stopped, let the air back in and remarked with a content smile: "Videtur, est slavus" (It is obvious, he is a Slav)[199].

III. 1. Political goals

III. 1. 1. The Slovak gymnasium in Veľka Revúca

Daxner shared with the majority of the national movement the political goals formulated in the *memorandum*: re-constitution of the language rights, autonomy in the *okolie* and peaceful co-operation with the ruling Maygars. None of these goals were realised. The establishment of the Slovak gymnasium in Veľka Revúca in 1862, however, was his personal goal and most probably his biggest success.

Since the pressure of the assimilation could fully unfold only on a constitutional basis, the national movement enjoyed a window of opportunity in the years preceding the nationality law of 1868. In 1867 and 1869, before the constitution of the *Ausgleich* took full effect, two more Slovak gymnasiums were established in Turčiansky Sv. Martin and Kláštor pod Znievom; national interest groups or societies (*spolky*) emerged, such as the Catholic *Spolek svätého Vojtecha (Society of the holy Vojtech)* and *Živena*[200], the association of the Slovak women, named after *Živa*, the Slavic mythological goddess of the earth. The societies distributed literature in Slovak, organised reading circles, engaged in social welfare and generally cared about the nation's culture and education. Both managed to survive until 1918; they were "the last success stories of the national movement"[201].

Daxner's view of education as the pillar of an enlightened and educated nation originated in Štúr's Hegelianism, which had led the 'father of the Slovak language' to

---

[199] Juliuš Botto recounts this anecdote in his biography of Daxner, referring to Francisci's autobiography. Botto's Slovak translation of the professor's praise reads "vidno, že je Slovák" (It is obvious, he is a Slovak); Botto, *Životopis Štefana Marka Daxnera* (Rimavská Sobota: Matica Slovenská, 1922), 18-19. Francisci remembers the praise in the original Latin as "videtur, est slavus", which is in English "It is obvious, he is a Slav", Francisci, "životopis", 77. I consider Francisci's version closer to the truth.

[200] Kováč, *Dejiny...*, 135.

[201] Kováč, *Dejiny...*, 136.

the codification of Slovak. One could say that Daxner carried across the Hegelian idea of the spirit of the nation into the phase of *institutionalised higher education*. It would certainly be incorrect and an exaggeration to say that he laid the grounds of a system of modern national education. But his efforts for the Slovak gymnasium led to the opening of two more which provided high school education in Slovak (at least for a couple of years, until the government closed them in 1874). Let us have look at Daxner's description of the education in Upper Hungary, which he was eager to change.

In his famous text *Hlas zo Slovenska* (*A voice from Slovakia*) Daxner described the history of the relationship of Slovaks and Magyars up to the year of the *memorandum*. On the last pages, he presented an analysis of the empire's ideological icon 'equality of nations' and its realisation in the Hungarian kingdom. He pointed to the gap between constitutional text and constitutional reality as clear evidence of the systematic injustice committed by the authorities. After having addressed in four paragraphs the administrative and political areas where that inequality was realised on a daily basis, he addressed the situation of high school education:

> "Fifth: What is there to say about the equality of nations in the schools and educational institutions? ... As regards the educational institutions established by the Imperial Government ... we have officially 4 Slovak gymnasia [podľa mena 4 slovenské Gymnasia máme], located in Trenčín, Nitra, Banská Bystrica and Levoča. We use the term 'official', because the language of scientific instruction in all these gymnasia is German."[202]

Daxner explained the importance of the Slovak gymnasium in Veľka Revúca by referring to education as a common national task for all Slovaks. The gymnasium had already two classes of students; although the majority of the population in the Gemer-Mala honta *župa* was Lutheran, the Catholics had also supported the school. They had provided financial means in a truly national and enlightened spirit[203]. But one gymnasium was not enough: without a stronger intellectual elite, the nation's future would not improve. If the people did not know themselves and their interests, it's lack of education would be used by its enemies. Daxner's reference to the schools

---

[202] Daxner, *Hlas zo Slovenska* (Pest: Trattner-Károlyi, 1861), 29. Daxner's brief foreword bears the title "Na dorozumenia!" hinting at Palarík's critical article about the gathering at Martin. He dedicated the text to the *narodovci*, who submitted the *memorandum* to the emperor. His treatise was later published under a different title: Daxner, *Slovenská otázka od konca 18. stoletia* (Turčiansky Sv. Martin: Náklad kníhtlačiarskeho účastinárskeho spolku, 1912).

[203] Daxner, "Národnie školy", *Pešťbudínske Vedomosti III*, č. 17, 27. 2. 1863, 1.

and the church – which he described as both being institutions that expressed the nation's enlightened spirit – reveal his Lutheran faith:

> "... we know that only education and schools can be our best weapon! ... Not with the sword, but with education did the Christians defeat the pagan gods ... Education, however, is being achieved in schools – if we truly want to win, we have to care about national schools established in our spirit."[204]

The strength of a nation corresponded to its level of education and enlightenment. The schools served as institutions that integrated family life with the lives of the public and the church; they received the youthful from their families to instruct them morally and intellectually and to return them to the communities and the church as citizens prepared for the tasks of life[205]. After some lengthy comments about the gap between the constitution and the reality of the educational system in Upper Hungary, Daxner concluded his article with general information about the gymnasium.

> "Our current situation is that we, in the territory of Gemer and Mala Honta, are encircled by four Magyar schools. This forced us not to postpone our work, but to make a start ... As per now, we have secured two professors – but we will have to elect two more professors to teach the third and fourth gymnasial classes. We know all too well that we cannot reach this goal without the help of others. It is therefore up to the nation and particularly the educated [na národu a hlavne na vzdelancoch] to acknowledge this school as a child of the nation and the church and to recognise their duty to help and promote its growth and development with all possible sacrifices and financial donations."[206]

If Daxner's tone was full of hope and his perception of the future pre-university education in Slovak modestly optimistic, he could not have foreseen in 1863 that the Slovak gymnasiums would not survive beyond 1874.

III. 1. 2.   The closure of the Slovak gymnasium in Veľka Revúca

The most thorough account of the gymnasium's history and institutional organisation is certainly August Horislav Škultéty's *Memoirs of the Slovak evangelical gymnasium of the Augsburg confession,* to which Daxner contributed a chapter of concluding remarks[207]. We will not go into the organisational details and statistics of

---

204   Daxner, "Národnie školy", 1.
205   Daxner, "Národnie školy", 1.
206   Daxner, "Národnie školy", 3.
207   August Horislav Škultéty, *Pamäti slov. ev. a. v. gymnasium a s nim spojeného učiteľského semeniska vo Veľkej Revúci,* (Ružomberok: tlačov Karla Salvy – nákladom vydavateľovým, 1889). Škultéty (1819-1892) was an evangelical pastor and the spokesman of the gymasium.

the gymnasium; nor will we address the constitutional ramifications of the church in educational issues. What interests us here is how Daxner perceived the circumstances of the gymnasium's closure.

He addressed in brief paragraphs the opposition of the Magyar and Slovak aristocracy against the February patent of 1860; the aristocracy, both Catholic and Evangelical had joined forces since the patent limited their privileges and dominance in church and school matters. The Magyar aristocracy aiming at re-establishing autonomy and the values of 1848 used Vienna's weakness after the war against Prussia to prepare the constitutional changes in the Hungarian parliament, which became the *Ausgleich* of 1867.

> "In these years, the gymnasium in Veľka Revúca blossomed ... the gymnasiums in Sv. Martin and Kláštor were founded, the Matica slovenská established – all the institutions supportive of the awakening of the moral and intellectual powers of the oppressed Slovak people. The programme to destroy these powers wouldn't be long in coming."[208]

While the Magyar aristocrats had been using the concept 'equality of nations' to oppose Vienna's centralist absolutism under Bach, their programme changed according to the German model as soon as they gained power:

> "Equality of nations became bereft of sense, tearing the country apart, 'state in the state', anticonstitutional plans, in short: high treason, dakoromanism, panslavism."[209]

The fate of the gymnasium was sealed not only because the Magyars introduced constitutional changes according to the *Ausgleich,* but also through the abuse of the election system in the local administration of the Gemer-Mala Honta *župa.* The highest authorities representing the state and the church arranged for the elections in such way that they accepted only opponents of the gymnasium as candidates on the lists. The system of *virilism* – we could call it perhaps 'public office gerrymandering' allowing only loyal citizens to occupy positions of local power – ensured that those supportive of the gymnasium could not run for the offices of the administration. The consequence of that practice were the rigged elections to the town council:

The close personal relations between Daxner, Škultéty and others involved with the volume is evident in the choice of the publisher Karol Salva, whom Daxner had defended and financially enabled to found a publisher's house.

[208] Daxner, "Poznámky", in *Pamäti slov. ev. a.* ... , 262-270; 264.

[209] Daxner, "Poznámky", 265.

"The elected town council consisted mostly of citizens opposed to the gymnasium or dependent persons [depending on the favour of the powerful, add. JB] or persons lacking an opinion of their own. This council then elected the town's magistrates – naturally it voted only for persons who were eligible to the higher positions of the church administration and known as convinced opponents of the gymnasium."[210]

The inherent discrimination of the virilist system dominated the affairs of state and church in the *comitates* and ensured that the policies issued in Budapest would be realised in the kingdom's regions. For the minorities, this practise proved fatal, as the electoral procedure and the agendas of how to run the *župa* and the towns were already pre-determined by those in power. Critical citizens did not stand a chance of being elected to the councils, while citizens loyal to the Hungarian state and the nationality law of 1868 were rewarded with powerful positions that enabled them in turn to enlarge their personal network. Accusations of Panslavism in Slovakia and Dakoromanism of the Romanian minority in Transylvania, respectively, could also lead to personal enrichment.

Daxner recounts how the magistrates fabricated arguments against the gymnasium to justify its closure and then to confiscate the property, including the building, estate, library and financial means. Apart from the practise of randomly imposed inquiries by state and church officials that investigated professors' and students' alleged Panslavist activities, the gymasium's opponents used petty accusations, wrong assumptions and plain lies:

"Dušan Abaffy, a student of the VI. class, had died; to commemorate their friend, his classmates hung up in the library his aristocratic coat of arms that displayed a red shield adorned with arabesques in silver and white on a blue background. Above the shield, there was a yellow-golden crown and within the shield symbols of military prowess in the same colour. Pavol Szontagh, a member of the investigating commission and former delegate to the town council held that the picture (the coat of arms of the Abaffy family) was based on the Panslavist colours (white-blue-red) and thus presented clear evidence of the Panslavist and anti-patriotic thinking, hence the evil spirit that ruled in the gymnasium. And the entire commission gave him right!"[211]

The supporters and the patronate, the founding and managing convent of the gymnasium, did not stand a chance against the Ministry of Religious Affairs that closed the gymnasium by a decree issued by his Royal highness on 24 of August

---

[210] Daxner, "Poznámky", 266.

[211] Daxner, "Poznámky", 266. The Panslavic colours Szontagh referred to, blue, red and white, originate in the flag of the Russian Empire, displaying the same colours turned upside down.

1874. There was no possibility of appeal. Representing the dissolved patronate, Daxner pressed charges to save at least the property of the gymnasium. The court rejected the charges, arguing that the property remained confiscated by the authorities, because the patronate had been dissolved; it was no more a legal subject and therefore in no position to sue. Daxner appealed with the argument that the patronate was dissolved only as an educational institution, but remained the legal owner of the property that belonged to their confession. He came forward with the records of the *gruntovna kniha*, the land register, to prove the patronate's ownership of the high school, its buildings, library and financial means[212]. Violating the most basic property rights, the authorities ignored the appeal and, in doing so, robbed a group of citizens of their rightfully achieved possessions. They would also confiscate the entire property of the *Matica* in 1875, which, like the gymnasiums, had been financed exclusively by private donations and collections. Kováč speaks of "the peak of cynicism", since the property theft was followed by using these means to finance Magyar national associations in Upper Hungary[213]. Daxner, who recounted these events, referring to himself matter-of-factly in the third person, still seemed quite shocked remembering the violation of positive law. The lawyer, used to precise, sober and issue-relevant wording, spoke sharply of "Magyar chauvinists" and concluded his remarks saying that the people had a long and truthful memory[214]. Let us now have a closer look at his political legitimating.

III. 2. Political legitimating

III. 2. 1. Natural Law and Positive Law

We have mentioned above that Daxner adhered to the superficial Hegelianism of the Štúr generation in his thought of education as the expression of the nation's enlightened spirit, hence its materialisation through language, culture and science. The Christian idea that the pen would defeat the sword gave evidence of his Lutheran faith. We have not found any passages in the selected texts where he analysed or promoted the ideas of a particular philosopher or thinker, such as Palárik, Šrobár and Vajanský did. Daxner mentioned the names of authors, thinkers, teachers and poets

---

212 Daxner, "Poznámky", 269-270.
213 Kováč, *Dejiny...*, 140.
214 Daxner, "Poznámky", 270.

of earlier generations, such as the less known Adam Kollár (1718 - 1783), Ján Kollár (1793 - 1852), Ján Hollý (1785 - 1849), Pavel Jozef Šafárik (1795 - 1861) and Štúr[215], yet only to stress his point that his generation and those to come should continue what the early *narodovci* had begun. He did not present critique or analysis of their ideas. We could therefore say that Daxner, much as Francisci, was a pragmatist. While Francisci managed the movement's journals, subscriptions and finances, Daxner provided the legal expertise. He was an expert in the distinction of rational natural law and positive law and his argumentation focussed on making this distinction clear to his fellow Slovaks.

> "... first, we have to briefly explain what we understand under the term 'law' [právo]: The word 'law' expresses the idea that applies to the most holy of humanity, guiding it from the rule of blind natural needs to the kingdom of freedom and the soul. Lawlessness is opposed to law. The law guarantuees the personal independence [osobnú samostatnosť] of a free individual (as is the nation) in the interaction with other free individuals, – it enables the freedom of the individual and the freedom of other individuals; – it is the harmony and the order of rational beings [bytností rozumných] that live together. Man has the holy, unlimited and eternal origins of that law in himself ... in the faculties of his reason given to him by the will of the almighty."[216]

The problem with natural law originating in human reason was its application on the levels of the state and the international system. Natural law could not effectively realise the freedom of the individual within a large group and that of nations within an empire, since it proved also too weak to defend itself against those who destroyed the development and spirit of a nation. The founders of the *Code Napoléon* had understood that no legislator could defy the spiritual power of a nation that out of free will defended the perpetual laws of humanity against the personal opinion of just one legislator[217]. Daxner empasised in his conclusion that the assimilation pressure against the Slovaks presented a violation of their natural right to express their language and culture, hence a violation of natural law. Like the *narodvci* of his generation, he did not use natural law to claim for sovereignty or a Slovak independent state, but wished to make it perfectly clear that the Magyars violated the very rights of the nationalities they so vehemently had claimed for themselves. In that, they violated their own state building principle of 'equality of nations':

---

[215] Daxner, "Národnie školy", 3.
[216] Daxner, *Hlas...*, 30.
[217] Daxner, *Hlas...*, 31.

"If we now express ourselves in regard to our neighbours: Hungary exists for us only to the extent that we exist in her; – we acknowledge her only to the level we are recognised by her ... the recognition of our nationality [národnosti našej] presents the basic condition of Hungary's true and real, not only visible unity. We are convinced that ... that unity can only be established in one way: When the *ethnographic border line* that is really separating both tribes [oboma plemenama] is recognised and guaranteed also by positive law, and when each nationality in *acceptance of the proportional size of both groups* established by that line [v objemu tejže čiary] enjoys the very same rights and duties."[218]

Daxner's claim for recognition of the Slovak nationality by positive law was of course identical to what the assembly in Martin a couple of months before had agreed upon: that the Slovaks had to have autonomy in a clearly defined territory where they formed the majority of the population – the autonomy of the *okolie*. Unlike Palarík, who strictly separated natural and positive law, Daxner's aim was to have the natural rights granted by positive law. Since the Magyars did not recognise the language and church rights guaranteed in the constitution of 1791 and had repeatedly violated these, a new formulation of the natural law, a new legislation was needed. This would have been a 'double guarantee' – natural rights granted by positive law of a new legislation – only on a superficial glance, since the governments had only paid lip-service to the nationalities' natural rights before. As a lawyer, Daxner naturally pinned all his hopes on positive law; only a new legislation – and that was the focus of the discussions about the October diploma and the February patent in the years following the end of the Bach regime – would grant the equality of nations in the kingdom. Although he referred to the Magyars as nationality, he did not *expressis verbis* mention a future joint rule; we can only assume that he had a future constitutional arrangement in mind when insisting on the same rights and duties. If the situation in 1861 did not look unfavourable for the Slovak demands, Daxner's optimism was visibly shattered in 1868.

---

[218] Daxner, *Hlas...*, 33; italics JB.

III. 2. 2. Slovak Democratism

"The word democracy – in Slovak government of the people [národovláda] – designates the status of a nation, in which it governs itself, and not a single person or some privileged caste [privilegovaná kasta]. In this sense democracy opposes the absolute monarchy and aristocracy."[219]

Man gifted with reason carries the origins of natural law in himself, as Daxner wrote in 1861. A few months before the emperor would sign the nationality law and some months after the *Ausgleich*, he saw fit to explain the difference between a true democracy and a false one. His article has an unusual pedagogical tone, with simple examples and a few phrases that sound somewhat populist – he obviously wanted to be understood.

After a brief paragraph on the moral goals and principles of social democracy, Daxner went on to distinguish between a pure, abstract democracy [čistý a odťažený demokratismus], which expressed the understanding of the idea itself, and the applied or practical democracy [demokratismus srostený] that had grown within a particular nation[220]. The pure democracy was inherent in every man, because it originated in human reason. In the past, the Slovak and Magyar democrats had understood this very well and lived in peace with each other. Here, Daxner clearly contradicted himself: referring to the history of Hungary before Magyarisation set in and claiming that both nations had lived peacefully side by side because of their true understanding of pure democracy is an anachronism. Most probably led by a hasty mental leap, he created a theoretical confusion of pure democracy with natural law. He held further that the notion of the practical or applied democratism was completely different: it consisted of as many different aspects or variants as much as men distinguished themselves from each other.

"The grown democracy is different in every nation because some nations did not protect their individuality and their various characteristic features. It is therefore obvious that the Slovak democracy is as distant from the Magyar one as the endeavours of the Slovak nation from those of the Magyars. ... It is obvious thus that even the worst tyrants can talk about freedom, equality of rights, democracy – in an abstract fashion – while in reality they torture and oppress the nations by despotism, murder and tyranny. In North America, for example, the people wanting to maintain slavery consider themselves also as democrats.

---

[219] Daxner, "Slovenský Demokratismus", *Pešťbudínske Vedomosti VIII*, č. 36, 5. 5. 1868, 1.
[220] Daxner, "Slovenský Demokratismus", 1.

> This remark applies in general to the understanding of [practical, add. JB] democracy, and in particular to the Slovak and Magyar notions of democracy."[221]

After the brief, hastily put down and somewhat confusing definitions of two different notions of democratism, Daxner revealed the main issue he addressed: his critique of some members of the *nova škola* that had founded the *National-democratic association* (*národno-demokratický spolok*) in Budapest. Prominent members were Daniel Lichard, Ján Bobula and Slovak entrepreneurs, journalists and teachers who shared the political interests of the *nova škola*[222]. To the less informed reader, his short paragraph on social democracy now made sense as it was directed against the Slovak entrepreneurs as "some capitalists that squeezed the nation" like a lemon[223]. Daxner did not mention any names, but referred to the opposing party as "the despotic party"[224]. The Slovak nation considered the understanding of democratism and freedom as the origin of the division into two political parties: the first one was honest and truthful, the second one loved domination, despotism, arbitrariness and secrecy. While the democratic and liberal party respected the motto "that which you do not want to suffer yourself, do not do to others", the despotic party kept to the rule "take from others and gather for yourself"[225].

> "Just go from house to house and ask the citizens: Do you, like your fellow citizens, want to have the right to elect to the assembly rightful and educated men whom you trust, so that they can establish how many taxes you have to pay and how these taxes should be spent?
> ... Do you want that the administrative offices to always address you in your own natural Slovak language? Do you want only men to become ministers, who enjoy the trust of the nation, the delegates, the assembly, so that nobody can rule the country, whom the assembly does not consider capable and honourable?[226]

---

[221] Daxner, "Slovenský Demokratismus", 1.

[222] http://www.luno.hu/mambo/index.php?option=content&task=view&id=7890; accessed 23.4.2009.

[223] Daxner, "Slovenský Demokratismus", 1.

[224] Daxner, "Slovenský Demokratismus", 1. In this context, the word "party" [strana] does not yet connote to political parties in the modern sense. Daxner used the term to address the rift in the *Slovak national party* (*Slovenská národna strana*), which was emerging after 1868. The members of the *New School* founded their *Slovak party of compromise* (*Slovenská strana vyrovnania)* in 1872.

[225] Daxner, "Slovenský Demokratismus", 1.

[226] Daxner, "Slovenský Demokratismus", 1.

The party of Slovak democracy, which is what Daxner called the adherents of the *memorandum*, had many such honourable men at its disposal, whom the majority of the population supported. The despotic party, by contrast, was the adversary of freedom and the rights of the Slovaks. The absolutist party, how he further addressed the members of the *nova škola*, used various and ignominious means against the liberal party, which gained them modest success among the population. Daxner voiced serious critique of his fellow citizens that followed the despotic party or were prone to do so. In a rather populist fashion, he accused those who did not share the opinion of the *stará škola* of lazyness, lack of education and political shortsightedness. He called for unity:

> "... and partly also because the friends of Slovak freedom on both sides – as they emerged due to a misunderstanding [of the true Slovak democracy, add. JB] – are separated according to whatever stories they cooked up and often go against each other out of petty reasons. One betrays the other and so they help the adversaries of Slovak freedom to win."[227]

Daxner's tone, as we mentioned above, was unusual in its sharpness, simple wording and somewhat populist appeal. We had the impression that the otherwise sober lawyer was really furious at the fellow Slovaks, who did not share the view of the majority of the movement. He thus created a theoretical paradox, since true democratism – and we are convinced that he knew this – allows always different opinions to be voiced. By linking the democratic idea exclusively to the majority of the movement and defining the Budapest dissidents as despots and absolutists, Daxner did not exercise tolerance. However, in the given circumstances, his anger is understandable – which is a psychological argument and not a philosophical-theoretical one. How could they stab their own people in the back by founding an association in the capital, networking and doing business with the oppressor, and then have the insolence to call themselves democrats and nationalists? It might have been a small comfort to Daxner that the *Slovak party of compromise* that grew out of the association lacked any political significance. It had no political influence on behalf of the Slovak nation and vanished after a couple of years. That the authorities had dissolved the national-cultural institutions and confiscated their property was one thing. The *narodvci* had learnt to deal with injustice and humiliations. Quite a

---

[227] Daxner, "Slovenský Demokratismus", 1.

different issue was to target the sons of the movement's prominent members – and with that the young generation.

III. 2. 3. Distributive justice and moral death

When his sixteen-year-old son Štefan was dismissed from the Pressburg lyceum on accusations of Panslavist anti-government activities in 1882, Daxner reacted with his well-known *Sachlichkeit*, objectivity and careful wording in this matter, which was hopeless from a legal point of view and emotionally painful. The *Národnie Noviny*, the 'house news' of the *nova škola* founded by Ján Bobula, published his protest letter in full, yet not without the brief editorial remark that the newspaper considered Daxner's version of the event as "not comprehensible" [nedostupné][228].

According to a letter sent to the editor of the *Národnie Noviny* under the title "one hand washes the other", Daxner's son was accepted at the gymnasium in Rimavská Sobota only because his father had acquaintances on the board and was on good terms with the *podžupan* of the Gemer-Mala Honta district. The writer thus accused the school and Daxner of Panslavist nepotism. Daxner countered these accusations with the statement that the board of the gymnasium had first made inquiries at the Pressburg Lyceum to check whether the dismissal applied only to the lyceum or to any other gymnasium in Upper Hungary. The lyceum replied that young Daxner was dismissed only from their institution and that there were no legal reasons that would prevent his admission to the gymnasium at Rimavská Sobota[229]. Neither the *podžupan* nor Daxner had, as far as he knew, any say in this matter and it was also incorrect to state that he had received favours from Daxner in exchange for the son's entry to the gymnasium. So much for the author of that letter.

Only three weeks after the Rimavská Sobota gymnasium had accepted young Štefan as student, the board informed Daxner that his son was dismissed on the grounds of a document issued by the senate of the Pressburg lyceum and the Royal Ministry of Religious Affairs. Young Daxner had been found guilty of membership in a secret circle committed to Panslavist and anti-government activities. He was therefore banned from all educational institutions in the state; furthermore, the diploma and credentials he would earn from schools abroad would not be

---

[228] Daxner, "K našim dejom", *Národnie Noviny VIII*, č. 64, 3. 6. 1882, 1.
[229] Daxner, "K našim dejom", 2.

acknowledged in Hungary[230]. This was, to put it in modern terms, *pro-active discrimination*. Whatever young Štefan would study, he would not be allowed to work in that profession in the kingdom. So, young Daxner had two options: either go abroad, into exile – or work jobs that did not require higher education. Needless to say, he would not have stood any chance to enrol at Pest university.

Daxner repeated word for word the report of the investigating commission he had requested. According to the report, the circle *Zora* (*sunrise*) was led by three students, among them young Štefan, who acted as librarian; it had fourteen members. The activities of the circle consisted of training in the Slovak language, reading, and critical reviews of texts [posudzovaním prác][231]. The money found when the circle was detected was used to pay for journal subscriptions, books and the hosting of the weekly meetings. The circle had already existed for a couple of months.

Daxner critically assessed each of the points with his own interpretation and made it perfectly clear that he was relieved: according to the positive law of the kingdom and the contents of the report, the accusations against his son and the *Zora* members were groundless. That *Zora* was not a secret circle was evident and common knowledge since everybody at the Pressburg lyceum knew that it existed since 1876. The reading, writing of critical comments on Slovak literature and having weekly get-togethers were no evidence of the secrecy of the group; these activities did not violate positive law but were normal activities of young students eager to acquire personal knowledge and education outside the curriculum. The fact, Daxner argued, that the Magyar and German student groups at the lyceum enjoyed the continuous advise of a professor, while *Zora* did not, was no evidence of the group's Panslavist activities. The lyceum had had educated students at the chair for Czecho-Slavic languages and literatures since Professor Juraj Palkovič had been appointed in 1803. Why thus did the board not advise the Slovak circle that they would need the supervision by a professor? The parents sending their children to school expected the school to comply with its responsibilities. In regard to the accusation of anti-government and Panslavist activities, Daxner defeated the report with one sentence:

"The members of the secret circle hold further that they did not pursue goals directed against the government, but that their goal was to educate themselves in the usage of their

---

[230]   Daxner, "K našim dejom", 2.
[231]   Daxner, "K našim dejom", 2.

mother tongue. They did not ask the professorial board for approval since they knew in advance that they would not receive it; that they destroyed their protocols is evidence of their dishonesty. The positive evidence for the anti-government and Panslavist activities would therefore be that they read the yearbook of the Matica [matičné Letopisy] and the journal *Slovak views* [Slovenské pohľady]."[232]

Daxner, the lawyer, now directed his pen against the government; he was defending his son, stressing that the authorities committed systematic discrimination of the minorities:

"This *distributive justice* is beyond comprehension. For membership in a club that lacked the approval of the school, fourteen students were condemned ... for the very same activities, five randomly selected youngsters are condemned to a moral death [k mravnej smrti] and the expulsion from their country [k vyhosteniu zo svojej vlasti]. The five were so cruelly punished in that they were denied the most basic rights given by god – the right to educate themselves in the country of their fathers and to become, on the basis of their scientific education, the supporters of their parents, successful members of the human society and good citizens of their country."[233]

Daxner had, to conclude, fought in the 1848 revolution, worked as a lawyer for the Hungarian government in various high positions and contributed immensely to the legal defence and financial support of the national movement. He never tired of fighting injustice; his efforts provided the movement with a new and modern identity, the identity of professionalism and legal expertise.

---

[232] Daxner, "K našim dejom", 2.

[233] Daxner, "K našim dejom", 2; italics by JB. Daxner's use of the term "distributive justice" might be somewhat confusing, since the term connotes primarily modern theories of justice, such as John Rawls' *A Theory of justice* (Cambridge, MA: Belknap Press of Harvard University Press, 1971). While Rawls investigates the procedure that is required to establish a fair distribution of goods and rights in a society, Daxner addresses the unequal distribution of justice in the sense of deliberate and systematic discrimination.

Young Daxner enrolled at the Czech University in Prague to study medicine, where the young Vavro Šrobar met him in the student circle *Detvan*. Šrobar, who was also banned from all gymnasiums in Hungary, finished his gymnasium in Přerov in Moravia. Šrobar writes that Daxner did not openly explain why he left Hungary. He seemed to have serious examination nerves and did not finish his medical studies. He later returned to Hungary and somehow managed to gain a position in the local administration in Rimavská Sobota. After the foundation of the Czechoslovak Republic in 1918, Šrobár made him the speaker of the local administration of the new government; Vavro Šrobár, *Z môjho života* (Praha: Fr. Borový, 1946), 264-266.

Štefan Marko Daxner – life in brief

26 December 1822 Born in Tisovec in the Banská Bystrica district of Middle Slovakia, where he went to primary school. His family was wealthy and well-established in the local state and church administration. Štefan's godmother was the wife of superintendent Dr. Pavel Jozeffy, the Lutheran pastor of Tisovec. Štefan started the lower classes of gymnasium at the Catholic school in Oždany and Spišska Nová Ves, from where he left for Rožňava.

1840-42   Studied philosophy, physics and mathematics at the Evangelical lyceum in Pressburg, where he became acquainted with the followers of Štúr.

1842-43   Auditor at the law faculty of the Evangelical lyceum in Trnava.

1843-46   Worked as legal secretary in law firms in Rimavská Sobota, Tisovec and in Pest.

1846   Passed the exams of the Law faculty of Pest university and opened his own legal practice in his native Tisovec.

1848   The Magyar authorities arrested him in October, charged him with treason and sentenced him to death, but commuted his sentence to a prison term.

1849   After his liberation from prison, he joined the Slovak voluntary national guards in the rank of captain and participated in the Austrian campaigns against the Magyar revolutionary army.

1861   Worked as administrator and lawyer in Rimavska Sobota, Košice, Nové Město pod Šiatrom (Sátoraljaújhely) and Nagykálló. He formulated the final text of the *memorandum* at the national gathering at Turčiansky Sv. Martin.

1861   He returned to Rimavská Sobota, where he became the second *podžupan* (vice-governor) of the Gemer-Malohotský župa.

1862   Owing to his initiative, the Lutheran Church opened the first Slovak gymnasium in Veľka Revúca, which enabled the pre-university education in Slovak.

1865	Appointed chairman of the constitutional court in Debrecen.
1872	The government allowed him to retire from his position and issued a pension, upon which Daxner and his family moved back to his native Tisovec.
1874	After years of inquiries by a governmental commission, the emperor declared the gymnasium in Veľka Revúca as closed. Dissolution of the *matica slovenská*. Daxner fought the authorities to maintain the building and finances of the *matica* as property of the national movement.
1881	Invited the pastor Daniel Lauček, whom the church had unjustly dismissed because of his views to stay at his farm in the mountains. Daxner supported him until 1885, which enabled Lauček to finish his philosophical œuvre *On human consciousness* (*Ľudské povedomie*).
1882	Daxner's son Štefan was dismissed from the Evangelical lyceum in Pressburg for his membership in the student circle *Zora (sunrise)*, which the authorities suspected of panslavist activities.
1887	Publication of the *Domový kalendár (house calendar)* in Klenovec in Central Slovakia. The authorities of the Evangelical church, giving in to the pressure of Magyarisation, suspended the editor Karol Salva (1849-1913) from his function because of the contents of the calendar. Daxner defended Salva publicly; with the financial support of the Daxner family, Salva founded his own publisher house in Ružomberok. The citizens of Klenovec protested openly against Salva's dismissal and were charged with the so-called *riots of Klenovec* (*Klenovské vzbury*).
1889	Daxner took care of the legal defense of the Klenovec citizens.
1891	The Evangelical Church dismissed Daxner from all his functions. He started to draft a law suit against the church, which he would not finish.
11 April 1892	Daxner died in his native Tisovec. His remains were transferred to the National Cemetery in Martin in 1979.

Michal Miloslav Hodža,
1811—1870.

Ľudovít Štúr,
1815—1856.

Jozef Miloslav Hurban,
1817—1888.

„My chytili sme sa do služby ducha a preto prejsť musíme cestu života tŕnistú."

The three codifiers of the written Slovak language.

The text below the pictures means: „We dedicated ourselves to the care of the soul and therefore must go the way of a hard life." To the memory of the 100th anniversary of the codified Slovak language (1843 – 1943).

Painting by J. Česnek, featuring Francisci, Daxner and Hurban in a Hungarian prison in 1849, awaiting their death sentences. The person in the centre, dominating the painting's composition, is Lajos Kossuth, the leader of the Hungarian revolution.

PETER BOBÚŇ : Ján Francisci ako dobrovoľník-kapitán.

Ján Francisci as captain of the Slovak volunteers in 1848. Section of the famous oil-painting 'The volunteers' camp' (1849 – 1850) by Peter Bohún (1822 – 1879).

Ján Francisci with his son Fedor, Fedor's wife and grandchildren.

Portrait of Ján Palarík with signature.

PRIATEĽ ŠKOLY a LITERATURY.

Číslo 49. Ročník II. *(Príloha k Cyrillo-Methodovi.)* **Budín, 8. Decembra 1860.**

Vychádza každú sobotu. — Predplatná cena: Na celý rok 3 zl. 20 kr., na pol roka 1 zl. 60 kr. rak. čísla. — S „Cyrillom a Methodom" spoločne: na celý rok 6 zl. 2 kr., na pol roka 3 zl. 1 kr. rak. čísla. — Predpláca sa u redaktora a vydávateľa Dr. Ondreja Radlinského (Festung, Georgi-Platz, č. 214).

„Žiadna škola bez života, žiaden život bez školy!"

JÁNOVI PALÁRIKOVI

na článok: „Čo máme očakávať od konštitúcie uhorskej pre našu národnosť?"

Vedľa povesti — zakliate pole,
Vedľa nich klas očarený,
Tlejúce v prsiach zdusené bôle,
Národ v duchu omarený, —
Nezmenia kliatbu lúčou, balvánom,
Ani orlami, ani Kriváňom,
Ani brál príkrych prielomom;
Inak to ide. inak sa mení,
Keď sa smrti dávna k životu lieni,
Hrob sa otvára len — slovom.
A toto slovo už dávno v ume,
Tak blízko duši bývalo,
A len sa zase ztratilo v šume,
I len sa ďalej snívalo:
Tebe jednomu dunajské víly
Moc jeho plnú čarov sdelily,
A Ty si sdelil i nám slasť;
Bez dlhých rečí, čiernej mystiky,
Strhnuls kabaly podlé riadiky,
Dal si nám život v slove „vlasť!"

Čaják.

Toast.

Videl som vás, duše moje!
V predu som vás vidal všade;
Škola, život — kdo zatají?
Stáli ste tam prví v rade.
Mnoho môžte, bratia moji!
Všade vás Boh v láske vodí,
Len ten zhynie v našom sieti,
Kdo sa jak kúkol zrodí.
Len si troje zachovajte:
Boh Otec, Syn i Duch Svätý,
Vlasť, ktorá nás vychovala,
Národ, v ktorom sme počatí!
Tvoelto troje nech vás spojí
V láske, jako vlastné deti,
Tak vám i nám — všetkým spolu —
Večny žitia deň zasvieti!

Čaják.

Slovenský ohlas na maďarský szózat.

Ohlás sa, duša slovenská! v slovenskom „szózat"u!
Zem slovenská je tvoja mať, miluj zem tú svätú;
Zem tá je krásna, slavná časť v sveta desatine:
Jak dá trpieť, zhynúť nedá Boh toľkej rodine!

Pred tisíckou vtrhli k tebe Árpadovcov voje;
Svet nepamätá, odkedy máš ty meno svoje *).
Tvoji dedovia sadali k prestolu Štefana.
Jich junač pri Ostrihome ubila pohana **).

Sloboda! hoj, jaké časy ty si tu už mala!
Keď priateľskú ruku do pút nevďaka sbíjala!
Chceli, by jích veľa bolo, nás nič lebo málo;
Národ náš sa rozveľadil, jích málo zostalo.

A svet národov našinskych hlasom hromu veté;
„Kdo chce žiť, nech vloží ruku v ruku miäch deti!"
Za mnohú krv vylievanú, za toľko vzdychanie
Vybojcov synovia, už raz učiňte pokanie!

Žije Boh! večne verná je svätá jeho vôľa;
Kliatba rabstva pravde jeho navždy neodolá;
Svitne — hej, zasvitnúť musí tam lepšia hodina,
Millionov sto kde za to prosí Hospodina;

Bo keďby raz veľnároda predca ztiekly žily,
Prúdy krve jeho by svet celý zaplavily.
A kdo veľkému národu potom hrob vykope,
Keď ľudstvo celé utonie v slz vlastných potope?

Nuž, k Bohu oko povdačné a modlitbu svätú!
Slovenskú zem, tú svoju mať, žehnaj, ľúby bratu!
Sveta šíreho ona je slavná desatina:
Trpieť môže, leš zhynúť nie slovenská rodina! *(Sokol.)*
S.

*) Od nepamäti, dávno pred príchodom Maďarov z Azie obývali našu krajinu Slovania, a mali, keď Árpad vtrhol, už vzdelané polia, role, dediny, mestá, jako i Nitru. Velehrad na Morave, Počoň (Bratislavu) a Devín pri Dunaji. Velehrad (Mosaburg) za Dunajom.

**) Sv. Vojtech, ktorý krstil sv. Štefana, z Radla, Vojtechov pomocník a potom arcibiskup Kaločský pod menom Anastazia, boli Slovania rodom z Čiech. Požňan a Konce boli hlavní vodcovia sv. Štefana v bitke pri Ostrihome proti Kupovi, vodcovi maďarského pohanstva, svedenej r. 998. V bitke tejto porazené bolo pohansko čiste Maďarstvo, soprevšie sa Štefanovi a spolunéma s ním krestanskému Maďarstvu a Slovanstvu. Slováci tedy boli verní pomocníci a priatelia sv. Štefana, zakladateľa uhorského kráľovstva, pamiatka tohoto žije podosiaľ v nasledujúcej prostonárodnej pieśni ľudu.

Stála bitka stála, za Štefana kráľa.
Takej viac nebude, kým svet svetom bude.
Stála bitka stála, v tej uhorskej zemi;
Bili sa junáci a pohanní Slováci.
Bola bitka bola vyše Ostrihoma.
Červená krv tiekla polovicou Hrona.
Červená krv tiekla k blízkemu Dunaju,
Tých kliatych pohanov kresťania rúbajú.

49

Birthplace of Ján Palarík in Raková pri Čadci.

Catholic church in Majcichov, where Palarík served as Catholic priest.

Štefan M. Daxner with his wife Paulina, née Štepanová.

Family home of the Daxners in Tisovec, 1943.

Birthplace of František V. Sasinek in Skalica.

František V. Sasinek, Catholic priest and professor at the lyceum (gymnasium) in Banská Bystrica.

Young Vajanský, as actor.

Baťko (Vajanský).

Pozdrav z Turčianskeho Sv. Martina.

Baťko Vajanský in 1912.

Birthplace of Vajanský in Hlboka.

Birthplace of Vavro Šrobár in Liskova.

The patriotic student association *Detvan*, Prague, 1900.
Vavro Šrobár is in the second row, third sitting from the right.

Vavro Šrobár and his first wife Berta, née Kučová.

Andrej Hlinka (1864 -1938).

František Sasínek, © SNK

IV. František Víťazoslav Sasinek (1830 - 1914). History and eccentricity.

IV. 1. Political goals

At the beginning of my research, I found that Sasinek had published countless articles about the history of Hungary and the origins of the Slavs, which immediately reminded me of František Palacký (1798 - 1876). Richard Marsina and Peter Mulik's collection of studies published in 2007 is the only study known to me that assesses the historical, religious and social aspects of Sasinek's works[234]. Matúš Kučera states that Sasinek's contemporaries had compared him to the Czech historian[235]. Palacký and Sasinek shared an unprecedented talent and passion for history and a lifelong concern for their nations' political liberties. But while Palacký is widely known in the Czech Republic and Europe, Sasinek is less well known, even in his native Slovakia. This can be explained by the distinct development of Slovak historiography.

Slovak historiography emerged in 1919 with the foundation of the Comenius university in Bratislava and developed in three phases[236]: the first was characterised by the perception of Slovak history as a part of the larger Czechoslovak history. Daniel Rapant represented an exception among the first generation of mostly Czech professors, who had to face the difficult task of investigating Slovak history from the perspective of a joint Czech and Slovak history. The second began in 1953 with the foundation of the Slovak Academy of Sciences and its Department of History that started to undertake serious research on distinct epochs, but was subject to the ideological constraints of Marxism-Leninism. The third phase began in 1989 and represented the third attempt to research Slovak history. This third attempt featured a new direction for Slovak historiography that involved taking up relations with international historiography and enjoyed a new professional framework without any ideological constraints[237]. In regard to the 19th century epoch of "praise and defense

---

[234] Richard Marsina and Peter Mulík, eds., *Franko Víťazoslav Sasinek. Najvýznamnejší slovenský historik 19. Storočia, 1830-1914* (Martin: Matica Slovenská, 2007).

[235] Matúš Kučera, "Koncepcia slovenských dejín v diele F. V. Sasinka", in *Franko ...* 9-20; 9.

[236] Dušan Kováč, "Popoluška slovenskej historiografii – vlastné dejiny," *Historický časopis 52*, č. 2 (2004): 233-237; 233.

[237] Kováč, "Popoluška...", 234

of the Slovaks"[238], the first historiographical phase accomplished historical descriptions and pinned down topical areas, but failed to fill in the historiographical lacunas, such as critical biographies of historians like Sasinek. He simply became forgotten in the collective memory due to the mentioned lack of historiographical research.

While Francisci, Palarík and Daxner's political perspective may be interpreted as egalitarian in the sense of proto-democratic, Sasinek's views were diametrically opposed to the most modest call for civil rights. He spoke with contempt about Socialism[239]. His suggestions of how to resolve social misery, brought about by the economic system established by Hungary's nobility in the preceding centuries[240], did not include political or economic reforms, let alone social or civil rights. Sasinek suggested faith as a cure: the poor should believe in the rightfulness and wisdom of the Church's leadership, since Socialism would only lead to damnation. The lord had created poverty and richness – it was not for the people to correct this divine segregation. To him, social mobility was blasphemy and attempts to establish a better life for oneself without the guidance of the Catholic Church was a godless endeavour doomed from the beginning. His outspoken tolerance of the Slovak Lutherans originated in his nationalism, which was language-based. As regards social issues, we could say that Sasinek adhered to the motto "Caritas instead of political rights". *Caritas* would ascertain the Catholic Church's power, in particular in the conservative countryside.

Making a sharp distinction between social issues and politics, he considered history to be the politics of yesterday. I shall try to show on the following pages that Sasinek did not separate history from politics, as Michal Otčenáš contends[241]. On the contrary, I think that Sasinek consulted historical documents to craft his political arguments. He developed from a loyal Catholic monk into a fervent Slovak patriot,

---

[238]   Kováč, "Popoluška...", 234.

[239]   Franko V. Sasinek, "Sociálná otázka," *Katolické Noviny XXV*, č. 10, 14, 21-23, 1894.

[240]   For a detailed analysis of the political-economic system in the Hungarian kingdom see Jenö Szücs, "The three historical regions of Europe," *Acta Historica Academiae Scientiarum Hungaricae 29*, no. 2–4, (1983): 131-184.

[241]   "František Víťazoslav Sasinek sa snažil poukázať na spoločenské poslanie dejín a striktne oddeľoval históriu od politiky." Michal Otčenáš, "Vedecko-organizačná a bádateľská činnosť' F. V. Sasinka", in *Franko...* 21-29; 25.

equipped with scholarly skills acquired in the seminary. As much as he criticised the Magyars for their assimilation, he did not utter a critical word about the Catholic hierarchy. And yet he insisted on surprisingly modern, objective methods in historical research; the study of sources had to entail linguistic and etymological analysis of the key concepts. Sasinek published in Latin, Slovak, Hungarian, German and Czech and often used the pseudonyms *Chvojnicky* and *Slovákovič*, especially in newspaper articles attacking Magyar politicians in a sarcastic and condescending tone. His etymological explanations of 'Hungar' and 'Magyar'[242] were lengthy and somewhat repetitive. What were his views about the language?

IV. 1. 1.   Language of communication

What were Sasinek's political goals? We hold that he had two: first, the status of *language of communication* for Slovak in the Slovak *župy* and second, the *power sharing* of Slovaks and Magyars. While the second goal was of course completely unrealistic, even in the years before the *Ausgleich*, the first represented one of the demands of the *memorandum* of 1861. Let us take a closer look at Sasinek's conception of 'language' and 'nation', from which his claim for the communication status was derived.

> "The Slovak sons are sons of the country ... Concerning their language, they are the sons of Slovak parents, who have the god-given right to demand of their sons and daughters that they honour them and keep alive *branch and language* ... What would those Hungarian 'trained pedagogues' say, if somebody suggested talking to a Magyar [student, add. JB] in English, so that he would understand [the concepts of science, add. JB]?"[243]

Sasinek's notion of the nation was the traditional one he shared with the majority of the members of the national movement: nationhood was based on Slovak. We have found no references to Herder or Hegel's philosophies in Sasinek's texts. That is the reason why we think that he subscribed to *rational natural law*, which for him was a part of the Catholic catechism. As a Christian nation and gifted with human reason, the Slovaks had the natural right to use their language. To forbid Slovak to be spoken was blasphemy and equated to cultural genocide, to use a modern concept. Education was an important issue to him. If the Magyars were serious about building a modern

---

242   Sasinek, "Uhor a Madar," *Slovenský Letopis I*, (1876): 96-111.
243   Sasinek, "Škola a maďarisácia," *Národnie Noviny IX*, č. 128, 31. 10. 1878, 2, italics by JB.

state through scientific and economic progress, they should understand the crucial importance of instruction in the mother tongue.

> "A Slovak student, ignorant of even the most basic Hungarian word, incapable of properly reading Hungarian, carries in his belt Hungarian school books, of which he has as much understanding as of Arabic, and, coming to school, he listens to a Magyar professor's lecture, which he understands as much as a Chinese would a comedy in a German theatre. ... do these Hungarian 'trained pedagogues' know the meaning of a 'circulus vitiosus' in education? It means that the Slovak youngster has already to understand Hungarian in order to learn Hungarian ... Is this how 'scientific knowledge' should be achieved?"[244]

Sasinek conceived of national identity as a natural thing the lord had extended to all nations. For the believers, rational natural law was the idea that human reason was a god-given gift; the non-believers conceived of it as a law of nature originating in a sphere beyond human understanding. Sasinek naturally understood rational natural law as a gift from the lord: all nations should be equal in their right to express their true self. The nationalities based their defensive demands for cultural rights, that then turned into demands for political equality, on rational natural law, a powerful moral weapon against positive law laid down by the ruling Magyars and Austrians. Practically all claims, the entire 'catalogue' – starting with language rights extending to territorial autonomy with local self-government and ending with sovereignty – could be justified through natural law that derived its moral power from a transcendent realm inaccessible to the human mind.

> "Equality of rights! ... There is no doubt that a two-fold law of nations [právo národu] forms the essence of nationality and language: a) that a nation can develop naturally in its own language and environment; b) that it is run in its own language and surroundings. A nation whose lower and higher education is conducted in a foreign language, in which judicial process is conducted and court sentences are read out in a foreign language, is being directly deprived of its language and national identity, its education and general good, its freedom and character; to such a nation, law, freedom and justice mean nothing."[245]

In accordance with rational natural law, Sasinek's political goal was the constitutionally granted use of Slovak as stipulated in the *memorandum*. He saw clearly that equality of rights meant that a nation should also be ruled in its language. This involved the areas of the judiciary and the political institutions, where positive

---

[244]   Sasinek, "Škola a maďarisácia," č. 130, 5. 11. 1878, 2.

[245]   Sasinek, "Rovnoprávnosť," *Pestbudínské Vedomosti VIII*, č. 53, 3. 7. 1868, 1.

law, set by the Magyars, determined the use of Hungarian. Courts and diets were the *foci* of social life; they were equally important for national progress. They had to be subject to rational natural law too. Sasinek thus called for the status of *language of communication*, which the Magyars had to reject. They logically anticipated that the demands for linguistic autonomy would lead to claims for territorial autonomy and eventually result in *secession* – which the Slovaks did not have in mind. From the Magyar perspective of the Hungarian political nation, the nationalities' language claims formed only the beginning of a longer process towards their projected status of sovereignty. The Magyar elite's own experience in negotiating the *Ausgleich* convinced them that any concession made to the nationalities would evoke demands that would eventually lead to a substantial loss of territory.

We think that Sasinek would have been content with the status of language of communication for Slovak – for the time being. It would have boosted the nation's economic and educational progress and enhanced the administrative and diplomatic skills of the urban elite. But we encounter here a contradiction in his thought: how to sustain conservatism and the Church's power under the conditions of economic and social progress? He must have been aware of the fact that development would bring about a critical amount of pluralism and intensified contact with trade partners, of whom the Magyars were the closest. Sasinek does not give us an answer; the following interpretation thus remains speculation.

He would have accepted progress unfolding in the clear confinements of the towns and insisted on the Church's leading role in the countryside. He might have undergone a modest correction of his aversion to social mobility, but would most certainly have spoken out for a Slovak Catholic university in Pressburg. The population in the countryside would benefit from the developing towns and send their sons to the seminaries and the university, which would offer higher education in Slovak. Students would not have to enrol at Pest University anymore. After some years, the Slovaks would be aptly prepared for local self-government in their *župy*.

Not surprisingly, Sasinek never addressed the minority issue, the *litmus test* of true equality of rights: he failed to elaborate on how to determine what language(s) should be used in the towns with a mixed population of Magyars, Slovaks and Ruthenians, or towns, where the Magyars formed the majority.

In his concern for the language, Sasinek defended the *Matica slovenská* against its critics. In his article *What is the Matica slovenská and what is it not?* he sharply opposed the critique of the association's opponents. He described the existing confusion about the association's goals and *raison d'être* as a misunderstanding owing to false information, lack of knowledge and malevolence[246]. Many would think of the *Matica* as the representative organ of the Protestants because the first chairman had been the Protestant superintendent Karol Kuzmány. Martin was a Protestant town insofar that the majority of the inhabitants adhered to the Lutheran confession; but the confession of the people had certainly no influence on the publication plans of the association, whose position was inter-confessional. The *Matica* was a national organisation, which was concerned with the Slovak language, culture and the nation's education, regardless of confessional aspects. Others believed the association to be a kind of enterprise, involving various national projects such as a bank, publisher's houses, gymnasium, dance clubs or folklore groups. The association had nothing to do with the *sporiteľna* (savings bank) just because the two institutions were located in Martin; nor was there a connection with the gymnasium, the publishers and other various citizens' groups. Sasinek condemned those referring to the *Matica* as a political organisation with sharp words:

> "Had the 'Magyar academy' ever been a political institution just because its chairmen had been Magyars? ... I had to fulfil my duty as patriot, because the malevolence of our enemies is deepening the errors and misunderstandings that alienate the public from the Matica slovenská ... they know very well that misinformed and uneducated people can, like an ox, be easily put under the yoke; a well-educated and critical people, however, understands its rights, failures and interests."[247]

In an emotional tone, Sasinek almost implored his readers to differentiate: The association was neither a "Jesuit bogy" [jezuitské strašidlo] as some Protestants believed, nor an Evangelical institute, as some Catholics thought[248]. He concluded with one of his biting and aggressive comments, addressed to the Magyars.

> "But you, you selfish vultures, who would like to feed on the dead and defeated Slovak nation, stop to malevolently accuse and aggressively damage the honour of the 'Matica

---

[246]   Sasinek, "Čo nieje a čo je 'Matica Slov.'?" *Národnie Noviny*, č. 32, 15.3.1873, 1.
[247]   Sasinek, "Čo nieje...", 2.
[248]   Sasinek, "Čo nieje...", 2.

slovenská'. Its only guilt lies in the fact that the scientific and cultural texts it publishes ... are in Slovak."[249]

IV. 1. 2. The idea of power sharing

If Sasinek called for equality of rights and the language of communication status in the 1870s, one has the impression that he had undergone a correction of the claims expressed in the *memorandum* in the 1860s. But his thought was erratic and lacked a coherent development of single ideas. His concerns were many-fold and not always logically coherent. It seems to me that he feverishly published what came to his mind changing from theme to theme and making up his own mind in the process of research. A look at his political statements leaves one confused as he contradicted himself several times. In the early 1860s, he called for the joint rule of Magyars and Slovaks – which was not a point of the *memorandum*. We could understand his demand for joint rule as the essence of the idea of *power sharing*. Yet, we are reluctant to use the term 'power sharing arrangement', as Sasinek did not go into details about the organisation of such a government. He was interested in the big picture, in the essential truth of history and deemed it his task to educate the nation about its past. Sometimes, we had the impression that he literally intended to hammer his particular views into citizens' heads, repeating some of his arguments, adding new ones, thereby creating a rather confusing blend of the terms 'autonomy', 'freedom', 'civil rights' and 'joint rule'. Sasinek could not be bothered by petty details about constitutional stipulations or legal wording. As precisely as he described historical events of the 9th and 10th century, he was vague in regard to nationality rights. History herself, or so he must have thought, spoke through him as the nation's principal historian, who once and for all unmasked the Magyars' continuous distortion of Hungary's history. His increasingly radical nationalism bordered on chauvinism; it was taking possession of him in the mid 1860s to such extent that he published a contortion of the concept and notion of 'historic rights':

"From these words of Mr. Eötvös follows his subjective opinion that only the Magyars are entitled to historic rights [historické právo] in Hungary, the Slovaks and the other nationalities, since they lacked these rights, would have at their disposal only natural law

---

[249] Sasinek, "Čo nieje...", 2.

[prirodzené právo] and the principle of nationality [zásada národnostná] ... upon which to base their demands."[250]

"If the Magyars consider themselves as the ruling nation in Hungary, what version of history do they justify their leading position with? ... The Magyars did not subject the Slovaks, but agreed on becoming associates [smluvne so sebou spojili]. The Slovaks were *socii* of the Magyars, not *gens subjecta*: that is why the Slovaks are as much entitled to Hungarian historic rights as the Magyars."[251]

Sasinek's interpretation of 'historic rights' was mistaken. We cannot say for certain that he undertook it deliberately to convince his fellow nationals of their former equal status with the Magyars. But, considering his education and, above all, the command of Latin that enabled him to study the historical documents, we are inclined to believe that he consciously corrupted the historical facts – with the noble intention of defending Slovak language rights. Let us explain how we think he did it.

Sasinek was confusing *rights based on rational natural law* with *rights originating in positive law*. The concept *historic state rights* was a well-known issue in the Monarchy after the failed revolution of 1848. Sasinek read and wrote Czech. We think that he was familiar with Palacký's draft constitution of 1848 and his later defence of the historic state rights of the lands of the St. Wenceslas crown[252].

In the first quote, Sasinek referred to the historic rights the Magyars enjoyed in the kingdom. To convince his readers and stress his point of what historic rights should be, not what they actually were, he delivered a misinterpretation. He interpreted the *historic state rights,* originating in positive law, as linguistic and cultural rights, originating in rational natural law, which they were not. It was a decisive fact that the Slovak *župy* had never been elevated to the status of a *crown land* or *a historical-political individuality*[253], because the Hungarian kingdom had been a multi-ethnic state with various ethnic groups as state-building nation. Magyar

---

[250] Sasinek, "Historické právo," *Pestbudínské Vedomosti V*, č. 58, 21. 7. 1865, 2.

[251] Sasinek, "Historické právo," 3.

[252] Palacký's most important political texts: "Idea státu Rakouského", first published in *Národ*, 1865, no. 96, 99, 106. Also in František Palacký, *Radhost. Sbírka spisův drobných z oboru řeči a literatury češské, krásowědy, historie a politiky* (Praha: B. Tempsky, 1873). František Palacký, *Geschichte von Böhmen: groesstenteils nach Urkunden und Handschriften* (Prag: Kronberger & Riwac, 1836-1867).

[253] See footnote 16 for a definition of "crown land" and "historical-political individuality".

nationalism started only later to constrain the multi-ethnicity of the population. The nationalities' language rights derived from the constitutionally granted freedom of religion, which Emperor Joseph II considered as a fundamental institute of his *Rechtsstaat*, his rule-of-law state. Joseph's political reforms originated in *Enlightened absolutism*, which should help to modernise the Monarchy. Every national group enjoyed the liberty to choose its liturgical language. Sasinek must have known that the language rights regulated the language issue *within* the kingdom, but never equalled, let alone overruled, the historic state rights, which determined the kingdom's rights and duties in its *external relations* with the Empire. The language rights had been crafted as an internal right that allowed the national groups to exercise their free expression of their religion. The language rights were *territorially neutral and apolitical* in the sense that they did not stipulate a group's political dominance over its territory. The use of the nationalities' vernaculars had been valid only within and for the group, while Latin had been the language of communication until Hungarian began to replace it in the first decades of the 19th century. The language rights were not designed as an external representation of the national groups in their relations with Vienna, as Sasinek pretended, but to grant their freedom in confessional matters.

In the second quote, Sasinek created a contradiction. He was right in pointing to the ethnic bias of recent Magyar historiography, but he failed to explain *why* the Slovaks had never been granted *historic state rights* in the first place. Why were the Slovak *župy*, established in the 14th century, never elevated to the status of a crown land? This was the weak point in his argument, but nevertheless a historical fact, which must have caused considerable distress to him. If the Slovaks, as he claimed, had had a distinct identity already four hundred years ago when they ruled jointly with the Magyars, why had they not been granted a historical status of their territory equal to the Magyars?

We think that Sasinek instinctively knew the answer and decided not to mention it: in the 14th century, the population of the Hungarian kingdom identified itself primarily as Christians and citizens of the kingdom. A national identity based on ethnic and cultural origins did not yet exist; identities were formed mainly through religious adherence and social provenience. Time and again, Sasinek blamed the Magyars for 'pushing the nationalities against the wall' – which they did. He portrayed the Slovaks as victims – which they were. But the fact that Slovak – and Magyar – national identity had started only with the renaissance of their languages around 1830 and 1790 respectively, considerably weakened his argument of a former joint rule of Slovaks and Magyars.

Nevertheless, Sasinek would express the same demands for a power sharing or joint rule in the 1890s. In his critical account of the preparations for the celebration of the Hungarian millennium in 1896, he used historical arguments to prove that 896 was not a historical date[254]. In a sarcastic tone, he went into the details of the settlement of the Pannonian plateau in the 9 and 10 centuries and accused the Magyars of having deliberately distorted the historical truth. Politicians and non-politicians would now equate current Hungary to the times when Arpad and his tribe settled at the Danube. Yet, this did not amount to objective and truthful historical research, as there were many non-Magyar tribes that had settled there before. Sasinek listed these tribes, among them the Chazars, Turko-Bulgarians, Polovcians, Germans and Romanians and, repeating his rhetorical question about who should celebrate that 'invented millennium' [to obmýšlané tisícročie], he followed with lengthy details about their relations with the Arpads. Referring to the *Tripartitum*, the codification of law by the Hungarian statesman Stefan Verböci (1458-1542) and the old-Slavonic Chronicle of Nestor, he dated the settlement of the Arpads on 891, when they first arrived in Pannonia with their Turko-Bulgarian and Chazar tribes. Sasinek stressed that the Arpads were already mixing with the ancestors of the Slavs in the 9th century, when they were fighting the Great Moravian state of Svatopluk I. In Sasinek's view, the year 896 was not a decisive date for Hungary; several battles were fought contesting the territory of Svatopluk I until 899, when Arpad's victory against Bracslav established his rule over lower Pannonia. His point was not only that the date of the millennium 896 was not historical, but also that there was no millennium to be celebrated at all, since the Arpads had not been the only tribe to settle and conquer the territory they later referred to as Hungary. The Slavs' ancestors had governed higher Pannonia, the region of future Slovakia. The millennium was the ideological result of the national chauvinism of the Magyars and the Slovak *Maďarony* currying favours with them. Sasinek himself, however, was not interested

---

[254] Sasinek, "Millenium," *Národnie Noviny XXII*, č. 141, 1. 12. 1891, 2.

in their petty views borne from their narrowmindedness, but in the true voice of history:

> "Endlessly, one can hear and read about the millennium that will be celebrated with a Hungarian state exhibition in 1896. But nobody answers the crucial question: who should celebrate this millennium? ... The historical truth doesn't depend ... on declaring as truth that which is generally accepted ... in uneducated circles it can still be heard that the sun is spinning around the earth ... Now, I don't see a nation in Hungary that the true voice of history would elevate to celebrate the 1896 millennium ... I would quite openly advise people to keep silent about this anti-historical celebration [ta oslava proti-historická]."[255]

IV. 2. Political legitimating

IV. 2. 1. Anti-Liberalism

Sasinek's fight against Magyarisation illustrates not only his nationalism, but also his contempt for liberal values, save for the abolition of serfdom[256]. His conservative perception of the female as perennial seducer was revoltingly misogynist and he was not shy to declare liberalism an ideology that spoiled the nation's sons (sic!). Loss of faith led to a betrayal of the nation, psychological and emotional distress and ended in financial fraud and imprisonment. In his essay *Liberál*[257] he delivered an illustration of the dangers Liberalism would bring down on the nation:

> "In our times we often hear one word: liberal. ... The basic principle of the liberals is: I believe and do as I please and leave others to believe and do as they please. They are free-thinking [svobodomyseľní] as regards religion; selfish [svevoľní] as regards the way of life; indifferent [ľahostajní] as regards the faith and way of life of others."[258]

The peasant Filip Horák was a brave, dutiful and hard-working man, who despised the pub and went to church. He had not enjoyed higher education, but was naturally intelligent; he could read, write and count. He subscribed to the *Catholic News* and the *Putnik (pilgrim)*, which informed him about the news in church and community. With the *Obzor* (*Horizon*), he improved his agricultural skills, while *Hlásnik* (*Watchman*) provided news about domestic affairs and the outside world. One would

---

255   Sasinek, "Millenium," 2.
256   Sasinek, "Poddanstvo v Uhorsku," *Kalendár Národni II* (1894): 130-147. He concluded declaring Magyarisation to be a new form of political serfdom the Magyars had subjected Hungary's nationalities to.
257   Sasinek, "Liberál," *Katolické Noviny XXV*, č. 6, 8, 9, 1894.
258   Sasinek, "Liberál," č. 6, 1.

not find a drop of *palinka* (brandy) in his house. This brave man was married to the peasant Jozefina, who gave birth to the sons Ondrej and Edmund. Ondrej took after his father; he was modest, faithful and hard working. Jozefina, influenced by the false flattery of an old woman, saw more in Edmund, to whom fate had assigned the future of a real gentleman. Ondrej was his father's son, Mundiček was hers. She arranged for private lessons to prepare him for higher education. Filip first rejected her suggestion to divide the inheritance, which rightfully belonged to Ondrej as the elder, but she kept insisting until he caved in. With finances secured, Mundiček enrolled in the gymnasium and started to call himself Ödon, greeting people in Hungarian instead of Slovak. Ondrej worked in the fields and grew up under his father's loving care. The village priest was not enthusiastic about Ödon's intellectual gifts and told Filip as much. Jozefina, however, made sure that Ödon enrolled in the law faculty of Pest University. In his letters he kept requesting funds. Also, he called himself Hegyi to conceal his Slovak origins. In the capital, falling into bad company, Ödon became a true liberal: he liked what was good for him and disliked what was not. During the day, he worked as a clerk in the office of the advocate Dr. Hladár (he who seeks); at night, he frequented pubs, drank and wrote political pamphlets about liberal and social issues. In four years he never once visited his parents. When he finally came home at Easter, in middle of the school year, Jozefina happily expected to see the diploma. But Ödon had never graduated. He lied that the diploma would be sent soon. He refused to say his prayers, ate, slept late into the day and read. When the shocked Jozefina tried to talk some sense into him, there was a knock at the door. The local notary and two gendarmes entered and arrested Ödon, whom they suspected of having counterfeited a cheque made out for one thousand gold ducats at the advocate's office in Pest. Jozefina then understood how badly she had been neglecting Ondrej and his bride Alžbeta and apologised to both. Ödon was transferred to Budapest, tried and sentenced to prison, where he caught a fever. The news of his death arrived with the request of a payment still outstanding. Touched by Ondrej's generous offer to pay for half of the debt, Jozefina paid for the other half and transcribed her widow's pension to Ondrej. Some days later, they received an official letter from the prison informing them that Edmund had rediscovered his faith in his last hours. He had begged the priest to extend his apologies to all his family and died in peace.

Sasinek's contempt for liberal values was further visible in his critique of the opponents of the *memorandum*, whom he called *antimemorandisti*; their prominent figure was the liberal Ján Palarík[259]. Using a religious metaphor, Sasinek compared the adoption of the *memorandum* at the gathering in Turčiansky Sv. Martin with the mercy of St. Martin, who had cut his coat in two and given one half to a beggar, who was cold. The sword of unlimited patriotism and devotion to the language had cut from the coat of the nationality rights the *memorandum*, which protected Slovakia in unjust and fatally threatening times. But what happened? Immediately, a Herodes showed up, who sought the *memorandum's* death, arguing that the demands would threaten Hungary's integrity. The voice of "Magyar pseudo-liberalism" divided the nation into two camps: those who contested the *memorandum* and those who defended it[260].

Sasinek delivered his critique in four points assessing what he believed were the arguments of the protesters. First, the *antimemorandisti* would not acknowledge the legality of the gathering in Martin, because no government had empowered them to attend. This was simply not true, so Sasinek, as the diet and the *župan* had been informed. Furthermore, everybody who truly cared about national issues had learnt about the meeting. The argument of legality was irrelevant here anyway, since the gathering did not convene in order to adopt new laws but to formulate the demands of the nation. With populist and simplifying retorics, Sasinek defended the legitimacy rather than the legality of the gathering.

Second, lacking any reasonable argument, the opponents would wash their hands in innocence only to conceal the fact that they did more than was necessary to support *Magyarism*. They argued that they could not send their own delegates. This had to be rejected too, since the gathering had been announced in all Slovak newspapers. Did they know about the meeting or not? If they failed to show up, it was their mistake and only demonstrated their malevolence toward the nation's good.

Third, should the gathering have consisted of administrative personnel of the towns rather than of the population? The meeting was organised to give the population a voice, to enable the nation to freely express its demands and critics of the administrative institutions that were carrying out the illegal Magyarisation; it was

---

[259]   Sasinek, "Memorandum a protesty," *Peštbudinské Vedomosti I*, č. 40, 2. 8. 1861, 2.
[260]   Sasinek, "Memorandum a protesty," 2.

by no means conceived as forum for the administration [ľud a jeho žiadosti, nie ale úradnikov]. Or would one expect the administrators to criticise themselves in front of everyone? The gathering was planned in the spirit of democracy, not to display aristocratic rule once more [demokraciu a nie aristokraciu][261].

Fourth, the opponents protested only because they had nothing serious to contribute. In his fourth point, Sasinek quite explicitly accused the *antimemorandisti* of malevolence and treason. They were eager to violently down-level the nation to the status of a "political beggar" [politického žobráka], who should content himself with the few bare bones thrown at him[262].

Sasinek stated in the second part of his article that the protests, however, also had a positive side, since they were proof of four facts. First, those enjoying the *memorandum's* sun shining brightly in Martin had expected a "storm" [burka] clouding the nation's unity anyway[263]. They were thus not surprised when such an outburst evolved surrounding the issue, whether the demand for the *okolie* should be integrated to the text of the *memorandum* or not. Second, the protests were necessary for the nation to see what was really happening. The opponents thus indirectly helped to advance the nation's political development and maturity as they forced it to open its eyes and distinguish those who cared about it from those who did not. Third, the protesters had, against their own wishes, contributed to the promotion of knowledge about the Slovaks in Europe. Some referred to a figure of eighty thousand, others of three hundred thousand Slovaks living in the lands of the crown of St. Steven and lacking equal rights with the Magyars[264]. Although they supported Magyar liberalism, the protesters unwillingly unmasked the alleged equality of rights in Hungary as a satire. Fourth, the protests taught the nation that freedom in the sense of political rights would not come for free, but had to be fought for in a continuous struggle. The nationalities in the Hungarian kingdom had had civil rights and political liberties [práva občianskej a národnej slobody] until 1836[265]:

> "From these times on, one son of our common mother-state Hungary, the Magyar, started to claim for himself alone the legacy of freedom of equality, the very same equality of

---

[261]   Sasinek, "Memorandum a protesty," 2.

[262]   Sasinek, "Memorandum a protesty," 2.

[263]   Sasinek, "Memorandum a protesty," *Peštbudínske Vedomosti I*, č. 41, 6. 8. 1861, 1.

[264]   Sasinek, "Memorandum a protesty," 2.

[265]   Sasinek, "Memorandum a protesty," 2.

freedom all Hungarian nationalities had inherited from their fathers. Yet, we Slovaks shall not allow this legacy to be taken from us by those who are entitled to their own freedom, but have no right to lay claim on our legacy [nie ale k nášmu dedictvo má]. ... Our fathers gave their blood for our common state of equality [jednu vlasť rovnopravnostnú], in which the equality of rights ruled, for the freedom of the citizens and the nations as much as for the Magyars ... For more than eight hundred years we have been the brothers of the Magyars, and so we shall be in the future; but only brothers, not a tribe dependent of their benevolence like the Israelites in Egypt!"[266]

Identifying in a simplicist fashion liberalism with the Magyars and condemning the Slovak opposition about the *okolie*, Sasinek nevertheless concluded his *phillipic* on behalf of the *memorandum* with conciliatory remarks that show his deep hope for an understanding between the nations – apart from his desperate need to represent the Slovak viewpoint.

"To you, our Magyar brothers! (yet not to those ugly fellow Slovaks that alienated themselves from us [ošklivým odrodilcom]) If the Hungarian nationalities extend their brotherly hand to you, take it. If you stepped together with them to the level of equality of rights, their motto would be 'We love each other!' Yet, if you won't extend your hand guided by the intention of equality of rights [rovnoprávnenu ruku], lest be assured that a true Slovak shall always remember his motto 'We shan't give ourselves up!' and he will persist against your absolutism."[267]

As conservative and simplistic as Sasinek's view of liberalism was, he was a generous and loyal colleague. In spite of his sharp rhethorics he was tolerant of different views among his fellow *narodovci;* when addressing the simple people for whom he wrote his religious texts, however, he was the conservative clergyman the Church expected him to be. In his obituary for Ján Palárik, an outspoken liberal and critic of the Church hierarchy, Sasinek showed his loving respect for the "enfant terrible" of Slovak Catholicism. After a brief and precise summary of Palárik's life and works, he concluded:

"As regards his politics, even though he worked with us on the foundation and management of the Budapest News, he maintained his own highly exclusive views, ... even though he did not approve of some of the steps we had taken while formulating and finalising the Memorandum, for the sake of the unity and good of the nation he never attacked us loudly or aggressively ... he could fulfil his task of mediating between the nation's various

---

[266] Sasinek, "Memorandum a protesty," 2.
[267] Sasinek, "Memorandum a protesty," 2.

standpoints. That, behold, was our dear Janko Palárik as priest, author and politician being in all these matters a role model of the true Slovak national character."[268]

IV. 2. 2. Constitutionalism or absolutism?

We mentioned above that Sasinek's thinking was erratic and not particularly coherent. He was certainly very knowledgeable when it came to historical issues. Unlike Palárik, however, he failed to address the nationality rights in detail. He did not suggest a political programme other than the repeated legitimating of the goals of equality of rights and joint rule. Nor was he very clear about the conditions of the *okolie* he had supported as a member of the *stará škola*. In his article *Absolutism or a constitution?* he presented a rare contribution to constitutional issues. One would expect the arch-conservative Sasinek to favour absolutism in at least its enlightened form, as his anti-liberalism would not support a liberal goal such as a constitutional state. However, at a second glance, the egalitarian facets in his thought, his patriotism and anti-aristocratism, might explain his preference for a constitutional state that allowed, at least in theory, the representation of Slovak interests.

He started with a general and brief definition of absolutism and constitutionalism and delivered his critique of Hungary as being *de facto* an absolutist state. The government would only accept into the diet those delegates, who supported the Deak party[269]. That was why the Slovak towns were sending a large number of "humiliated servants" [velký počet 'ponížených služebnikov'] to the diet, who just sat there, "silent like fish and with hanging heads like dried lentils"[270]. They would not represent the interests of their people, on the contrary, they voted against them. If the government was dependent on such delegates, it betrayed itself; any state, whose fundament was bad, would sooner or later collapse. That which was made to last, had to have a sound basis and that basis were the demands and just views of all Hungarian nations [žiadosťach a spravodlivých nárokov všetkých národov Uhorska][271].

Sasinek stressed that a constitution that respected the rights of the population only on paper would not last a thousand years. His allusion to the Hungarian

---

[268]   Sasinek, "Ján Palárik (Nekrolog)," *Národnie Noviny I*, č. 116, 11. 12. 1870, 3.
[269]   Sasinek, "Či absolutism alebo konštitúcia?" *Národné Noviny III*, č. 39, 30. 3. 1872, 1.
[270]   Sasinek, "Či absolutism...", 1.
[271]   Sasinek, "Či absolutism...", 1.

millennium was followed by a critique of the *Ausgleich*, which was similar to Palarík's statements elaborated upon above. Sasinek compared the discontent of the population in both parts of the Monarchy and the governments' reactions against these sentiments to the misogynist metaphor of a stupid mother, who beat her hungry children to stop their crying. The Czechs, Moravians, Poles, Slowenians and Dalmatians in Austria, and the Croats, Slovaks, Serbs, Ruthenians, Romanians and Germans in Hungary were equally disappointed. The state might have been lingering on from day to day, but it would not be capable of granting a safe future. Premier Andrassy should condemn the bad aspects of the current situation not only because they were already damaging the state, but also because they would continue to do so in the future. Owing to its size, the state was less flexible than an individual; any reforms and changes would be in effect only after a couple of years.

> "Such a mistaken step in Austro-Hungarian politics took Beust, changing the Hungarian-Austrian Empire into a Magyar-German state, which was based upon the principle of 'pushing the Slavs against the wall' ... Count Andrassy should understand ... that a true consolidation and strengthening cannot be carried out through a Magyar absolutism here, neither through a German there, but only through the laws of the constitution."[272]

IV. 2. 3. Slavic solidarity

A further interesting aspect of Sasinek's political legitimating can be found in his solidarity with the Slavs. He was not only a patriot eager to improve his nation's life, but showed a deep concern for all nations living under foreign rule. The most cruel event of the Balkan crisis of 1875 and 1876 was the crushing of the Bulgarian April Uprising in 1876, which became known as the *Bulgarian horrors*; he defended the Slavic viewpoint and accused the Western nations of hypocrisy. His article *The disgrace of the XIX century!*[273] can therefore be considered a testimony of his loyalty to the Slavs, all the more as we think it safe to assume that he knew Kollár's text *Slavonic reciprocity*.

Sasinek began his article stating that deeds counted more than words. This applied also to politics. If one had a look at the 19th century's values of freedom, civilisation and culture, one would first consider it as a century of mankind's progress toward the good and an era of humanity. A closer look, however, revealed its failure:

---

[272] Sasinek, "Či absolutism...", 1.
[273] Sasinek, "Haňba XIX. storočiu!" *Národnie Noviny VII*, č. 11, 27. 1. 1876, 1.

the 19th century was rich in theory but poor in practise: theories of freedom, civilisation and culture were being realised only in part. Humanity suffered not much more under the barbarism of the middle ages than now, considering in particular the situation of the Slavs. Like other nations, the Slavs had anchored the ideas of freedom, civilisation and culture in their hearts eager to effectively realise them in their national lives. They had assumed that the more advanced nations, which had proclaimed these values in the first place, would assist them in putting these values into practise; yet, a look at the reality confirmed the opposite: The Slavs were everywhere oppressed and bereft of their freedom. The selfishness of certain nations was so great that they were not content with the masses they already called their own; they had to overwhelm and incorporate the Slavic nations, as if they were some material that served for their gaining of political and economic weight. The Slavs, by contrast, had never been aggressive and conquering; they had always been and still were content with what they had.

The so-called civilised and Christian Europe did nothing to help the South Slavic nations that were being extinguished by the cruel barbarism of Muslim fanatism [muhamedánskym fanatismom barbara][274]. The Slavs in the South, forced to use the most desperate measures in order not to be treated as cattle, but as human beings created in the image of the lord, had been forming a wall protecting Christianity and Europe's civilisation from the sword of the vandals. Sasinek's allusion to the medieval concept *antemurale Christianitatis* formed the basis for his harsh critique of Western Europe's hypocritical stance. No science about freedom and civilisation would guide the European diplomats in their attempts to find a solution to the Balkan crisis, only selfishness and their hatred of the Slavs. They looked at the horrors evolving in the Balkan region in a calculating fashion that lacked the human values they were so proud of having declared.

> " … we would hear the following argumentation: it was not possible to unite them [the South Slavs, add. JB] to Serbia and Montenegro, because this would create two strong Slavic states. To give them sovereignty was not possible either, as it would pour oil into the fire of Slavic awakening. Now what? To introduce conditions, under which they were able to limit evil, but not to grow wings that would let them fly to the fields of civilisation and culture."[275]

---

[274] Sasinek, "Haňba…", 1.
[275] Sasinek, "Haňba…", 2.

The Western European nations should therefore stop bragging about freedom, civilisation and culture, if they were not willing to admit that they held the privilege and monopoly on these values, while the Slavic nations were condemned to buy with their blood only poor alms of freedom, civilisation and culture. As long as the West was trampling on the Slavs' freedom, keeping up the lack of education and burning the "origins of culture" [ohniská kultúry] in their lands, they should not praise themselves as "the apostles of freedom, civilisation and culture" [apoštolmi svobody, civilisácie a kultúry], but as the "medieval knights of slavery, barbarism and stupidity" [ritiermi stredoveku za otroctvo, barbarstvo a hlúpotu][276]. Sasinek had signed his article with his pseudonym *Chvoinický*, most probably for the following three reasons: First, he directly accused the Western nations, among them of course Austria-Hungary, of deliberately sacrificing the South Slavs to the Ottoman Empire owing to their perennial hatred of the Slavs. This could draw the administration's suspicions of a call for Panslavist activities that would sooner or later involve the Russian Empire, by then Austria's opponent in the Balkans.

Second, the combination of the words 'apostle' and 'freedom' immediately recalled the spirit of the secret revolutionary movement *Mlada Evropa (Young Europe)*, which was inspired by Giuseppe Mazzini's (1805 – 1872) liberal and national circle *La giovine Italia*[277]. Mazzini had formulated his revolutionary ideas of *Young Italy* in the 1830s. His goals included the Italian unification on a national-democratic basis. Mazzini further considered the Slavs living under foreign rule as allies, who would be supportive of his ideas. Mostly Polish emigrants joined the movement *Young Europe*, whose motto was 'God and the nation'. In Slovakia, Štúr and Hurban became inspired by the revolutionary ideas in their teenage years; their adherents shared the democratic and national goals of *Young Europe*. Yet, for educational and political reasons, the early national movement started to focuss on the preeminent language issue. The secret society *Vzájomnosť* was founded by Alexander Boleslavín Vrchovský (1812 - 1865) in Pressburg in 1837, but never gained a foothold strong enough to establish a steady co-operation with *Young*

---

[276]   Sasinek, "Haňba…", 2.
[277]   I would like to thank Anna Procyk for drawing my attention to Mazzini, the *Young Europe* movement and its relation to the Slavs in the early 19th century.

Europe[278]. We think that Sasinek deliberately repeated 'apostle' and 'freedom' to stress that the West had forgotten its former ideals and goals. His ironic tone should convince the reader of the West's biased views of 'freedom, civilisation and culture'.

Yet, the words also recalled a positive meaning: they reminded those readers familiar with Bulgarian history[279] of the fate of Vasil Levski (1837 - 1873). Levski, a deacon of the Orthodox Church, had been a principal figure in the early struggle of the Bulgarians against the 'Ottoman yoke'. His strategic and military skills helped the national movement to organise themselves, until Russia liberated Bulgaria in 1878. Levski was betrayed to the Ottoman authorities and his execution made him a national hero and legend. Until today he is referred to as the 'apostle of freedom'.

Third, Sasinek's allusion to the concept *antemurale Christianitatis* could be understood as inciting the Croats against the Hungarian government. Apart from the traditional Western fear of Panslavism and Russia's involvement, a union of the Croats, Serbs and Bulgarians against the Ottoman Empire would have wider political implications that would destabilise the entire region – which would prove to become reality in the two Balkan wars from 1912 and 1913.

---

[278] On *Young Europe,* Mazzini's influence on the *Štúrovci* and the group *Vzájomnosť* see Františka Čechová, "Štúrovci v mladej Európe," *Historická revue 14*, č. 4 (2003): 20-22; Ján Béder, "Tajný spolok slovenských radikálov," *Mladá tvorba 2*, č. 12 (1957): 374-376; Viliam Mruškovič, "Neznámy list 'vzájomnostných novín'," *Literárny archív 27*, č. 90 (1994): 37-54.

[279] One of Kollár's demands of *Slavonic reciprocity* to work was the Slavs' familiarity with other Slavic cultures, histories and languages: "We do not think that each Slav should speak or write perfectly in all dialects, but he should understand every Slavonic speaking Slav and master the dialects to a level that allows him to read books in their original dialects. Neither do we demand that every Slav should purchase all books and journals published in all dialects, for nobody could afford to do so. But the excellent books, the classics and those of pan-Slavonic contents (that are universal and of concern to all Slavs) he should be able to acquire. ... How many Poles speak, read and write perfectly foreign, non-Slavonic languages like French – and not a word Czech or Serbian! How many Czech libraries are full of the works of all German novelists – and not a single Polish or Russian book! How many Russians translate flawlessly from English, Italian --. Fairly, one should first know one's own blood and kin, and then the foreign. To forget one's own issues or to look contemptuously at one's close tasks while courting the foreign, alien and remote, is always a sign of a nation's degeneration." Baer, *Preparing Liberty...*, 20-57; 27, 37.

IV. 2. 4. The historical catechism for the Slovaks

In his text *Historický katechismus pre Slovákov* (*The historical catechism for the Slovaks*)[280] Sasinek summed up sixty points that should educate the nation about its own past. United by a strong national feeling and their own history, or better, what Sasinek believed they should consider their past, the nation would gather momentum to fight for equality of rights in Hungary. Sasinek's critique of the dominance of the Magyars in Hungary was the result of his historical research. A crucial point in his text is the question how the Slovak territory had become part of the Hungarian kingdom of Saint Steven (1000 - 1038)[281]. Sasinek's answer drew on the *topos* of an agreement: Mečislav II, the Polish king, had married his daughter to Imrich, successor to the throne of Hungary. Slovakia was the bride's dowry and her territories formed a separate principality [údeľné kniežatstvo] within the kingdom of Saint Steven[282].

We think that Sasinek's interpretation was based on a myth. The integration of the Slovak territory into the Hungarian kingdom lacks evidence, which gave rise to polemical debates between Slovaks and Magyars that had started in the 17th century[283]. In view of the lack of sufficient documentary evidence, myths arose that were used to explain the co-existence of the two national groups in the kingdom. There were two main theories: The Magyar viewpoint held that the Magyars, i.e. the Arpad dynasty, had subjected the Slavs. Some tales referred to Svätopluk I (871-894), the most influential emperor of Great Moravia, who had allegedly sold his lands to the Magyars in exchange for a white horse[284]. The Slovak view portrayed the ancient Slovaks, the Slavic ancestors of the Slovaks, as hosts, who had welcomed the Magyars as guests in their lands and concluded a treaty on joint rule with them. Both positions reflect the national ideologies about the past. We could circumscribe these views, which were based on legends and folk tales as myths inculcating the basic feature of the national-ethnic character. One could say that these myths created and

---

[280]   Sasinek, *Historický katechismus pre Slovákov* (Ružomberok: Glačou a Nákladom Karla Salvu, 1906 (3)).
[281]   Sasinek, *katechismus...*, 15.
[282]   Sasinek, *katechismus...*, 15.
[283]   Kováč, *Dejiny...*, 32.
[284]   Kováč, *Dejiny...*, 32.

confirmed each group's characteristic behavioural features. We think it could be called a process of identity-formation based on mythological perception of one's group. The Magyars wanted to see themselves as powerful conquerors, while the Slovaks liked to portray themselves – in Herder's sense – as peaceful and hospitable people that concluded in a rational fashion a treaty with their new neighbours. The characteristic features of both nations thus reduced the complexity of historical facts into the simplicistic views of one's characteristic national feature that subsequently legitimated one's political claims. Magyar vs. Slovak became identical with conquest vs. agreement, or military prowess vs. peaceful negotiation. The integration of the Slovaks to Hungary presumably evolved in a process of violence and agreements, which was a characteristic procedure of the Middle Ages[285].

Sasinek was a multi-faceted personality with an iridescent character, who used his considerable skills not always to his own advantage. His political goal was the constitutional guarantee of Slovak as a language of communication in the Upper Hungarian *župy*: schools, gymnasiums, judicial and political institutions should communicate in Slovak. He first used rational natural law to attack the positive laws the Magyars had laid down. Later, he published a deliberate misinterpretation of the 'historic rights'. He did not comment on this change of mindset from rational natural law to positive law. Furthermore, he failed to offer a solution for the towns and areas with mixed population.

Because of censorship, we can only speculate whether he had an independent Slovak nation-state in mind. We think that he would have backed the *okolie;* he had after all signed the *memorandum* whose main demand had been the *okolie*. A Slovak county ruled directly by Vienna and provided with territorial autonomy and internal self-government could have led, in a second phase, to the federation of the kingdom. Yet, federation was a liberal idea; to our knowledge, Sasinek did not mention a federation as the solution for the Empire's nationality problem.

He was too intellectual, elitist and eccentric to garner a wide following. We think he was aware of his lonely position within the national movement. His nation's situation was hopeless: the Slovaks would have to endure the ongoing assimilation, but they had one weapon: the continuous intellectual engagement for the national cause.

---

[285]   Kováč, *Dejiny...*, 32.

Should or could one call Sasinek the Slovak Palacký? Reluctantly yes, as regards his general merits in historiography. No, considering his old-fashioned views about social problems and his failure to fight for liberal values. He deserves respect for his scholarship and life-long commitment to the national cause. The defence of his nation must have caused him to take up the desperate act of distorting the historic rights. His eccentricity and increasingly radical nationalism added up to his neglect of reality. He did not care about a serious discussion of nationality rights and was simply not interested in giving serious thought to the minorities – but then such thought was obsolete anyway. He was a fervent patriot, who was increasingly losing touch with his own people. This might be a further reason for the general ignorance about him. But he defended Slovak rights with his considerable intellectual gifts and gave the nation a sense of its own past.

> "They [the Magyar patriots, add. JB] perceive the Magyarness of Hungary as the only binding expression of legality, the good of the country and patriotism. ... Our love for our sweet language is the reason why they hate us ... We are not demanding that the Magyar children should learn Slovak; but that in the gymnasiums of Slovakia, Slovak should at least be compulsory, ... so that the Slovak youth could prepare itself for its future participation in the life of the community ... We do not consider patriotism related to the Magyar language as a *conditio sine qua non*, but as love for the country and the development of the sciences, as love for education and the general good of all citizens."[286]

---

[286] Sasinek, "Patriotismus," *Národné Noviny III*, č. 121, 10. 10. 1872, 1.

František Víťazoslav Sasinek – life in brief

(Pseudonym: Franko Chvojnický, Slovakovič)

11 Dec. 1830	Born in Uherská Skalica in North-Western Slovakia. After primary education, he went to gymnasium in Skalica, Szolnok and Bratislava.
1846	Joined the order of the Capuchins. Sasinek studied philosophy in Pezinok, Tata and Pressburg, and theology in Scheibbs in lower Austria.
9 Oct. 1853	Ordained as Catholic priest in Raab, today's Györ in Hungary. After leaving the monastery, he was appointed priest of the diocese of Banská Bystrica, a position the famous bishop Štefan Moyses (1797-1869), founder and first chairman of the *Matica slovenská*, had held before him. Besides his duties as priest, Sasinek held a professorship in dogmatics and taught at the seminary as well as the local gymnasium.
1857	Priest at the diocese in Rača.
1860s	He published regularly on national culture, literature and politics in the *Peštbudinské Vedomosti (Budapest News)*, the Catholic newspapers *Cyrill a Method*, *Katolickej Noviny (Catholic News)* and *Priateli školy a literatury (Friends of school and literature)*.
1863	Foundation of the *Matica Slovenská* in Martin. Sasinek supervised the organisation's editorial and publishing activities, and founded the educational journal *Slovesnosť (Grammar)* with Andrej L. Radlinský (1817-1879) in Uherská Skalica.
1865	He was appointed editorial manager of the Matica. Together with Radlinský, he started to write the two volumes of *Archiv starých československých listín, písemností a dejepisných pôvodín pre dejepis a literatúru Slovákov (Archive of old čechoslovak fragments, texts and historic origins for history and literature of the Slovaks)*, which was published in Turčiansky Svätý Martin in 1872-73.

1869	Appointed secretary of the Matica. He edited *Slovenský letopis pre historiu, topografiu, archaeologiu a ethnografiu (Slovak journal for history, topography, archaeology and ethnography)*, published in Uherská Skalica from 1876 to 1883. Until his death, he published mainly books on history, such as *Dejiny drievnych národov na území terajšieho Uhorska (History of the nations living in the Hungarian countryside)*, 1867, 1878 (2) in Turč. Sv. Martin; *Dejiny počiatkov terajšieho Uhorska (History of the origins of contemporary Hungary)*, 1868 in Uherská Skalica; *Dejiny kráľovstva Uhorského (History of the Hungarian kingdom)*, vol. I in Banská Bystrica, 1869, vol. II in Turč. Sv. Martin, 1871; *Dejepis všeobecný a zvláštny Uhorska svetský a náboženský (General history with particular attention to the secular and religious history of Hungary)*, manuscript published by Radlinský in Vienna, 1871; *Dejepis Slovákov (History of the Slovaks)*, Ružomberok, 1895; *Država Velkomoravská (The Great Moravian state)*, 1896. Besides some collections of religious songs and prayer books, he published also in German, f.e. *Die Slovaken (The Slovaks)*, in Turč. Sv. Martin, 1875, 2nd edition Prague.
1870	Corresponding member of the Royal Bohemian Society in Prague.
1888-92	Editor of the Catholic news *Čech (The Bohemian)*. He was expelled from Upper Hungary for his patriotic ideas and lived for some time as spiritual counsellor at the monastery of the Sisters of Mercy in Prague, and later in Algersdorf in Styria.
1901	Lived until his death at the monastery of the Brothers of Mercy in Graz, Austria.
17 Nov. 1914	Sasinek died in Graz. In 1930, his body was transferred to Skalica, where it was buried in the crypt of St. Anne's Church.

Svetozár Hurban Vajanský, © SNK

V. Svetozár Hurban Vajanský (1847 - 1916). Messianism, Panslavism and the superiority of art.

"If, in our country, a man pulls at the yoke, he must be everybody: poet, author of cover articles, novelist, proof-reader and so on. There is no other way."[287]

Vajansky's description of his work mirrors his life-long commitment: the volume of his poetry, critiques, cover articles, novels and letters is overwhelming. He published very extensively, almost frantically, it seems, about art, literature and politics. His preferred genres were poetry, prose, novels and political comments. Naturally, I do not claim that this chapter presents a comprehensive assessment of his works, as I shall be focussing on his political articles, the major part published in *Národnie Noviny*. Because of the scope of my investigation, I cannot take account of Vajansky's poetry, novels, translations and literary critiques. For an overview and introduction from the perspective of literary studies I recommend the works of Ivan Kusý and Ján Juríček[288]. Excellent on Vajansky's thought about history is Karol Hollý's recent study *The negation of event history and historical optimism. The historical ideology of Svetozár Hurban Vajanský*[289].

In spite of Vajansky's high standing as the *uncrowned poet laureate* of the Slovak people and his intellectual focus on literature and art, I deem him nevertheless an important thinker of the national movement: he and his followers represented a political faction that had taken up the *legacy of the memorandum generation*. He found a way of peaceful resistance that would, so he believed, constitute the existential meaning of Slovak nationhood. The Slovaks had not yet reached the level of nationhood, because their literature and art were still underdeveloped. Art, literature and poetry were thus the means to become a nation, to develop a true Slovak identity. To him, nationhood was not a question of language rights and parliamentary representation, but a burning issue of an *inner spiritual disposition*, an

---

[287] Svetozár Hurban Vajanský, *Zápasy a hľadania v zrkadlení času. Život a dielo v dokumentoch* (Martin: Osveta, 1985), 74.

[288] Ivan Kusý, *Zrelý Vajanský* (Bratislava: Tatran, 1992); Ján Juríček, *Vajanský. Portrét odvážneho* (Bratislava: Obzor, 1988).

[289] Karol Hollý, "Negácia událostnej histórie a historický optimizmus: Historická ideológia Svetozára Hurbana Vajanského, (1881 – 1897)", *Historický časopis 57*, č. 2 (2009): 243-269. I would like to thank Daniela Kodajová and Gabriela Dudeková for recommending this study to me.

inner socio-cultural and psychological connection of a people with its literature. In his focus on art and literature, he distinguished himself from the Martinists, who had been following Štúr's romanticist emphasis on language as the worldly expression of the nation's spirit. Vajanský's thought is Šturovian in the sense that he adhered to the romanticist idea of cultural pluralism as the opposite of enlightened universalism. However, the usage of one's codified language was not enough; one had to go a step further and make the language an artistic instrument, a tool of art. Blunt everyday communication would not do – language was the means to express art, and only art was proof of a cultured and civilised group – a nation in the sense of a *Kulturnation* as the very opposite of the *political nation* the Magyars adhered to, at least in theory.

One could say that Vajanský dealt with the political legacy of his father's generation with unpolitical means: he went back to the pure romanticism of the 1848 generation. He could not be bothered with the political aspects of the failure of the *okolie*, since he was never really interested in politics. In his 'political' articles, he did not refer to constitutional questions or issues of rights, but stressed the importance of art and culture. His passion was literature and poetry, which he started to write at the age of six. While his father supported the memorandum that presented a transition from 1848 romanticism to the politics of Martin in 1861, his son would witness the entire political development from 1861 to the 1880s and 1890s, when the assimilation peaked. The issue of Slovak autonomy was therefore not a lost cause, as it had never been an issue for him in the first place. He committed himself to the struggle for the language in order to use it as a tool to establish the true sign of nationhood: a Slovak national literature. In that sense of literature and art, he was a political figure. The scions of the memorandum generation, Francisci, Daxner and Sasinek, had oriented themselves toward Vienna, while Palárik, the *enfant terrible* of Slovak liberalism, had supported Buda. Except for his Panslavism and slavophile Messianism that remained unclear in terms of a political programme or goal, Vajanský had no political orientation; his point of orientation was Slovak literature, which had to be defended against assimilation – and became a political issue only because the Magyar authorities brought charges against him several times for his articles.

An introductory overview of Slovak intellectual history of the 19th century, as this investigation attempts to be, has to include Vajanský, all the more so as he did not represent an intellectual bridge connecting the memorandum generation with the modern Realists-Hlasists[290]. He was not as isolated and contested as Palarík and the members of the *nova škola*, but his thought did not bring about any changes either. Politically, he made two steps back joining the Štur generation in their focus on language, but in terms of art he presented a revolutionary new idea to the Slovaks, linking their nationhood exclusively to literature. We could therefore say that his thought presented a regression in political terms and, at the same time, a revolutionary advance in artistic terms. I think that Vajanský had no real understanding of politics, but then he was not interested anyway. That the national movement was broken into two factions was of less concern to him, as he did not think in terms of a united political movement. On the contrary: the only movement he deemed worthy of engagement in was literature. Literature was the embodiment of the nation, enabled the nation to become what it should be, led by insightful and prophetic leaders such as himself. Therefore, he rejected the Hlasists-Realists because of their worldliness, their focus on negligible and lowly everyday issues and, above all, their ignorance of art as the expression of the nation's soul. To him, their focus on socio-political and economic issues was alien; their attempts to import Czech political thought into Slovak life was ridiculous, to say the least. He was simply not interested in the conditions and issues the Hlasists were occupied with. From the perspective of the Hlasists, the national movement was being crucially endangered by Vajanský's promotion of an 'elitist intellectual ivory tower' that called for passive resistance. From Vajanský's point of view, the Hlasists-Realists were fighting a lost battle; they concentrated on wordly issues that were of no relevance for the Slovak level of civilisation. The fact that they promoted ideas originating in Czech political thought was just a further proof that they had no real understanding of the Slovak national spirit.

Vajanský's anti-Semitism was directly linked to his critique of Magyar liberalism, hence originated in his nationalism. He reproached the Jewish citizens their economic successes and loyalty to the Magyar elite. I have found no passages in the selected texts where he called for violence against the Jews or professed a belief in the 'blood libel'. In his anti-Semitism, he would, much like Vavro Šrobár later, criticise them for their alleged complicity with the Magyar assimilation. He addressed

---

[290]   For the political goal and thought of the Hlasists-Realists see chapter VI on Vavro Šrobár.

the Jewish citizens as "internal enemies" and "traitors"[291] at a time when the assimilation was most brutal – which, of course, does not alter the fact that he did not want to understand that the Jews were an oppressed minority themselves. I shall elaborate more on the anti-Semitism around the turn of the century in chapter VI. Vajansky was a fourteen-year-old when the text of the memorandum was formulated in 1861. As a young adult he experienced the *Ausgleich* of 1867 and the adoption of the nationality law of 1868. The fresh ideas of the Hlasists-Realists, led by Vavro Šrobár, entered Slovak intellectual life in 1898, when he was fifty-one years old and already a famous poet. One could therefore say that Vajanský represented the 'memory of the national movement'. How did he use his experience, or rather, what suggestions and goals did he have?

V. 1. Political goals

V. 1. 1. The Slovak Messianism

By 'political goal' we usually understand a clearly determined action, based on rational thinking and leading to a visible and noticeable result. Vajanský, we hold, pursued a goal that was not quantifiable in the sense of being measured. I identified his goal as the *collective inner nation-building* through art and literature. The Slovaks would have reached nationhood, could call themselves a nation only when they, as a group, could claim to have created a high-standing literature. The proof of being part of the world's civilisation was that literature. The individual intellectual in this process of nation-building was held to promote the goal, while the masses should follow. I did not find any passages in which Vajanský determined the function and role of those who were not intellectuals. Therefore, I think it safe to state that he was an elitist intellectual: Save for him, nobody could really know when that goal would be reached. We shall deal with his legitimating of that goal and his justification of the intelligentsia's anti-egalitarianism in the following chapter. Now, we shall have a closer look at his suggestions, or rather what he considered necessary to lay the grounds for a development toward that inner nation-building.

---

[291] Vajanský, "Vnútorní nepriatelia", *Národnie Noviny XXIX*, č. 64, 19. 3. 1898; "Zradili ľud", *Národnie Noviny XXXI*, č. 36, 27. 3. 1900.

Vajanský set all his hopes on a particular Slovak and Slavic messianism, which he conceived as inextricably bound to Panslavist ideology. In his Russophile hopes and Slovak Messianism, he followed the romanticist traditions laid down by Kollár and the late Štur. His Slavophile and Russophile focus experienced a distinct strengthening through his personal contacts with the Slavophile circles he was introduced to in Russia[292]. How did the future of the Slovaks look?

Messianism as a subcategory of eschatology is a system of beliefs that originates in the Judaeo-Christian world; it includes a wide range of Christian and Hebrew thinkers from the pre-Christian times until the 21st century. For the purpose of this chapter, a general definition of *Messianism* is most helpful[293]. We understand Messianism as *a movement of collective redemption or utopia, which conveys the future arrival of a saviour or messiah, who will unburden the group from its sufferings.* Until the appearance of that saviour, the group has to accept its suffering as its fate; it is told to believe and hope. In 1874 Vajanský described the heroic suffering of the Slovaks:

> "They threw all institutions of the government, the judiciary and the administration into the vandalising den of mongolism ... But God shall be my witness – I do not know what other means they still have at their shameful disposal they would not use against the Slovak people. But we shall be quiet and law-abiding [tichí a zákonní]! ... You beat the oxen and water our mob [luzu] with the glory of our destroyed schools. But we shall be quiet and law-abiding! ... The bile is overflowing in the viscera of our youth, a bitter and sharp bile! But we are being quiet, law-abiding! ... And even if God bestows upon you a hundred more years of unlimited rule and you will, in each of these terrible hundred years, invent new means to murder our life – we shall prevail, because the truth and the law are shining under our flag."[294]

Vajanský made obvious, if not shameless use of his rhetorical talent to call for a peaceful and law-abiding passivity. The only solace the people had was the belief in the future and the help of God. The Slovaks, however, would be mistaken if they considered themselves alone. He used the *Eastern question* to demonstrate the

---

[292] Juríček, 137.

[293] For detailed definitions and explanations of the various forms of messianism see http://plato.stanford.edu/search/searcher.py?query=messianism; accessed 27 June 2009; http://search.freefind.com/find.html?id=5355294&pageid=r&lang=de&mode=ALL&query=M essianismus&Find=Suche; accessed 27 June 2009 and http://www.britannica.com/EBchec ked/topic/192308/eschatology/247643/Messianism#ref=ref846793; accessed 27 June 2009.

[294] Vajanský, "My budeme tichí, ale vytrváme", *Národnie Noviny V*, č. 139, 24. 11. 1874, 1.

situation of the Slavic tribes, which, with the exception of powerful Russia, were experiencing incredible suffering under foreign rule. At the core of the Eastern question stood the *Slavic Cinderella*, the half-dead tribes; the Eastern question was therefore "a purely Slavic question" [čistoslavianskou otázkou][295]. The Slavic tribes were territorially disunited and lacked a centre, which had made it easy for foreign powers to conquer them. The Italians ruled in Trieste, in Istanbul the Turks, in Pest the Magyars. The taxes paid by the Serbs, the Slovaks and the Ruthenians financed the Magyar museums, theatres, the opera and the academy. German marionettes bought large estates in Bohemia and colonised them with Germans. As if this were not severe enough, the Slavs fought each other, tearing themselves further apart. The diversity of religions, literatures, dialects and writing was a direct threat to their existence. Only a grand and common idea, a uniting spark could overcome the mountains that separated their territories, block the foreign elements in their midst and enable them to develop in freedom:

"We don't know if this will ever happen, but it is a fact that the Slavic Cinderella came forward and the world is now talking only about her, whose biggest sacrifice had been to be forgotten."[296]

That the *Eastern question* addressed the main problem of the European balance of power that was being threatened by the slow decay of the Ottoman Empire was of no concern to Vajanský[297]. He wore 'Slavic spectacles', considering every political issue a Slavic one; after all, he was a poet and artist, not a historian occupied with boring facts, eager to find petty solutions and rushing to pragmatic steps that would peter out anyway. While he saw quite clearly that there was no immediate solution to the painful situation of assimilation, he nevertheless wasted no thought on what could be done on a daily basis. The Masarykian *drobná práce* (*small works*) was alien to him, since he was a representative of Romanticism and occupied with one grand idea, like Štúr before him. Pragmatism, feasible solutions or activities that would bring about a real improvement of the Slovak situation was not what their dire situation required. Vajanský was quite sure that he had found the right way to foster nation-building and

---

[295] Vajanský, "Slavianska popelka", *Národnie Noviny IX*, č. 140, 28. 11. 1878, 1-2, 1.

[296] Vajanský, "Slavianska popelka", 2.

[297] Hollý calls this aptly "the tendency of fully rejecting (event) history as scientific programme to promote ethnography" [tendencie k úplnej negácii (událostnej) histórie ako výskumného programu v prospech pestovania etnografie]; Hollý, 258-259.

the subsequent inner freedom of the Slovaks. His elitist introductions lent a distinct eloquence and the impression of serious scholarship to his articles. Often, he started his articles with a sharp critique of others who, so he thought, lacked a proper education. His article on *Nihilism* illustrates not only his intellectual elitism, but also his Russophile defence of the Empire's politics.

> "Today, as every little simpleton [hlupáčik] has the brazeneness to babble about Russian nihilism and the dangers threatening Russia from that side, let us, once and for all, enlighten this matter that equals an epidemy from Astrakhan as much as one egg looks like the other. We are in the lucky condition to sketch our opinion, not from stupid slices of alleged wisdom but based on the pure sources ... "[298]

To mention the pure sources was one thing; another one was how he dealt with them. Vajanský was not shy to drive home his point of a solid loyalty to Russia, representing the Russian government's view. Those, who considered the nihilists a political force the Empire should take seriously, knew the Russians as well as they knew the inhabitants from Uranus. It was utterly absurd to expect the Nihilists Kropotkin and Mezencov to garner a wide following in the imperial administration[299]. One dead Russian was immediately replaced by hundreds who were committed to the government. The Russians' courage was legendary; they would not fear canon fire nor thousands of theirs being killed in war. The rumours that the Russian people were so stricken with fear and panic that they would not hinder those wishing to emigrate lacked any substance. The passivity [nečinnosti] of the Russian nation originated not in panic, but in one common and absolute indifferent peace of mind [jedine úplná ľahostajnosť][300]. That peace of mind, or rather, temperance, was the Russian nation's grand contribution to mankind. These sentences reminded me immediately of Tol'stoi's great novel *Voina i mir* (*War and Peace*). Vajanský would go on his first trip to Russia only two years later in 1881, but his admiration for the greatness of the Tsarist Empire had already no limits. Nothing could unsettle his optimistic belief that Russia would one day liberate the Slavs.

Commenting on the German and the Russian press about the Eastern question, he, referring to himself as being impartial [nestranne], described the German party in

---

[298] Vajanský, "O nihilizme", *Národnie Noviny X, č.* 42, 10. 4. 1879, 3.
[299] Vajanský, "O nihilizme", 3.
[300] Vajanský, "O nihilizme", 3.

a condescending tone[301]. The German newspapers, so Vajanský, would often forget themselves, use unbased allegations and cheap witticisms overheard in the streets. The Russians, however, remained calm and never used low language. They reacted with objectivity, determination and fairness. It was typical that the Magyar press joined the German side; they were guided by shortsightedness and blind hatred. The journalists from Pest were trying to meddle in that war of the journalists, completely overestimating Hungary's minor role in world affairs. The great nations, however, did not care about the support of the smaller ones, as they, to put it in modern terms, were playing in a different league:

> "Great nations share a variety of problems that can easily evoke disputes. But the great nations that have the immense task of responsibility for the world do not let themselves guide by temporary sympathies and antipathies ... Little detours and leaps will not make a great nation leave its direction. That is the way how *Russia works since three hundred years for the liberation of the Slavs* [osvobodení Slavianstva] and no temporary changes in daily politics will distract her from her path."[302]

Vajanský did not further elaborate why Russia had been working on the liberation of the Slavs for three hundred years. Three hundred years ago, in 1579, the Slavs in Central Europe had lived in quite different circumstances: both the Bohemian kingdom of Saint Wenceslaus and the Hungarian kingdom of Saint Steven were ruled by the Habsburg Rudolf II, who made Prague the capital of the Holy Roman Empire of the German nation. The Balkan Slavs had been the European part of the Ottoman Empire since the Middle Ages. Why would Russia want to liberate a populace that did not yet consider itself a nation, let alone an unfree one? Why should Tsar Ivan IV, the Terrible, think in 19th century terms of national liberty and national identities? If Vajanský, however, alluded to the apocalyptic idea of *Russia as the third Rome*, the rightful follower of the Byzantine Empire, the liberation of the Slavs would have to be understood in Christian spiritual terms – which would make sense only if the Slavs converted to Orthodoxy as the true Christian faith. Some Orthodox adherents of the idea of Russia as the third Rome had considered Catholicism and Protestantism as heresy[303]. I think that Vajanský's assertions originated in his Panslavist hopes that

---

[301]   Vajanský, "Novinárska vojna", *Národnie Noviny X,* č. 100, 28. 8. 1879, 2.

[302]   Vajanský, "Novinárska...", 2; italics JB.

[303]   An excellent introduction to Orthodoxy is Thomas Bremer's *Zwischen Kreuz und Kreml. Kleine Geschichte der Orthodoxen Kirche in Russland* (Freiburg: Herder, 2007).

had been nourished by Nikolai Danilevskii's famous *Rossiia i Evropa* (*Russia and Europe*)[304] and the Russian liberation of Bulgaria in 1878, which seemed to confirm Danilevskii's views. Vajanský was obviously not interested in delivering an explanation; he concluded his article in his characteristic elitism, which, however, demonstrated his absolutely admirable mastership of rhetoric. Russia had come down on the Ottoman Empire, that principal murderer of the Slavs, like an avalanche. Germany's main task was the unification of the Germanic states. Both great nations were determined in their political direction and nothing could hinder them in their chosen paths. The red-blooded little strugglers in Pest, who overestimated their role in world politics should learn this lesson from him:

> "'Sit in your nice little house, you have enough work and dirty linen to wash!' Do not meddle into the disputes of the powerful, which did not call you for help. 'Sit down in your petty hut, Loydaček, if I need you, I'll find you.'"[305]

Naturally, Vajanský reacted sharply on the assassination of Tsar Alexander II in 1881. The Tsar-liberator had been murdered by a band of subjects that were comparable to wild animals[306]. Even the Western states that opposed Russia

---

[304] Nikolai Y. Danilevskii, *Rossiia i Evropa* (Moskva: Kniga, 1991). Nikolai Yakovlevich Danilevskii (1822-1885), a biologist by profession, published *Rossiia i Evropa* in 1868. Russia had saved Europe from Napoleon in 1812 and from the liberal revolutionairies in 1849. She, so Danilevskii, did not receive any gratitude or respect, and the West's protection of the Ottoman Empire was clear evidence of Europe's anti-Russian tradition. As the only independent Slavic State, Russia had thus to protect her fellow Slavs not only against the infidel Turks, but also against the political and cultural dominance of the West, against Austria-Hungary in particular, where millions of Slavs were being forbidden to use their language in the administration even in districts where they formed the majority of the population. Considering in a nationalistic fashion the Western *decadence* as a vital threat to mankind, Danilevskii predicted that Russia, by virtue of her moral superiority and political unity, was the only empire capable of saving mankind from the *apocalypse*. Danilevskii's book is a masterpiece of Panslavist ideology, a milestone in Russian political thought, whether one agrees or not, a good introduction to Russian imperialist nationalism legitimated by Orthodoxy and an exemplary text of apocalyptic literature. Danilevskii's claim that Russia would have a future leading role as the only true Christian state raised immediate fears in the West of her perennial aspirations for world leadership, which, to some extent and in certain circles, last to this day – even if the global reality speaks quite a different language.

[305] Vajanský, "Novinárska…", 2. With the term "Loydaček", Vajanský referred to the journalists of the *Pester Lloyd*, a German daily newspaper published in Budapest. The diminutive suffix "-aček" expressed contemption in the sense of "little scribbler of the Pester Lloyd".

[306] Vajanský, "Cár osvoboditeľ", *Národnie Noviny XII*, č. 32, 17. 3. 1881, 1.

expressed their sorrow about the Tsar's death. Alexander II had served his people by liberating the serfs in 1861; his reforms modernised the army and the Imperial administration. He had freed the Bulgarian brothers from the Turkish yoke and died a martyr. The murderers had, however, only killed a man who was mortal – they could never destroy the holy greatness of Russian Tsarism:

> "It originates in the solid and healthy Russian nation of eighty million which is of the same blood than we. 'Oh my God' called the deadly wounded Tsar, 'Oh my God' call also our people, with the same sounds, the same words, their souls and bodies oppressed by grief. ... Look at our grief, oh Lord, redeem us."[307]

The poet expressed his Slovak messianism and his Panslavistic belief in Russia's liberating role in a lecture in August 1884. The text is also an excellent illustration of his main theme: Slovak nation-building through literature.

The sense of literature and art was the expression of a nation's soul. What was a general or a statesman, compared to a poet, architect, artist or a sculptor? Art was the sum of a nation's wishes, it's life. Art was a world on its own, independent, followed its own rules and laws and goals. Many artists, however, misunderstood this simple truth, because they confused the independence and freedom of art with the self-determination of the individual.

> "They consider themselves as members of an international cosmopolitan republic, whose cardinal law is constituted by the caprices and fancies of each member. But such understanding is the complete opposite of art and its highest principle of the harmony of contrasts."[308]

Art had thus the unifying function of accommodating contrasts, of overcoming oppositional views. It was not a petty game to spend one's spare time with; that was why the greatest men in the history of mankind had committed themselves to art with their soul.

> "Art must be the inner need [vnútornou potrebou národa] of a nation, express its ideas, mirror its feelings, revive its hopes. Art must be the extraordinary sacred expression of a nation's intimate being, in one word: art, in its function as an all-embracing vessel must be the independent image of a nation and its highest thoughts."[309]

---

[307] Vajanský, "Cár...", 1.
[308] Vajanský, "Umenie a národnost'", *Národnie Noviny XVII,* č. 115, 5. 8. 1886, 2-3, 2.
[309] Vajanský, "Umenie...", 2.

Art was the expression of the idea of the nation. Naturally, it had still the function of expressing creativity, but national individuality appeared in it like in a crystal prism, explaining itself and showing its soul. Art was much older and had always been of a higher significance than nationality. Christianity was the original source of art and mirrored its changes and appearances through the centuries. Vajanský referred to the historian Jacob Burckhardt (1808 – 1897) in his thoughts about the perfection of Doric columns[310]. Without the great works of art, the basilica of St. Peter, the works of Raphael, the statues of Michelangelo, the conservative Roman curia could not have defended itself against the successful new thought:

"... against the liberation of the spirit, sent from England, the Czech lands and finally from Germany."[311]

Until today, so Vajanský, the Protestant churches had failed to find their own expression through art; but times were in motion, and art had ceased to be the exclusive domain of religious reverence. The idea of nationality was replacing religion. What he had been hinting at with references to the Rumiantsov museum in Moscow and the "thoughtless verism and naturalism of the contemporary Western nations", he revealed in his conclusion: Vajanský united Slovak Messianism with Panslavist thought and his view of art as the only nation-building element. The Slovaks should expect their liberation through Russia; until Russia deemed the time as right to liberate the Slavs, the Slovaks should be creating their nation through art. He thus suggested a *two-folded process* toward freedom: the *inner freedom* of the Slovaks could be achieved only by becoming a nation through art and literature, while the *outer, political freedom* was the task of the mighty brother-nation in the East, which had preserved its essence of life and would replace the decadent Western nations as the true leader of the Christian world:

"No direction is outlivened as quickly as that one [the Western naturalism that lacks ideals, add. JB]. It is the dead point of the wheel [of life and art, add. JB] Who shall replace it? That nation, that branch, which preserved its basic essence of life [pôvodnej šťavy]. That branch is the Slavic one. If it is its fate, as we firmly believe, to fulfil this task because of its

---

[310] Vajanský, "Umenie...", 2.

[311] Vajanský, "Umenie...", 2. Vajanský referred to the Protestant movement starting with John Wycliffe in England, who inspired Jan Hus in Bohemia and Martin Luther in Germany.

numerous population and the territory that populace lives in, it must assume leadership in art [vodcostvo v umení]."[312]

Slovak Messianism and Panslavism expressed in art – Vajanský's goal seemed convincing. After a paragraph of 'bashing the decadent West', followed by an appraisal of the greatness of Tol'stoi, Dostoievskii, Gogol' and Turgenev[313], he concluded his lecture with a romanticist critique of the universalism of the Enlightenment:

"Also, art is becoming a human right in the world [dostáva právo občianske všade na svete], wherever a human heart is beating and a human brain is thinking. ... The idea of an absolute and universal humanity [všeľudstvo absolutne] equals the absolute absence of humanity [absolutnym neľudstvom]. We are looking for a type, a colour and an individuality in a human being and a nation; ... Universal poets and artists are either plagiators or brutes."[314]

Shakespeare's *Maria Stuart* and his other dramas that played in Venice (*The merchant of Venice*), at the coast of Bohemia (*The Winter's tale*) and in Denmark (*Hamlet*) were considered to be world literature by the mistaken thinking of universalism; they were, first and foremost, an expression of the British spirit [ducha brittanského][315]. The Slovaks had to defend their individuality that was inextricably linked to their inner freedom, the freedom of creativity and art.

V. 2.   Political legitimating

V. 2. 1.   Insights and outlooks

If the Slovaks wanted to become a nation in the only acceptable meaning of nationhood, a civilised cultural entity that had created a literature of its own, then there was one way to achieve it: the intelligentsia had to claim for leadership in national life – which was not identical with politics. On the contrary: Vajanský's disregard for politics seems, at first glance, similar to the Masarykian *a-political politics* Vavro Šrobár would adhere to. The poet, however, suggested a perspective that one could describe rather as *a-political art*, since it did not include any other

---

[312]   Vajanský, "Umenie...", 3.
[313]   For a good introduction into Vajanský's relation to author of *Fathers and sons* see Andrej Červeňák, *Vajanský a Turgenev* (Bratislava: Vydavateľstvo Slovenskej akadémie vied, 1968).
[314]   Vajanský, "Umenie...", 3.
[315]   Vajanský, "Umenie...", 3.

pragmatic activities than artistic creativity in the field of literature. He was neither modest nor shy and wanted the people to understand that egalitarianism had no place in national life. In his treatise *Insights and outlooks* he made it perfectly clear that first, there was no such thing as objectivity or an objective view of things in national matters, and second, that the intellectuals were entitled to lead the masses, owing to their particular spiritual and artistic disposition[316]:

> "Objectivity will always and only depend on the condition that the novelist, either through chronology or reflection, is seeking to tell the truth according to his own thoughts, his own perspective and understanding, without any *tendency* ... To have inclinations means to be short-lived. ... Only a homunculus doctissimus could exercise a balanced objectivity, but his works would remain dead and lack the recognition by and the influence on the thinking and feeling world."[317]

Vajanský's conviction that there is no objectivity, that it is impossible to be free of preferences, bias and inclinations, might remind one of the Critical Theory of the founders of the Frankfurt School, Theodor Adorno and Max Horkheimer; they established a new system of sociological, psychological and philosophical thoughts that Jürgen Habermas developed further into his theory of discourse ethics[318]. The similarity, however, is only a very superficial one; we would be gravely mistaken to assume that Vajanský, who rejected both liberalism and socialism, any modern politics indeed, would intellectually anticipate a theory that was partly built on Marxism and attempted to make modern democracy more human. His *subjectivism* was fascinating in his rejection of scientific thought; he deemed any approach or theory as biased – the contemporary historians who were investigating events, origins and directions would just not admit it. An exception was Jacob Burckhardt's work about the culture and art of the Italian Renaissance, since the great German scholar [veľký učenec nemecký] had studied the entire literature of that epoch; that was the reason why his œuvre provided a truthful and artistic image of that epoch [pravdivý, umelecký obraz][319]. Apart from the fact that the famous historian was Swiss, a

---

[316] Vajanský, *Nálady a výhľady* (Kníhtlačiarsko-účastinársky spolok: Turčiansky Sv. Martin, 1897), 3-7. The volume is a collection of Vajanský's texts published in the *Národnie Noviny*.

[317] Vajanský, *Nálady a...*, 3-4.

[318] For an excellent summary of the Frankfurt School, its philosophers and the Critical Theory see http://plato.stanford.edu/entries/critical-theory/; accessed 29 June 2009.

[319] Vajanský, *Nálady a...*, 4. Burckhardt's *Die Kultur der Renaissance in Italien. Ein Versuch*, was published in 1860 and introduced a new approach to historiography, investigating art,

negligible detail he could not be bothered with, Vajanský explained that Burckhardt's book was purely scientific on the inside, but inspired by an artistic feeling. The principal task of every writer was therefore not to be afraid of the closeness of events and perspectives, but to paint a honourable and truthful image of the currents of thought and spiritual characteristics of his times. The truth lay in the eye of the beholder, or the intellectual, respectively. He would now try to unveil the insights and national characteristics of Slovak life and culture for one principal reason:

> "Because we would not believe how limited the knowledge about us is, what an unfinished and concealed nation we are being considered even by those who love us and want to know us better. ... We are terra incognita to everybody."[320]

He refused to write about the Slovaks in a scientific manner, so the poet, since his task was to explore the spirit and character of their times. He was certain that the Slovaks lacked the feeling for art, artistic judgement and preservation of their own being. They had always been active, labouring and working, but the sense of art and artistic creativity was absent in their lives. The people were waiting for the sense of nation coming to them from the outside [až národnosť prijde k nemu z vne]; the inspiring and initiating work of their fathers, the first generation, was therefore the beginning of a difficult struggle [počiatok toho ťažkého boja][321]. Vajanský's declaration about the future illustrates his elitism and his claim for the leadership of the intellectuals in the spiritual sense of nation-building. It would be a crazy undertaking to try teaching the masses the characteristic elements they did not have. But, since they had a latent, sleeping sense of their national characteristics, it was a duty to awaken these elements:

> "Even if we wanted to, we can no more join [pripojiť sa] that unmoving human conglomerate [nedvižnému konglomerátu ľudovému] and keep sleeping with it. We cannot, because the spark of spiritual life is glimmering in us and moving us. The first Christians could not return to the pagan life. ... We are a recreation [novotvorbou] in our nation ... We are no political party, we are the nation, pars pro toto, like the head that guides the body."[322]

---

culture, institutions and social life. The work became famous also because of Burckhardt's lively descriptions and insightful imagination.
[320]   Vajanský, *Nálady a...*, 7.
[321]   Vajanský, *Nálady a...*, 11.
[322]   Vajanský, *Nálady a...*, 12.

He followed with some lengthy chapters about the intellectuals, authors and *literati* he deemed worthy of being part in the *canon of national literature and art* he was creating, among them Hviezdoslav, Hollý, Vrchovský, Daxner, Sasinek, Francisci, Paulíny-Tóth, Štúr and Kollár[323]. His descriptions of the development of their language, the controversies surrounding the codification and the period of the *Matica* are interesting to read: Vajanský presented his own very specific and sometimes unusual views of each epoch, much as if he wanted to put his own stamp on the entire Slovak cultural history, beginning with the Bernolák codification – and ending with himself. The *Matica*, for example, did not deserve his praise:

"The Matica, for the short period of its limited activities, did not create any literary, nor cultural-intellectual school [neurobila ani literárnu, ani kulturnó-myšlienkovú školu]. At the end of the day, neither the great and wealthy academies [in the world, add. JB] can create such a school. It [the Matica, add. JB] was an estimated, beautiful and serving representation of the entire nation, an organ that allowed the nation, from time to time, to come forward to the Slavic world ... "[324]

While they lived in very difficult times, enduring the assimilation that had bereft them of the most basic educational institutions, Vajanský praised the passive endurance of his people, the patient suffering of the masses. The Magyars might very well be playing *va banque* with the non-Magyar nationalities, but only a fool would believe that the national and political conditions in Central Europe were settled and fixed once and for all. The Slovaks had demonstrated their "inner justice, immaculate rightfulness and unquestionable lawfulness"; nothing, no politics, patriotism, brute force, neither plots nor dialectics could deny them their right to independent and individual national life[325]. Surprisingly modest, if not led by rhetorical tactics, the poet admitted that he might have made mistakes, exaggerating some issues while neglecting others, but he was quite certain on three points: First, that the Slovak nation was an individuality, second, that its spiritual world had emerged and third, that it had the right to appear in its existing particularity, in its own being. He would not make any appeals or compromises in regard of these points, all the more as appeals and compromises belonged to the world of party politics[326]. The Slovaks

---

[323] Vajanský, *Nálady a...*, 30-31.
[324] Vajanský, *Nálady a...*, 46.
[325] Vajanský, *Nálady a...*, 67.
[326] Vajanský, *Nálady a...*, 68.

were not a party, but a nation, whose membership extended to everybody sharing his opinion:

> "He, who acknowledges the three points presented above, is with us [je náš], whatever other thought, party or faith he adheres to. Since we are not a party, but an organic whole [organickým celkom], our house is large enough to include different spiritual systems [rozmanité duchovné systémy]."[327]

The idea of the nation as an organic whole, a branch blossoming on the tree of mankind, was a further illustration of the romanticist element in his thought. Considering his *Insights and outlooks* from my interdisciplinary viewpoint and scrutinising his way of argumentation, I hold that Vajanský delivered a *free reflection on nation-building*. I would not call it a nation-building theory nor a nation-building ideology, since the overall tone and conduct reminded me much more of the *liberty of the essay in the style of Montaigne*[328]. *Insides and outlooks* does not present a concise and logically coherent system of thoughts; the author himself stressed this point, denying any objectivism at the very beginning of his treatise. However, his legitimating of the intellectuals' leadership, his view of the people as 'masses' and his cast-iron definition of nationhood as art enforced my assumption that he created a *canon of Slovak literature and nationhood* to provide spiritual and artistic guidance to the movement – an undertaking he did not openly declare. He placed himself and his authority, however, at the end of that national-spiritual-cultural-development, at the end of his own *canon* – which made him *the prophet of Slovak Messianism*. Naturally, he did not openly declare himself as prophet, but, reading carefully between the lines, the readers would understand that he, the *uncrowned poet laureate,* was the only person to decide who was a member of the national intelligentsia and knew that liberation could come only from Russia. For the time being, before the liberation, his task was to guide the masses, inculcating the sense of nationhood through his poetry, novels and literary critiques.

Vajanský did not further elaborate on the intellectuals' superiority. After all, he did not have to justify himself, let alone his intentions. He was a poet and artist, gifted with talents that made him a leader in spiritual and artistic matters, not a petty

---

[327] Vajanský, *Nálady a...*, 68.
[328] Michel Eyquem de Montaigne (1533 – 1592), a French writer, philosopher and member of the aristocratic administration at Bordeaux. Montaigne created the essay as a new literary genre. He published three volumes under the title *Essays* in 1580.

party politician negotiating for crumbs, read language rights, from the Magyar table. If the Slovaks had to endure hardships, it would only be to their benefit, since the difficulties they experienced in their national life would, one day, be over. They would prevail until Russia would liberate them. By sketching a national *canon* of influential national intellectuals and putting himself at the end of that *canon*, Vajanský created an interesting treatise of nation-building, which was a rhetorical masterpiece and full of artistic *esprit* and verve – yet politically completely unsuccessful[329]. But then, politics were too. He rejected any definition of the nation that opposed his views. The masses would accept it or leave it. The great poet stuck to his task of being a prophet of the nation, much in the sense of the Greek princess Cassandra that warned of danger. Charles Darwin (1809 – 1882) and Friedrich Nietzsche (1844 – 1900) were thinkers that presented a danger to the nation.

V. 2. 2.   The rejection of modernity

Vajanský elaborated on his rejection of modernity in the fields of politics, science and philosophy. He topped his mocking views about parliamentarism with a critique of Darwin's theory of evolution and the rejection of Nietzsche's philosophy. Let me begin with parliamentarism.

Referring to *The correspondence of John Lothrop Motley*[330], Vajanský quoted from a letter of Bismarck to Motley from 1863; the Prussian minister spoke with contempt of the German parliament, comparing it to a *Phrasenhaus* (house of

---

[329] The conduct and the form, not the contents of *Insights and outlooks* reminded me of Masaryk's nation-building theory, presented in *Česká otázka*: both authors presented their interpretation of the past, Masaryk Czech history and philosophy, and Vajanský Slovak literature and art. Both identified a basic element that had been prevailing through time: Czech democracy was the sense of Czech history, while Slovak literature was the origin of national individuality. Both thinkers placed themselves at the last phase of the developments they had created; Masaryk at the beginnings of the phase of political democracy, sovereignty and Czechoslovakism and Vajanský as the national poet and prophet of Slovak Messianism, who foresaw the liberation by Russia. By doing so, Masaryk justified his authority in politics, and Vajanský his in matters of art.

[330] John Lothrop Motley (1814 – 1877) was an American historian, personally acquainted with Otto von Bismarck and from 1861 to 1867 Amereican diplomat to the Austrian Empire.

platitudes) and stating that such tirades could certainly not govern Prussia[331]. Vajanský supported Bismarck's views and criticised the Hungarian parliament.

"That which is, is reasonable [Čo je, je vraj rozumné], a German philosopher said! My God, that philosophical sentence is dead if one has a look at the parliament! The speeches are remarkable through that which they are not; and further: they are not literary, not artistic, not philosophical, not scientific, not beautiful, not informative, not actual, decisive in nothing..."[332]

Parliamentary sessions were quite a funny matter in themselves: the people shuffling in the corridors, the chairman ringing the bell, the parliamentarians attacking each other verbally, the students marching in the streets in protest, the gendarmes being called in – but it was not funny for those who had to foot the bill for that gay comedy, nor for the nations that were suffering the consequences of that violent outvoting and were dying a spiritual and physical death. The parliamentarians enjoyed good health and humour and, under the pretence of serving the state, they were playing parties, knights and statesmen. Vajanský concluded his article with a rather chilling warning: The house of platitudes was bustling and providing niceties to its slaves. But the time was running out and a great catastrophe was near. Yes, indeed, the oppressed nations' consciousness was gaining in strength, hidden and unobserved[333].

If parliamentarism equalled a house of platitudes that made cynical fun of the oppressed, the current anti-Christian theories, in particular *On the origins of species by means of natural selection* (1859) by Charles Darwin (1809 – 1882), were just another sign of the moral and spiritual decadence of their times:

---

[331]   Vajanský, "Parlamentarismus", *Národnie Noviny XX*, č. 25, 28. 2. 1889, 1.

[332]   Vajanský, "Parlamentarismus", 1. Vajanský seemed to refer to a simplification of Kant's Categorical Imperative: *Was gut ist, ist vernünftig und was vernünftig ist, ist gut*. (That, which is good, is reasonable, and reasonable is that, which is good). Kant created *The groundwork of the Metaphysics of Morals* (1785) that prepared his famous Categorical Imperative. Vajanský's reference was wrong; he did either not understand the sense of the *Imperative* or misquoted it. Kant's *Groundworks* ... are available on http://philosophy.eserver.org/kant/metaphys-of-morals.txt ; accessed 1 July 2009. The categorical Imperative: "We can now end where we started at the beginning, namely, with the conception of a will unconditionally good. That will is absolutely good which cannot be evil- in other words, whose maxim, if made a universal law, could never contradict itself. This principle, then, is its supreme law: "Act always on such a maxim as thou canst at the same time will to be a universal law"; this is the sole condition under which a will can never contradict itself; and such an imperative is categorical."

[333]   Vajanský, "Parlamentarismus", 1.

"Among these anti-Christian theories we can find the teachings of that outstanding [učenie výtečného] Darwin, who made such a noise around the world ... I refer to the *law of the struggle for the existence of the individuals* [zákon borby za jestvovanie individuumov]. That highly egoistic idea of the struggle for existence [idea borby za jestvovanie] (Kampf und das Dasein) is the basis of Darwinism. ... And there is no doubt that nature [príroda] and anthropology provide thousands of facts that allow the establishment of such a *one-sided* theory, *one-sided and narrow*, and therefore, all things considered, *wrong* [falošnú]."[334]

"Kampf und das Dasein" (struggle and existence) instead of "Kampf um das Dasein" (struggle for existence) could either be a simple typo or a mistaken translation, unveiling the poet's rather problematic relationship with the German language. I think it is a typo. However, Vajanský's summary of the theory of evolution or, what he considered Darwinism to be, would surely have made the great British naturalist turn in his grave. Vajanský delivered a thoroughly artistic misinterpretation of the theory of evolution: Progress was based on the development and perfection of the lowest and highest organisms. Therefore, it became a fact that, as the struggle for existence was forced upon by nature, the stronger individuals had certainly the natural, biological facilities [isté surové], but not the natural right [nevyhnutné právo] to destroy and humiliate the weaker ones in the higher interest of the perfection of the tribe or generation[335]. Vajanský equalled the a-Christian theories to a white host wafer: it did nothing while laying on the tongue, but started to poison the entire organism as soon as it entered it. Darwin's new teachings came in the form of natural science, the host wafer, and poisoned society's organism. There was, however a remedy: besides the struggle for the existence, there was the struggle for the life of the others, a high altruism that existed in the lowest organisms and extended to man, if he did not strip himself [nesvliekol] of his mirror image of God, his being the reflection of God and nature [podobu Božiu i prírodu samú][336]. Darwin's theory fostered egoism, contempt for the other and represented the denial of everything that was good and to the spiritual prosperity of man.

Vajanský did not mention the key concepts "evolution" and "natural selection", which are crucial for the understanding of the theory. There are, in my opinion, three possibilities to interpret his views about Darwinism: First, he did not understand the

---

[334] Vajanský, "Protikresťanské theorie", *Národnie Noviny XXIX*, č. 248, 29. 10. 1898, 1.
[335] Vajanský, "Protikresťanské...", 1.
[336] Vajanský, "Protikresťanské...", 1.

basic statements of the theory, second, he deliberately presented a mistaken summary to convince his readers of the 'anti-Christianism' of natural sciences in general, and Darwinism in particular, or third, he confused Darwinism with *social Darwinism*, which would make sense, given the conditions and social environment of Magyarisation. Social Darwinism conferred Darwin's biological theory to individuals, social conditions, nations and races; it was a current of thought of the late 19th century that used a simplicist and populist distortion of the theory of evolution to legitimate racial and national superiority. Much like organisms, individuals, nations and cultures prospered or vanished through the process of natural selection; the weaker would perish, while the stronger survived because they could better adapt to the environment of modern society, Imperialism and *laisser faire* capitalism. The cult of the *Herrenrasse*, promoted by the NSDAP, had its origins in social Darwinism. I am inclined to think that Vajanský refused to understand Darwin's theory; after all, he was a well-read intellectual, not a fool. Owing to his task of being the prophet of his nation, he touched upon social Darwinism to explain the victimisation of the Slovaks by Magyar assimilation:

> "They [the new teachings, novoučenie Darwinoho, add. JB] sanction straightforwardly the devouring of the weak by the powerful, the oppression of nations, classes, the extinction of entire races in the name and by the right of a greater power."[337]

Religion and its connection with art was all that was left to them, or so he must have thought; if the nation lost the basis of its individuality and humanity, it would loose itself. Vajanský rejected modernity as the legacy of the Enlightenment and repeated his romanticist argumentation: there was no universal rightful view or opinion, let alone a universal validity of the alleged results of an anti-Christian school of thought that called itself natural science. The bible had determined the primordial origins; the a-theistic materialism of modernity demonstrated only decadence and the lack of humanity.

He went into great lengths to describe the peak of godlessness, the decadence and dissolution of the Christian spiritual values in his article *Anarchia ducha (The anarchy of the spirit)*[338].

---

[337]   Vajanský, "Protikresťanské...", 1.
[338]   Vajanský, "Anarchia ducha", *Národnie Noviny XXXI*, č. 32, 17. 3. 1900, 1.

"In the highly educated West, philosophy, natural sciences, sociological systems and programmes are leading directly to the anarchy of the spirit. The opposites and contrasts in the lives of the nations have sharpened and, if we were not immensely optimistic, we had to say that distress, denial, evil, lies, lowliness, darkness and death will win."[339]

Vajanský struck out rhetorically to declare Western philosophy in its entirety as the source of the evil of their times. He touched upon the pantheism of Spinoza and Hegel and declared Hegel's dialectics as evil [zlo]; Schopenhauer's pessimism and naturalism were leading to a Buddhist Nirvana, while Darwin's naturalism justified putting power above the law [sila pod zákonom][340]. All these disruptive ideas and thoughts were crowned by Friedrich Nietzsche (1844 – 1900), who, by declaring that the *Übermensch* was above everything, brought the current spiritual chaos to perfection; his own tragic life, so Vajanský rather *ad hominem*, was the logical consequence [logickou konsekvenciou] of his philosophy – since 1889 he was in medical care in a Jena madhouse [v blázinci].[341] The poet continued his *philippic* against Western anarchism, which, under the pretences of 'enlarging the intellectual horizon', 'opening new perspectives' and 'rebirth of mankind' meant only degeneration. The spiritual chaos the Western philosophers and their epigones had stirred up was comparable to "moral insanity"; it destroyed the sense of nation as the work of the most noble and beautiful spirits and trampled on the ideals of the good, beauty and truth with its dirty feet. Radical individualism named *Übermenschentum* [nadčlovectvo] and eager careerism [štréberstvo] wanted to destroy the harmony of the grand unity, patriotism, love of the nation and the altruism of nation and family[342].

Vajanský continued his critique over six issues of the *National News*, portraying the actual currents of thought and art from his Panslavistic perspective. I shall not go into the details of his text, as a thorough assessment of his statements would require at least thirty pages. From the perspectives of philosophy, art history and literature, the text in its eclecticism is very interesting: he listed a high number of Western thinkers, artists, sculptors and authors to describe the spiritual anarchy they had helped to create with their works. Not even Charles Baudelaire deserved a

---

[339] Vajanský, "Anarchia…", 1.
[340] Vajanský, "Anarchia…", 1.
[341] Vajanský, "Anarchia…", 1.
[342] Vajanský, "Anarchia…", 1.

positive judgement; the author of *Les fleurs du mal* was so immersed in his "poetic I" [poetické ja] that his exaggerated individualism only contributed to the current destruction of the most basic moral values[343]. The English pre-Raphaelites had first discovered their admiration for the beauty of Medieval art [obľubu stredovekového], but they soon engaged in a free-floating subjectivism, influenced by the French: Baudelaire and Morris had found to each other via the channel[344]. Raphael was in fact one of the most famous painters of the Italian Renaissance, not the Middle Ages, another petty detail Vajanský did not care about. Walt Whitman was as much a Western decadent as Henrik Ibsen, Heinrich Heine and Richard Wagner. Nietzsche, eventually, whom he must have really despised, was the embodiment of that anarchical mood of the *fin de siècle*; his thoughts were nothing more than "obsessed scribbling" [grafomania].

> "The common characteristic of these philosophical decadents is to suggest to the young the creed of greatness. Three to four lessons, the reading of confused critiques – and the *Übermensch* is ready."[345]

Interestingly, the conduct and fundamental theme of Vajanský's text is very similar to Nietzsche's *Twilight of the gods, or how one philosophises with a hammer* (*Götzendämmerung, oder wie man mit dem Hammer philosophiert*) (1888)[346]: Nietzsche criticised German and European philosophers and artists, such as Darwin, Dante, Kant, Plato, Rousseau and Zola. He condemned their cultural decadence (!) from his perspective of the power of the will, spoke of a German 'beer culture' and praised the virtues of the healthy and strong: Caesar, Napoléon, Goethe and Dostoievskii had passed the test with his hammer. They were not shallow, their substance was healthy. Naturally, I cannot prove that Vajanský had read Nietzsches' *Twilight*. However, the similarity is a striking one: the flow of arguments, the eclectic perspective blending philosophy, art and religion and, eventually, the critique of decadence as the main theme. The poet was either inspired by the philosopher and

---

343   Vajanský, "Anarchia...", č. 37, 21. 3. 1900, 2.

344   Vajanský, "Anarchia...", č. 41, 25. 3. 1900, 4. William Morris (1834 – 1896) was an English architect and textile designer and one of the founders of the pre-Raphaelite brotherhood that oriented itself artistically in the early Renaissance prior to Raphael (1483 – 1520).

345   Vajanský, "Anarchia...", č. 46, 30. 3. 1900, 3.

346   For a good introduction and summary of Nietzsche's life and works see http://plato.stanford.edu/entries/nietzsche/; accessed 2 July 2009.

used Nietzsche's structure and composition to unveil his decadence, or then, the similarity was pure coincidence. I assume that the philosopher inspired the poet, who wanted to warn his nation of the dangers of a mistaken art. *The anarchy of the spirit* is also an excellent demonstration of Panslavist thought: a fundamental anti-Western attitude, paired with the firm belief in Russia as the liberator of Central European Slavs, the praise of Russian art, literature and poetry and the refusal of any critique of the great Slavic brother nation.

To conclude, Vajanský was a remarkable and elitist intellectual who was not shy to claim for the leadership of the intellectuals. His expertise in poetry and literature was higher than his knowledge of history and politics, which made his texts nevertheless interesting to read. He excelled in rhetoric and used his talent to create a *canon* of Slovak literature, art and poetry. His Panslavistic belief in the liberation by Russia could not be destroyed, certainly not by the political realities. The poet adhered faithfully to the Romanticism of the Štúr generation and praised his nation's peaceful endurance. He, the prophet of *Slovak Messianism* knew that their suffering would have an end. His *canon* and his continuous engagement for the nation's spirit brought him to prison three times and made him a kind of martyr. His Slavophile traditionalism came along with an utter contempt for the decadent West. Vajanský did not teach his nation what he considered inferior Western pragmatism but gave the gift of the characteristic traits of Slovak identity: peacefulness, belief, endurance in the harshest of times and lastly, the direction toward itself: the growing to a nation through art.

Svetozár Hurban Vajanský – life in brief

(Pseudonyms: Miloslav, Napreják, Starý Napreják, Škorpion)

16 January 1847   Born in Hlboka as Svetozár Miloslav Hurban. He was the first child of Jozef Miloslav Hurban, the hero of the 1848 revolution and confidant of Štúr, and Anna Hurbanova, born Jurkovíčova, the daughter of the *narodovec*, notary and teacher Samuel Jurkovíč.

1853-1857   Hurban instructed his elder children himself, preparing Svetozár for the gymnasium. Young Svetozár started to write poetry and diaries at the tender age of six, a profession he would excel in later.

1858-1861   He studied at the gymnasium at Tešin in Silesia, read Goethe, Schiller and Shakespeare, but experienced difficulties in Mathematics, Latin and German.

1861-1862   Svetozár continued his gymnasium in Oberschützen in Burgenland, Austria.

1863-1866   Studied at the Evangelical gymnasium in the Prussian Stendal, close to Berlin. The stay in Prussia was to prepare him for his later studies in theology. He read Heine, Uhland and Lenau, and visited Dresden, Berlin, Magdeburg and Rostock.

1866-1867   His lack of interest in studying theology was a disappointment to his father who nevertheless allowed him to enrol at the Catholic gymnasium in Banská Bystrica, after Svetozár had failed the exams at the Lutheran lyceum in Levoča. He graduated with the matura in 1867.

1867-1870   Studied law at the Istropolitana University at Pressburg. For his early literary merits, he earned a financial grant from the *Matica*. Met Palacký and Lamanskii at a student gathering in Vienna in 1868. From 1869 to 1870, he chaired the student circle *Naprej (Forward)*. After graduation, he worked as legal secretary at the office of advocate Vendelín Kutlik in Trnava, changing in 1871 to an advocate's office in Pest.

1873	Viliam Pauliny-Toth, then editor of *Národnie Noviny*, signed Hurban's cover article *Škola a život (School and life)* with the pen name 'Vajanský', connoting the Slavic mythological god Vajan. Hurban kept it as his official name.
1874	Passed the exams of the law school in Pest and opened his own office in November in Skalica. He was a regular contributor to *Národnie Noviny* and *Orol*. Married his fiancée Ida Dobrovitsova in 1875.
1876	Moved to Liptovsky Sv. Mikuláš and opened his lawyer's practice. Financial restraints did not hinder him from intensive study of Russian and Russian literature.
1878	Moved to Martin and took over the editorship of *Orol*, in spite of Francisci's warning of the difficulties of such a post. First trip to the Adriatic and the Balkans, which inspired him to produce his collection of poems *Jaderské Listy I (Notes from the Adriatic)*.
1879, December	His famous poems *Tatry a more (The Tatra mountains and the sea)* were published, dated as 1880. They were reviewed by Jozef Škultéty. In the following years, his poems about Russia, Russian poets, artists and Czech authors were published in various journals.
1881	Together with Škultéty he started *Slovenske Pohľady*, a journal for poetry, literature, art and politics. In October, he went on his first trip to Kiev and Moscow, where Lamanskii introduced him to Slavophile circles. Back home, he became the secretary of the Women's association *Živena*.
1883	Attended the opening of the National Theatre in Prague. Acquaintance with the Czech poet Jan Neruda, whom he sent his poems *Zpod jarma (Under the yoke)*.
1884	His novel *Suchá ratolesť (A dry sprig)* was reviewed by, amongst others, the Czechs Jan Herben and Jozef Vlček.
1885, April	Second trip to Russia; visits to Warsaw, Kiev and St. Petersburg.
1887	Third trip to Russia.

1888	Fourth trip to Russia with Pavol Mudroň and Ambro Pietor. In Kiev, they attended celebrations of the 900th anniversary of Russia's Christianity. 1892 Accompanied his daughter Olga to St. Petersburg, where she enrolled at the Mariinski Institute. Lamanskii and other Russian friends financed her education.
1893	The Slovak *Sokol* of Chicago nominated him as its first honorary member. Charged with anti-patriotic and Panslavistic activities, he started his one-year prison sentence in Szeged in February, where he received news, journals, and letters from Slovakia, Bohemia and Russia. His return to Martin in February 1894 was a public triumph.
1895	Attended the festivities of the centenary of Šafařík's birth, organised by the national student circle *Detvan* in Prague. In August he attended the congress of the non-Magyar nationalities in Pest, whose resolution failed to affect any political changes whatsoever.
1897	His fiftieth birthday was celebrated in domestic and foreign newspapers and journals.
1898-1899	Replaced Ambro Pietor as the editor-in-chief of the now daily *Národnie Noviny*, due to Pietor's prison sentence. Start of the polemical debates with *Hlas,* and later, the Czech *Čas* that would last until 1903. Vavro Šrobár criticised Vajanský's leadership of the N.N.
1900	Sentenced to five months in prison for "anti-patriotic activities". Imprisoned from September to February 1901 in Banská Bystrica.
1903	He served his third prison sentence of two months at the state prison in Vacs, near Budapest.
1906	Published an article in N.N. about the Ružomberok process against Hlinka, Šrobár and others. His full report appeared later as a brochure.
1907	Interrogated because of his article on the tragedy of Černova near Ružomberok, where Magyar gendarmes had shot into a peaceful

demonstration of Catholics, who wanted Hlinka to inaugurate their newly built church. Fifteen people were killed and a 105 hurt.

1908-1914 His poetry, novels and articles works focussed on Slavic issues and were published in Bohemia, Russia and the Balkans. His last trip to Russia led him to St. Petersburg in 1913.

1915 In his polemics with the Hlasist Anton Štefanek, he rejected a future Czechoslovak order and criticised the idea of introducing Czech as the written language in Slovakia.

17 August 1916 Vajanský died of a heart attack. He was buried at the national cemetery in Martin.

Vavro Šrobár, © SNK

VI.   Vavro Šrobár (1867 - 1950). Realism and Czechoslovakism

"Back in those times, there was no independent political movement in Slovakia. The brutal
regime of the liberal government [the Tisza government, add. JB] terrified the Slovak
intellectuals who, from year to year, were diminishing in numbers, and pushed them from
public into private life. An insurmountable divide opened between the Slovak population
and the intellectuals; the people lost their leaders ... The sad situation of the Slovak people
could not even be concealed by the publication of election manifests issued from time to
time by the 'leaders.' Informing the people and the country that the situation demanded not
to participate in the voting, the 'leaders' recommended passivity as the most successful
option."[347]

Compared to the conservatives Sasinek and Vajanský, Vavro Šrobár would prove
with his own intellectual development and, of course, enjoying a favourable
international situation that passivity in politics lead to nothing. In the last decades of
the 19th century the generation of the memorandum still adhered to the 'politics of
Martin', was paralysed by the assimilation and slowly dying out, while the younger
generation was left without orientation. The peculiar behaviour of the *Memorandists*
was to draw back into an ivory tower of literature and poetry while, at the same time,
insisting on a leading role as the nation's intellectual elite. They dogmatically and
sharply condemned any suggestions that differed from their own views. That
withdrawal from reality into one's own community that was threatened from the
outside reminded me, to some extent, of the behaviour Bruno Bettelheim described in
his essay *Freedom from Ghetto Thinking*[348]. Šrobár and his fellow Slovaks, who had
studied abroad and came back to Slovakia to initiate change had to fight three fronts:

---

[347]   Vavro Šrobár, "Počiatky slovenského obrodenia", in *Boj o nový život* (Ján Párička:
Ružomberok, 1920), 442-458; 443. The article was first published in *Sborník slovenskej
mládeže*, 1909. In the last decades of the 19th century, the term 'liberal' became synonymous
with 'Magyar nationalist', since the assimilation peaked under the rule of the Liberal Party.
Kossuth's legacy, the Magyar political nation, was the goal of the Liberals that justified the
assimilation of the non-Magyars.

[348]   "But it was not only lack of knowledge ... it was also an unwillingness to fight for themselves
... this unwillingness to fight was a direct consequence of ignorant innocence – ghetto
thinking. ... The Jews had not troubled to learn that things had changed, so they could not know
that this tempest was of a wholly new order. ... The reason they could not and did not fight
back lay in their inner feelings of resignation, in the careful eradication, over centuries, of
tendencies to rebel, in the ingrained habit of believing that those who bend do not break."
Bruno Bettelheim, "Freedom from Ghetto Thinking", in *Freud's Vienna and other essays*
(New York: Vintage, 1989), 243-271; 263, 267 .

the government's assimilation, the intelligentsia's conservatism and the passivity of the population. However, some of the *Hlasists*, named after the journal they founded, would play a crucial role in the *převrat* (toppling of the government, revolution, *Umsturz*) of 1918. They would form the Slovak political elite in the sovereign Czechoslovak Republic.

Note that I shall not present a detailed account of Šrobár's involvement in the foundation of the Czechoslovak Republic, or an account of the years he effectively ruled Slovakia on behalf of the Republic. For historical analysis of the years 1918 to 1938 I refer to the collection of essays *Muži deklarácia (The men of the declaration)* and Šrobár's memoirs of the years 1918 to 1920[349]. Leikert's collection of essays has a cultural studies approach and is recommendable as an introduction, in particular as regards Šrobár's role in the modernising aspects of Slovak cultural life[350]. The *Festschrift* dedicated to his 70th birthday is an interesting introduction to his political achievements and personality, containing mostly memoirs of persons who knew him from politics or the academia[351]. I am primarily interested in Šrobár's political goals in the years prior to 1918 and the arguments he used to legitimate his activities, all the more as his biography shows an interesting development, in regard of both goals and legitimating. Once he was firmly convinced that *Czechoslovakism* was the best – and only – way, he engaged for the common state.

I consider the state building theory of *Czechoslovakism* as a current of 19th century political thought because it included ideas of the 18th and 19th centuries that were partly realised in the 19th century: equality of nations legitimated by natural law, a democratic constitution including minority rights and anti-clerical and anti-aristocratic nationalism. *Czechoslovakism* as a set of ideas of the 19th century came to be realised in the 20th century, but its main philosophical principles originate in the rationalism and universalism of 18th century Enlightenment, on the one hand, and the liberalism and nationalism of the 19th century, on the other. I shall not deal with Šrobár's thought after 1938, or his activities during and after WWII, as they go beyond the scope of this investigation and require a critical analysis on their own.

---

[349] Dušan Kováč a kol., *Muži deklarácie* (Bratislava: Veda, 2000); Šrobár, *Oslobodené Slovensko. Pamäti z rokov 1918-1920* (Bratislava: Academic Electronic Press, 2004).

[350] Jozef Leikert a kol., *Kultúrno-politický profil Vavra Šrobára* (Nitra: Kulturologická spoločnosť, 2005).

[351] *Šrobárov sborník k 70. narodeninám* (Bratislava: Štefánikova spoločnosť, 1937).

Also, in terms of the political thought of the Slavic nations, the 19th century with its claims for the equality of nations, and, subsequently, autonomy or sovereignty, had come to an end only in 1918. The fall of Austria-Hungary, the Ottoman Empire, Tsarist Russia and Wilhelminian Germany led to the reconstitution of Poland and the creation of sovereign nation states in Central Europe and the Balkans. Political ideas such as Fascism, National Socialism and Communism that originated in 19th century and had since been developing, came to their fullest und most appalling realisation in the 20th century. To speak with Eric Hobsbawm, the long 19th century as the *age of empire* ended in 1914 and was followed by the *age of extremes*, the short 20th century[352]. We shall see in the following chapters how Šrobár's goals and political thought were affected by the historical break of 1914.

On a first glance, Šrobár's biography seems to mirror Masaryk's life, with a different timing, of course. Masaryk had been a professor of philosophy and sociology at the Czech university in Prague for six years, when the young Slovak arrived in the capital of Bohemia in 1888. Both had been born to poor families in the countryside; Masaryk's parents were servants to the household of an aristocrat, while Šrobár's family were peasants that had achieved some social standing because of the father's position as the local *richtar*, a representative position similar to the major of a small village. They were not wealthy. Masaryk's mother, an ethnic German, motivated her eldest son to get a good education, while Šrobár's father was very liberal about his fourth child's future. He praised his second son's wish to go to gymnasium. Both experienced difficulties in their efforts to acquire education at a gymnasium, owing to social and national discrimination. Both were, nevertheless, stubbornly steady in their wish to go to university and consequently emigrated. Masaryk graduated at a Viennese gymnasium, while Šrobár had to absolve the eight class of the gymnasium three times at different schools. He graduated in the Eastern Moravian town Přerov. Masaryk studied philosophy at Vienna University, and Šrobár enrolled at the medical faculty of Charles University in Prague. Both were religious and conceived of ethics as the pillar of modern politics. Masaryk was a believing Protestant and Šrobár a Catholic.

---

[352] Eric Hobsbawm, *The age of empire 1875-1914* (New York: Pantheon, 1987), 326; *Age of extremes: the short twentieth century, 1914 – 1991* (London: Michael Joseph, 1994).

To name him a 'Slovak Masaryk', however, would do both politicians injustice; I would rather speak of a professor-student relationship, since they were personally acquainted and in steady contact, but not close. Having learnt about Šrobár's first prison sentence in 1906, Masaryk sent him a brief note from Vienna, his sarcasm originating in his optimism:

> "Whether I regret it or not – this will be to your benefit, it raises your authority [vaši autoritu zvýší]."[353]

He described his last meeting with Masaryk in 1935, when the eighty five year old president was stricken with illness:

> "The president wanted to know, as always, about the current situation in Slovakia. The issues of Hlinka, the Pittsburgh agreement, the politics of the state, the fight of the parties [zápas strán] etc. came up. I explained that Hlinka was raging against the state, against the Czechs, and that his meetings were characterised by violent turmoil. The president asks: 'Did he personally suffer any crime?' I: 'Yes, he was not appointed bishop.' M: 'But we cannot make him a bishop, if Rome does not want him.' ... M.: 'Come again to visit, you see, we still have a lot to discuss.' The president was being ill and tired and I did not meet him again."[354]

Masaryk suggested to found the journal *Hlas* (*the voice*) that addressed seemingly a-political issues such as health care, social problems and economic progress, bringing fresh wind into Slovak public life. The idea behind the focus on social and economic progress was to prepare the nation for modernity. A superstitious, uncritical and uneducated people would lack the psychological resilience and civil virtues a modern state required – and for both, this modern state had to be a democracy as the only legitimate representation of the people. Also, Šrobár assumed Masaryk's principle of the *small works* (*drobná práce*), the daily, small, ethical and unspectacular efforts of every individual to lead a moral life and educate oneself. The *small works* were a practical guideline that would strengthen the morality of the nation and prepare it for future sovereignty. It is certainly an uncontested fact that Masaryk's intellectual power, political plans and his party of the *Realists* gave Šrobár the much-needed direction he had been seeking.

> "The first of the Czech university professors who took notice of the Slovak students of the *Detvan* club was professor Masaryk. One day, I think it was in 1889, he invited us ... to his

---

[353]   Fond Vavra Šrobára, Slovenská Národní Knižnica SNK, Martin, sig: 173 D 28.
[354]   Fond Vavra Šrobára, sig: 173 P 15.

apartment. He told us about the sad conditions in Slovakia, about the politics of the Martin
adherents, about the horrible national annihilation, about Magyarisation and Russophilia ...
It was the young Slovak generation's task to take up work, to shed light on these terrible
conditions and critisise them in a journal that was independent from the politics of Martin
... Masaryk was, I think, the first to point out the wrong Russophile or rather, Tsarophile,
direction of our Slovak politics ... "[355]

Although the Slovak students would need some more time and education until they
saw themselves fit to found *Hlas* in 1898, the new approach critical of the Martin
generation had set root. Masaryk's intellectual influence opened a new and fresh
perspective; while Šrobár followed the principles of Masarykian politics and was
familiar with the professor's publications, he was not a slave to his master. In the
early years of his studies he had tried to find answers in the works of Western
philosophers such as Schopenhauer, Kant and Voltaire[356]. The Slovak poets Holly,
Hviezdoslav, Vajanský and Kollár had awoken his enthusiasm for the nation that
turned into an admiration of the Russian nation by the works of Tolstoi and
Turgenev. Nikolai Danilevskii's *Rossia i Evropa* made him follow the theory of
Panslavism[357]. All these thinkers and works, however, could not provide practical
guidelines on how to improve the life of the Slovaks. The only body of thought that
provided feasible suggestions was the Masarykian, in itself an ecclectic blend of
Western philosophy, sociology and themes of Czech history. Šrobár was perfectly
capable of thinking for himself and aware that the basic principles of Masarykian
political thought – the meaning of Czech history, the current moral crisis of the
Czech nation and *drobná práce* as the remedy[358] – could not simply be transferred
and applied to Slovakia. The Czechs had successfully defended their language that
had led to the foundation of a Czech university in Prague, also because the Austrian
government was not pursuing a harsh assimilation like the Magyars. The Slovaks, on
the other hand, had been continuously up-rooted, not only by the Magyars, but also
by fellow Slovaks in high administrative positions, who had adopted the ruling
nation's state ideology, customs and manners by acts we might describe as *self-
colonisation*, that is an overly active, if not pro-active, adaptation of foreign thought

---

[355] Šrobár, *Z môjho života* (Praha: Fr. Borový, 1946), 159, 160.
[356] Šrobár, *Z môjho...*, 222.
[357] Šrobár, *Z môjho...*, 237-239.
[358] Tomáš G. Masaryk, *Česká otázka. Naše nynejší krize* (Praha: Svoboda, 1990).

to one's conditions without a critical assessment. While the generation of the memorandum had spoken of *Maďarony*, Šrobár – like Vajanský before him – used the term *odrodilec (uprooter)*, describing an individual who actively pursues the uprooting of Slovak identity and language. The *odrodilci* dominated the schools and the local administration. Šrobár's personal experience with one of his teachers at the gymnasium in Levoča gives us an insight into how that uprooting was carried out:

"Behyna had a choleric temperament, was deranged and his face was blue with anger. He literally flew into the classroom and shouted that the students were cowards and lazybones. That day he told me to wait in front of the gymnasium ... He advised me to forget about all that Slovak stuff [všetko slovenčenie] and to focus on Magyar. He would recommend me to famous professors in Pest, would supervise my studies, I could study philosophy, and a brilliant future would await me as a writer. ... 'There are three great poets in Magyar literature who are of Slovak origin: Petöfi, Madácha and Mikzsáta. In Slovak literature they would have been forgotten. As Magyars they became famous. Think about it! If you leave the right path, nothing will become of you. I give you three days.'"[359]

Šrobár's biography is a good illustration of the political situation of the young intellectual elite in the last decades of the 19th century. With literally zero chances for personal advancement – poor family background and the language of instruction being either German or Hungarian – he nevertheless completed his studies while educating himself in politics, graduating as a physician and returning to his native Ružomberok to open his practise. Had he stayed in Slovakia, he would have most probably become a Catholic priest, as it had been his mother's wish, or a local peasant, adhering to the passivity Vajanský taught. As a teenager, he had admired the Russophile poet, but only in Přerov and then in Prague he came to the conclusion that politics must be linked to activity. The *Martinists* were thus wrong in their passive obstruction of the government. While Šrobár was active in *Detvan*, the circle of the Slovak students in Prague, a man moved close to Ružomberok who would fatally influence Slovak history five decades later. In the late 1880s, the Catholic priest Andrej Hlinka was appointed to the parish Sliače. They soon became acquainted, since Šrobár came home from university every summer to spend the holidays with his family. As patriots they shared the resistance against the assimilation, but Šrobár soon had his doubts about Hlinkas' political ideas, method and the honesty of his character. They would co-operate, bound by their common political goals, even

---

[359]   Šrobár, *Z môjho...*, 115.

served their sentences at the same prison in Szeged, but kept their distance[360]. His memories of his early impressions of Hlinka's personality, published in 1946, are certainly influenced by the later events, when they became adversaries in the Czechoslovak Republic. However, we can read them as an illustration of Šrobár's psychological eye, trained by medical science:

> "Hlinka was a hasardeur ... he took risks without thinking about the consequences ... His role models were the young Catholic priests who stirred up the country against the church law ... He joined this movement and started to publish articles against the liberal law and especially against the liberal regime [proti liberálnemu režimu] ... Hlinka had a poor knowledge of philosophy and sociology, but he could not be bothered with worldly problems; his polemics were therefore always personal ... only arguments ad hominem. He used to hit home with people; he exaggerated their personal inclinations, stressed the rumours and anecdotes that surrounded them and portrayed them to the public in a simplicist and repetitive fashion until he himself believed these rumours to be true and important."[361]

Šrobár opened his practise in 1899, which did not do too well in the first couple of months, because the conservative and superstitious peasants were somewhat reluctant to ask for medical advise. He had time to edit *Hlas*. Because of his activities, the authorities sentenced the young doctor, some fellow Hlasists and Hlinka to a year in prison, which they had to serve in the south-eastern Hungarian town Szeged[362]. In prison, Šrobár made the acquaintance of young Béla Kun (1886 – 1939?), the future leader of the short-lived Bolshevik government of Hungary.

> "He sat on my bed, although there was a chair in my cell, and started to laugh. I disliked his dominant, aggressive and ruthless behaviour. I gave him the chair and asked him to sit down. 'In prison, there are no class differences.' 'You are right, but there is one difference even in prison: good behaviour.' ... 'What did you do in Pest?' 'I am a journalist'. 'And why are you here?' 'I called the metal workers to strike.' 'Until when are you here?' 'Until May'. We had a strange relationship until the end. I disliked very much his brazenness, lack

---

[360] A good overview of Šrobár's views about Hlinka and their co-operation is Jozef Leikert, "Životné a politické postoje Vavra Šrobára do roku 1918", in *Kultúrno-politický profil...*, 9-76.

[361] Šrobár, *Z môjho...*, 278-279.

[362] Vajanský attended the trial, which started 26th November 1906 in Ružomberok. He published a detailed report, which was based on his notes: *Ružomberský kriminálny process proti Andrejovi Hlinkovi a spoločníkom* (Turčiansky Sv. Martin: Kníhtlaciarsko-účastinársky spolok, 1906).

of personal hygiene, fanaticism and cynicism ... But, on the other hand, I respected his belief in the socialist programme."[363]

Trained in natural sciences and adhering to Masaryk's Realism, Šrobár had no interest in Marxism. We think that the believing Catholic rejected the theory's fundamental materialism and atheism. While imprisoned, Šrobár occupied himself with a task that expressed the very sense of Masaryk's *small works*: He wrote a medical reader that should educate the peasants about basic hygiene and first aid. Addressing issues such as poor nourishment, the fatal effects of alcoholism and the importance of clean houses, he gave further advice on how to deal with infections, broken limbs and skin diseases. The poor conditions in some of the villages were caused by a general ignorance and lack of public care.

"The people drank, frequented the advocate, quarrelled and beat each other up and had debts at the pub; the roads were impassable ... the people used to be drunk all the time did not care about keeping their huts clean. Neglected and desperate children were playing in the courts and the dusty roads. Their traditional garbs smelled of mould ... [364]

As much as Šrobár cared to improve the hygienic conditions of the peasants, the nation's enlightenment and economic progress, his sometimes negative, sometimes positive statements about Jewish citizens require careful and objective dealing within the historical context. Šrobár wrote in his memoirs, published in 1946, that he had become an *anti-Semite* in his teenage years because of a bad experience with a Jew in his native Ružomberok[365]. The usual Christian anti-Semitism of the Churches accused the Jewish citizens of usury and slandered them as wealthy exploiters and oppressors, since they were loyal to the ruling Magyars. Šrobár changed his views significantly around 1900, when he became a convinced democrat and adhered to the state building theory of *Czechoslovakism*. I selected the following quotes below to illustrate his early and later views of the Jewish citizens. Naturally, I tried to follow the principles of scholarly objectivity and fairness and would like to stress that in all his texts the negative statements about the Magyars were predominant. To my knowledge, Šrobár addressed the Jewish citizens only in regard to their economic

---

[363]   Šrobár, *Z môjho...*, 449. For a brief introduction to Kun see http://www.britannica.com/ EBchecked/topic/324824/Bela-Kun; accessed 10 June 2009; Kun's major texts are available on http://www.marxists.org/archive/kun-bela/index.html; accessed 10 June 2009.

[364]   Šrobár, *Z môjho...*, 274.

[365]   Šrobár, *Z môjho...*, 59.

power as the entrepreneurial minority and in the context of the miserable social conditions in the countryside. There is no passage known to me, in which he attacked them at length, referred to them in what we would call 'hate speech' today, nor did I find articles or essays dealing exclusively with the so-called 'Jewish question'.

In the context of his discussion with Masaryk about the Jews in Slovakia and in Bohemia in the mid 1890s, the young student still adhered to the 'classical' Christian anti-Semitism:

"Generally, Masaryk was no anti-Semite. He reproached the Jews that they are not capable of freeing themselves from the Old Testament, the Talmud and the ghetto despite living in a Christian world. They isolate themselves from the oppressed nations and are loyal to the ruling nations according to religious commandment; here, it means that they germanise and magyarise ... They have many good skills, are cunning in business ... they ... gave science many excellent experts ... I added that Schopenhauer does not recognise the Jewish spirit to extend any significant ethical influence on European thought, that in Jewish texts one smells the 'foetor judaicus'. Masaryk replied that it would be more appropriate to speak of 'foetorom ghetta', where neither the sun and the spirit of the new world, nor new ideas or the solidarity of the European people enter. ... (In ten years people would say he 'defended Hilsner'; but he did not defend Hilsner, the murderer, he fought against the terrible and uncritical superstition of the Czech people.)"[366]

---

[366] Šrobár, *Z môjho...*, 245-246. By 1946, Šrobár could not know that Hilsner was innocent. He had been accused of ritual murder; the populace believed the anti-Semitic fairy tale of the 'blood libel' that Jews killed Christian girls or children for their blood, which they needed to prepare the Pessah matzos. Masaryk's forensic evidence proved that the girl was not cut but stabbed to death, which turned the death sentence into a lifelong prison sentence. Hilsner was released in the general amnesty in 1916, issued by emperor Karl. In 1969, the brother of the murdered girl confessed on his death bed that he had murdered his sister.
The distinguished Slovak historian Ivan Kamenec views Šrobár's anti-Semitism in the broader context of what one could call 'tactical anti-Semitism': 'Srobar's anti-Semitism did not differ that much from the usual stereotypes that were dominant in the Slovak society and the political elite prior to 1918. Their relics can be felt, to some extent, until today. The verbal expressions of anti-Semitism differed only by the degree of radicalisation. As a Hlasist, Šrobár belonged to the moderates. At the end of the day, even T. G. Masaryk suggested to the Slovak Hlasists to use a distinct amount of anti-Semitism in their political fight; it should be directed against the Magyar national politics and the economic system of usery. Masaryk, with the full weight of his personality, gave these directions to the Slovak Hlasists at the very time he was engaging himself in the so-called Hilsner affair. History is full of surprising paradoxia.' I would like to thank Ivan Kamenec for his expertise; personal discussion of 25 June 2009, Bratislava, Slovakia.

In the first issue of *Hlas* in 1898, he criticised the passive obstruction of the older generation and described the social situation in Slovakia in the context of the reforms the Hlasists suggested:

> "In one word: the Slovak intelligentsia is dissipated between three and a half million people that is misled by the government, caught in a web by the Jew-spider [žid-pavúk], unaware of his civil rights, spiritually and materially neglected, forgotten in crime and poverty..."[367]

In his memoirs, he recounted how he tried to educate the peasants in his native Ružomberok by suggesting reading books instead of getting stone drunk every day. This memory dates back to the first years he had his medical practice, around 1909, when he gave a public lecture about alcoholism:

> "One of the youngsters asked me what to do on the holidays and Sundays when they were not working in the fields. I told him: 'Read books or the newspapers!' And I told him about the importance and need of newspapers, how one can learn from them about the world, politics, economics and various other beneficial things. 'Look: every Jew reads the news and that is why he is more intelligent than you. Learn something from them! You won't see a drunken Jew – learn also this from them!'"[368]

In the first weeks of the war in August 1914, Šrobár and some friends went to a beer garden in his native Ružomberok, where they had an argument with Jewish citizens about the war.

> "We found the local 'Magyar' intelligentsia sitting at a wooden and worn out table: 5 patriotic Jews. ... The advocate started; he was 45 years old, an intelligent, cunning and humorous man, who loved anecdotes. ... He had gone for some time to the rabbinical school and it seems that he had some remainders of Talmudian shrewdness, which he made fun of, but which had also shaped his arguments and way of thinking. Otherwise, he was a tireless narrator of rabbinical anecdotes and wisdoms."[369]

As was to be expected, the Jewish citizens and the Slovaks had different views about the war and the discussion took a sharp direction; the advocate ended up accusing Šrobár of high treason, upon which Šrobár and his friends decided to avoid discussions about the war with Magyar patriots in the future. The following excerpt stems from an unexpected visit and interrogation by the detective Duliškievič in Šrobár's house in Ružomberok on 22nd November 1917:

---

[367]   Šrobár, "Naše snahy", *Hlas I*, (1898): 1-6; 3.
[368]   Šrobár, *Z môjho...*, 383.
[369]   Šrobár, *Pamäti z vojny a z väzenia* (Praha: Náklad Gustav Dubského, 1922), 10, 11.

"D: 'I have to say that all Slovaks, not standing in front of the public, talk in private as if they had made an arrangement. And a second fact is that the Slovak intelligentsia called for a passive resistance against the Hungarian government. Why is that so?' ...

Š: 'The reason is that the Slovak intelligentsia does not believe the Hungarian government. A hundred times it promised and a hundred times it either disappointed or forgot us ... Do you recognise, Sir, the crime that is being done to us?'

D: 'Yes, I do.'

Š: 'The Magyar side acknowledges this crime in private, but is being silent about it in public.'

D: 'You know, the Jewish pressure is to blame for that ... '

Š: 'We have heard this excuse before ... '"[370]

After more than two years of tireless work in the barracks of Ružomberok, where he and his team were treating soldiers from the Carpathian front, Šrobár went on a holiday in January 1917. On his way to his beloved Prague, he stopped in Pest.

"Life in Pest seemed to run in a strictly zoological fashion: gone the business and gone the amusement. And, if Pest before the war had been Jewish – it seemed now that there were no other people than Jews. Even in the Lukacs bath where I healed myself and relaxed, the entire personnel was Jewish, the doctor, the masseurs and the vendors – all of them Jews. No wonder [Niet divu] that the Christian hatred boiled up against them and rumours circulated that this war was all about the Jews enriching themselves and pushing the Christians out of all positions ... Jews gained positions in the ministries, public offices, hospitals, everywhere one could hide from the military service and do some business [nejaký kšeft robiť]. Through these activities we can better understand all the events that happened after the fall of the Magyar state in the first days of November 1918 in Pest: The Magyars did not have citizens who could have enforced the belief in the sense of the state, enthusiastic people who were self-sacrificing, loving the common good more than themselves. That was why the Magyar empire fell so easily and that artificial instrument dissolved into pieces ... Careless amusement, cowardice, corruption, egoism, incapability and materialism buried the thousand years work of the Magyar nation in a couple of weeks."[371]

For the 'Panslavist and Czechoslovakist' speech, Šrobár gave at the worker's gathering in Liptovský Sv. Mikuláš on 1 May 1918 he was sentenced to prison in the Central Hungarian town of Cegléd. The gendarmes arrested him in the streets; he had a few of hours to collect his belongings.

---

[370] Šrobár, "Nečekaná návšteva detektiva Duliškieviča u Dra Šrobára", in *Boj o nový život* (Ján Párička: Ružomberok, 1920), 482-488; 485, 486.

[371] Šrobár, *Pamäti* ... 70-71.

"My detective behaved very decently. Some Jews from Liptov entered our wagon, traders and landlords. Among them, the citizens from Ružomberok W. Huncústky, a humorous person, and the landlord T. from Teplá. The latter offered me, out of free will, a sum of money; one would need this in these conditions. I thanked him for his good intention. The Jews have that instinct for pragmatic help. Often, it is a precious characteristic trait of theirs."[372]

In 1920, when he was the plenipotentiary minister for Slovakia, he remembered the following:

"At the end of June 1920 in Bratislava, I run into the notary from Ružomberok. He complained that the Jewry [židovstvo] was discontent with my regime. I explained to him the status the Jewry had had before the war and how it now behaves in the new state and how it did under Magyar rule. – You Jews enjoy more freedom today than we, the nation, used to. You can publish in newspapers and read whatever journal you fancy, you can work, trade, organise yourself freely, vote, run for the advocate's office, get rich and nobody hinders you. You are completely free and, do you remember the scene in the garden, how you shouted at me, poured evil words on me and how that fat advocate yelled at me? – Nem szabad! You cannot say this in public [neslobodno hovoriť]."[373]

Referring to these quotes I would like to describe Šrobár's views of the Jewish citizens as follows: As a teenager and student, he was a self-declared anti-Semite, owing to the socio-economic conditions in Slovakia. In Bohemia, he educated himself in natural sciences and acquired the rational, anti-clerical and democratic thought of Masaryk's Realists. He certainly did not support the personal discrimination against any citizen, Slovak, Magyar, Catholic, Jewish, Roma or Lutheran. He fiercely rejected violence against any citizen. His main political enemies were the conservative intellectuals around Vajanský and, later, Hlinka and his Peoples Party. His negative statements about the economic power of the Jews stem from the last decades of the 19th century and do sometimes express discriminating words. His anti-Semitic views, however, changed once he became convinced of the importance of ethics in politics and *Realism*[374]. Neither a liberal nor a conservative, he was a patriot in the sense of national awareness and used harsh words when addressing the Magyars, the Slovak intelligentsia and the conservative Catholic clergy. None of the five thinkers whose goals and thoughts I analysed,

---

[372] Šrobár, *Pamäti* ..., 121.

[373] Šrobár, *Pamäti* ... 13.

[374] Note that *Realism* refers to the thought of the Czech and Slovak Realists, while the small caps refer to the generally used term. On Realism see chapter VI. 1. 2. below.

referred to the Jewish economic power as often and directly as Šrobár. Their contact with the Jewish citizens were of a different character, since they lived in small towns in Western Slovakia and in times when the assimilation was not yet that harsh. In the 1880s and 1890s in the Slovak north-eastern countryside, however, the pressure to magyarise extended to all citizens, regardless of their religious adherence or national identity. I think that Šrobár's anti-Semitic views mirror his general perceptions of the social conditions, of which the Jewish citizens were a part; he certainly did not hate the Jewish citizens for their culture or faith. I have found no passages in his texts where he expressed a belief in the 'blood libel' or referred to other anti-Semitic fairy tales. In our attempt to present his goals and thought in the most possible objectivity and historical fairness, we hold that he had an anti-Semitic view of the Jewish citizens because of their entrepreneurial successes and their loyalty to the ruling Magyars. He changed his views in the first decade of the 20th century, influenced by *Czechoslovakism* and the goal of democracy.

Apart from medical care, which he considered an aspect of an educated and civilised nation, what were Šrobár's political goals?

VI. 1. Political goals

VI. 1. 1. Hlas – enlightenment, work and rationality

Before he founded *Hlas*, Šrobár published a couple of articles in the *Národnie Noviny*; he would, however, soon fall out with the editorial board about the direction of Slovak politics. As a student in Prague, he published under the pseudonym V. Lieskovan, indirectly opposing the passivity of the Martinists without openly critising them. He sharply condemned the liberal government of Koloman Tisza.

> "With the birth of the first generation of the XIX century great men led it and ... wrote these words in golden letters: 'Liberty, equality, fraternity [Voľnosť, rovnosť, bratstvo]' ... For twenty five years we have been living in liberty, equality and brotherhood with all nations of the *Hungarian* state. But we could barely enjoy the golden rays of the sun of freedom with our brothers, the Romanians, Serbs, Ruthenians and Germans, since in the Pest assembly, in the presence of all the delegates of Hungary, Minister President Kol. Tisza declared under a stormy applause and the enthusiasm of the entire assembly: 'There is no Slovak nation, I do not know any other nation in Hungary than the Magyar!'[375]

---

[375] Šrobár, "Voľnosť, rovnosť, bratstvo", *Národnie Noviny XXV*, č. 135, 15. 11. 1894, 2.

After explaining that Tisza's words were identical to those of Kossuth in 1848, he listed what the nation had to endure under the enforced assimilation. The non-Magyar people in Upper Hungary did not enjoy the goals of the Enlightenment the Magyar liberal government was so proud of, since its interpretation of the ideals of the French Revolution could be summarised as follows: Instead of liberty and equality – Magyar institutions and the prison in Szeged if anybody dared to protest. Instead of fraternity – the collection of taxes, of which 2% were used to finance the assimilation in the Slovak župy[376]. Šrobár appealed to the reader that, in spite of the difficulties of the current situation, there was still hope. As long as there were ideals, ideas and the will to pursue them, they would win one day. He suggested the *small works* as a means to overcome the discrimination. Eventually, he referred to the Czech historian Palacký and the moral principle of Czech history that would also apply to the Slovaks. Not by the sword, but by the word and a moral education was the nation's spirit to be rekindled:

> "Because (as Palacký speaks about the brother nation of the Czechs) we have to thoroughly acknowledge that whenever we won in the past, we did so because of our moral strength, not our physical power, and whenever we lost, we did so because of the spiritual inadequacies of our acts, the lack of ethical courage and moral bravery."[377]

The Hlasists, young university-trained intellectuals, would open up a phase of modernisation, bringing new options to the passive public. The Martinists of the elder generation, led by Vajanský, would fight them fiercely as competitors, accusing them of atheism and Czech cultural dominance.

> "We do not present a detailed programme. Quite openly we admit that we are not prepared to lead the young generation that is lost in the world and being torn between the influence of various societal, political and moral views. ... What are our aspirations? First and foremost, we want the Slovak man to morally renew himself."[378]

In his article *Our aspirations (Naše snahy),* published in the first volume of the new journal *Hlas,* Šrobár introduced the Hlasist movement in a brief sketch. The text was in its essence the signal for a struggle for intellectual leadership, directed against the elder intelligentsia. However, an openly declared power struggle would have divided the nation even more. That was the reason why Šrobár formulated the Hlasist

---

[376]   Šrobár, "Voľnosť ... , 2.
[377]   Šrobár, "Voľnosť ... , 2.
[378]   Šrobár, "Naše snahy", *Hlas I,* (1898): 1-6; 1.

programme in careful words. The movement should not be understood as a further political party that attempted to stand up against the assimilation and contesting the course of the Martinists, but as an internal *programme of reform*. In his analysis of current Slovak politics, Šrobár assessed first a rift between the Slovak people and the press that were divided into the society of the *Maďarony* and the national society[379]. On a second glance, however, the two camps were not that different. The *Maďarony* were generally considered as traitors, who treated the people violently and rudely; there was no vice they would not give themselves up to and no sin they would not commit. The national society was used to perceive itself as the very opposite.

> "... there is no difference between the current Slovak national society, meaning the national intellectuals, neither at home nor in public, and the Maďaronist group. If a Maďaron treats the people rudely, our intellectual is not an iota more friendly ... We are alike in every way ... Our people are fearing us no less than the ruling administrators and aristocrats ... How easy it is to blame the all-powerful enemy for our limited cultural and political status ... We do not address anything new here, as we have recently read ...: *We – the Slovak intelligentsia, are the nation, pars pro toto.*[380]

Šrobár identified the Martinists' self-declared entitlement of representing the entire nation not only as a numerical impossibility but also as the feudal thinking of aristocrats that look down on the masses of serfs. He criticised the elder intelligentsia's "egoistic" and "liberalistic opinions" – in the sense of Magyar liberalism that equalled chauvinist assimilation – and presented the alternative of the Hlasists:

> " Against which ... we counter the Christian origins of humanism [ľudskosti], the origins of social love. These are the origins of the equality of individuals, nations, the origins of brotherhood, love in the interactions with those close to us, the origins of the truth in thought and the appearance of the human soul. To put the life of a Slovak intellectual on these fundaments is what we call his rebirth [obrodením]."[381]

While he considered it natural that men first thought of themselves, selfishness proved to be fatal when it became a dominant feature in a nation's life. Šrobár accused the intellectuals, including the Hlasists, of neglect and indifference toward their own people. The "Slovak fatalism" [slovenský fatalismus] was just a blind

---

[379] Šrobár, "Naše snahy", 1.
[380] Šrobár, "Naše snahy", 2, 3, italics by me. Šrobár referred to Vajanský's text *Insights and outlooks*, 12. Vajanský's quote in the original: "... my sme národom, pars pro toto...".
[381] Šrobár, "Naše snahy", 3.

belief in the victory of the truth that lacked any effort, any activities. The moral reformation of the Slovak individual was the first of the Slovak Realists' aspirations; their second was to spread and deepen the works of the Enlightenment [prácu osvetnú][382]. Enlightenment work – the Masarykian idea of transferring theory into practise – required, above all, education and expertise:

> "We demand thus from the Slovak lawyers, doctors, ingenieurs, philosopher, priests, businessmen and artisans, and so on, not only to be well trained in their fields, but to achieve the most possible perfection ... We have had already more than enough amateurish work; what is now required is to go a step further."[383]

Enlightenment work had to be well organised: the Hlasists suggested forming expert groups and professional guilds that would take care of the training and education of the youth. The young generation should go abroad to acquire professionalism in apprenticeships, high schools and universities in Austria, particularly Bohemia, France, England and even in America, where their fellow Slovaks were very well organised. This second aspiration was the most decent work for the nation. After suggesting similar improvements to schools and economics of finance, Šrobár eventually addressed the issue of political activity:

> "To really work politically, we have to achieve first many other 'non-political' works. And these are exactly the small, unspectacular works in the areas of morality, enlightenment and national economics. Therefore, in our opinion, *political activity* in Slovakia means *any work*, which we achieve to the prosperity of the other close to us, his moral and intellectual rise and the protection of his material well-being. From this follows that we shall not expect salvation from the so-called 'high politics', *randomly bestowed* alms from abroad, which some of our 'politicians' consider the liberation from all poverties and societal insufficiencies."[384]

The suggestions of the Hlasists were identical to the *small works* Masaryk had formulated for the Czechs in the 1890s: 'work for the nation' entailed the daily, continuous and unspectacular efforts of every individual in a profession, science, education, economics and culture. The goal of the *small works* was to become a better person, to educate oneself according to the latest scientific findings, treat others well and by doing so, improve the moral quality of the nation. The key words are *love for the other,* in the sense of fraternal Christian love, and *non-political politics.* The

---

[382] Šrobár, "Naše snahy", 4.
[383] Šrobár, "Naše snahy", 4.
[384] Šrobár, "Naše snahy", 4.

term *non-political* was a stroke of genius of Masaryk, as he rightly saw that in the given circumstances, Czech party politics were stuck, owing to unrealistic goals, and also blocked by the intransigence of the imperial government. Unsuccessful party politics thus had to be replaced by a 'non-political' movement that united the nation and strengthened its progress in economics, science and patriotism[385]. *Non-political* and *small works* was the glue that kept the nation together in that it created civil discipline, individual responsibility and social cohesion – civil virtues required for a sovereign democracy. *Non-political* and *small works* was the only way the Slovak Realists deemed feasible for Slovakia, due to the low level of education, the power of the clergy, the absence of manufacture and industry and the poverty in the countryside. Suggesting a set of instructions how to do something for oneself that would also benefit the nation and stressing that each citizen was equal to the other meant a clear and sharp break with the Martinists. Such break would add only a further divide since the population was already separated along confessional lines so much so that "a Slovak Catholic trusts a non-Slovak Jew rather than a Slovak Lutheran."[386] Šrobár was fully aware of the potentially dangerous consequences of the Hlasist programme and he concluded his article with a very clear statement that left no doubt about the Realists' intentions:

> "From our views about Slovak politics follows that we have no intention to call for a schism [rozkol] in the nation, nor do we have plans to found a political party. On the contrary: we shall be treating every political party, which is working for the moral and material improvement of the Slovak people, *in an equally objective and honest way*, and we shall be glad to support any party in this matter with that which lies in our strengths – be it the Slovak National Party, the Slovak Social-Democratic Party or eventually, the so-called Peoples' Party [strane t. zv. ľudovej]."[387]

If he mentioned in a brief last paragraph that the Realists favoured the idea of the *cultural unity of the Czechoslovak nation* [kultúrnu jednotu naroda československého], he signalled to the yet undecided that the Hlasists were oriented

---

[385] Former Czech dissident and president Václav Havel spoke of 'anti-political' politics [anti-politická politika], describing the basic viewpoint of the members of *Charter 77* to make daily efforts for the human rights the Czechoslovak government had signed in the CSCE treaty of Helsinki; see my *Politik als praktizierte Sittlichkeit. Zum Demokratiebegriff von Thomas G. Masaryk und Václav Havel* (Sinzheim: Pro Universitate, 1998).

[386] Šrobár, *Z môjho…*, 271.

[387] Šrobár, "Naše snahy", 6; emphasis by JB.

towards Czech political thought that promoted Western ideas of anti-clericalism, democratic values and above all, a rational and realistic approach to political issues. The future, or so Šrobár must have thought, laid in Western political culture, all the more as the *Russophilia* of the Martinists had completely failed. The idea to expect salvation, read liberation from Tsarist Russia had never been a realistic alternative, not even in Štúr's times; the inherent romanticism of Russophilia lacked practical advise of how to improve the life of the population.

VI. 1. 2. Realism

"It is not that long ago that more than three quarters of the population in our villages could not read or write. ... Go around our villages during the school year and have a look at the basic conditions in the schools. In dark, run down buildings you will find a hundred to a hundred and thirty children, jammed together in foul smell and dust like in a stable, in winter like in an ice cubicle, in summer like in a leaden Venetian cell – and such a 'band' is taught by one teacher. One would not give a hundred and thirty horses to one herdsman's care and guide, but one teacher has to teach a hundred and thirty children!"[388]

The direction Šrobár promoted in the programme of the Hlasists was based on *Realism* as the fundamental perspective on social life. *Realism* meant, above all, to have a fact-based understanding of the nation's situation by assessing its inherent problems in an objective and dispassionate fashion. This would allow exploring how the problems were connected and what means one had at his disposal to solve them. That the passivity and arrogance of the intellectual elite would lead only to the widening of the rifts running through the population was one issue; another was how to initiate the change. If Šrobár had stressed the importance of national unity and the national work being individual acts of the Christian love of the next, the programme, however, should not be considered a religious one. In spite of his repeating the terms 'God' or 'Christianity', he did not address the Catholic Church. We could say that he remained a faithful Catholic until the end of his life, but was decidely anti-clerical and anti-religious in political matters. The clergy's claim of leading the nation and its mingling into politics had done nothing to improve the nation's life; his critique of the clergy was connected to his conviction that the Church and the state were separate entities with different tasks.

---

[388]   Šrobár, "Kus svetla", *Národnie Noviny XXIII*, č. 92, 9. 8. 1892, 1-2; 1.

To us, living in the 21st century, the term *Realism* sounds somewhat confusing, if not empty or obsolete; there was no European movement or party known to me in the 19th century that equalled the Czech and Slovak Realists. On the Czech party landscape in the late 19th century and in Slovakia around the turn of the century, however, *Realism* became a new body of thought, comparable perhaps to the beginnings of the ecological movement in the early 1980s in West Germany that led to the foundation of the *Green Party* (*Die Grünen*). The Realist movement was not very successful in the Czech lands nor in Slovakia, since it did not attract the masses, owing to its 'non-political' programme that was bereft of the populist and emotionally appealing slogans of the other parties. The Realists were mostly intellectuals who had enjoyed university education; their self-asserted lack of a political programme confused the people. However, *Realism*, if properly understood, accounted for three important features: *Simplicity, feasibility and egalitarian morality*. It would certainly be wrong to state that the Old and Young Czechs in Bohemia acted irrationally, nor could one say that the Martinists were not capable of rational thought. The problem was the transfer of theoretical statements into pragmatic guidelines: the elder generations did not have a method that would see them, or the nation, out of the political deadlock they had, to some extent, created themselves. Naturally, we do not claim that *Realism* brought about the political liberation for both nations, which was, first and foremost, negotiated by the exile government and the emigré communities with the winning allies. However, the new thinking prepared a critical faction of Czech and Slovak intellectuals for the regime change; many among them would be ready and capable to run the Republic in the aftermath of 1918. How did Šrobár conceive of *Realism* and how did he apply it to the Slovak conditions?

We have mentioned above that *Realism* did not promote atheism, but it certainly called for a critical view of the clergy as a powerful institution that was blocking progress and development.

"A certain representative of the Catholic Peoples' Party – I won't mention his name – sticks to the natural sciences from the times before Copernicus and Galileo Galilei, until these days he does not accept that the earth spins around the sun!"[389]

---

[389] Šrobár, *Politický problem Slovenska* (Praha: Svaz národního osvobození: Praha, 1926), 26. The person Šrobár refers to is Andrej Hlinka.

Realism meant to strive for education, scientific expertise and to look at society and politics from an objective and scientific point of view – of which the elder generation and, foremost, the dogmatically trained Catholic clergy was incapable and also unwilling. The issue-related and scientific method of the Realists was their pre-eminent weapon against the superstition and uncritical submissiveness the clergy created in the population in order to manipulate it more easily. The Realists thus came up with a method that first, stated a problem or question, second, assessed the problem according to the scientific principles of its genre or branch, sociology, philosophy, history, etc. and third, tried to find the best possible solutions that would be of a universal benefit, for the nation and mankind. The Realist approach had thus to follow the ethical guidelines of the love of the next and, subsequently, the democratic egalitarianism. Šrobár's articles *Magyarisation*[390] and *Lessons learnt from our mistakes*[391] give us an excellent illustration how he applied the Realist thought and method.

> "Nothing worries the Slovak intellectual more than that which we call Magyarisation. ...
> Let us now hear what one can say about Magyarisation in a dispassionate and calm manner.
> ... There is no nation in Europe that does not have its political 'religion' and its political
> 'faith'. This religion carries in itself the seeds of all national ideals, and its characteristic
> features are determined by the characteristic cultural status of its individuals ... the political
> religion does not constitute itself from reason ..."[392]

After quoting a lengthy excerpt from the British sociologist Herbert Spencer[393] (1820 – 1903), he analysed Magyarisation as a sociological and psychological phenomenon, coming to the conclusion that Magyarisation was the *Magyar political religion*. Magyarisation had its origins in the iconic idea of the one Magyar political nation of 1848. The expressions of loyalty to the Magyar nation could be heard, so Šrobár, in the churches, in public and in parliament. This loyalty was considered the nation's highest ideal and stood above the moral laws of humanity and the law of god[394]. Magyarisation was revered like an indicator that measured a citizen's morality or his lack thereof.

---

[390]   Šrobár, "Maďarisácia", *Hlas I* (1898): 65-73.
[391]   Šrobár, "Poučenia z chýb", in *Boy o nový* ..., 120-124.
[392]   Šrobár, "Maďarisácia", 65.
[393]   Šrobár used the Czech translation of Spencer's *The study of Sociology* (1873, 1896): *O studiu sociologie* (Praha, 1898).
[394]   Šrobár, "Maďarisácia", 67.

"Because the overwhelming majority of the Magyar intelligentsia is dominated in its will, actions, reason and, above all, moral views by the origins of Magyarisation, it considers the purely Magyar as superior than the purely human and Christian – that is why we call Magyarisation the religion of the new times."[395]

The Magyar political religion was nothing unusual or condemnable, since every nation had its own characteristic features, political ideals, set of moral values and culture; the problem was that the Magyar political religion was regarded superior to the universal moral laws that originated in Christian values and extended justice and equality to all national groups. Šrobár conceived of Magyarisation as an *"anti-Christian religion"* [náboženstvo protikresťanské][396]. Magyarisation violated the basic Christian values of peace and equality, thus respect for the different moral views of the kingdom's population; this egoism and violence turned the Magyar political religion into a superstition [povera][397]. It is fascinating how consistently Šrobár applied Realist principles to government politics, in particular to such an emotionally loaded term like Magyarisation: in an unparalleled logic, he named the assimilation first a political religion, then an anti-Christian religion and topped it by labelling it a superstitious belief. By doing so, he banned Magyar rule and politics into the realm of irrationality – superstition, after all, connoted also the ancient customs of pagan groups that had not yet achieved the civilisational realm of enlightened rationality. His scientific reference to Spencer gave his arguments validity. After the first two steps, that is, naming the problem and assessing it in a scientific method, he concluded with the third step that suggested a solution. The youth was the generation most threatened by Magyarisation and it "was falling under the influence of that religious egoism, violence, ... that new, anti-Christian and pagan [pohanskej] superstition."[398] He listed three fields where the Slovak youth could be protected: First, by the *book*, meaning extra-curricular self-education in the mother tongue that would widen the intellectual horizon. Second, through the upbringing in the *family*, where parents should not give away their children to influential Magyar institutions and persons because they mistakenly believed their offspring would have a better future. The parents were held to educate the young as good patriots, teaching

---

[395] Šrobár, "Maďarisácia", 67.
[396] Šrobár, "Maďarisácia", 67.
[397] Šrobár, "Maďarisácia", 68.
[398] Šrobár, "Maďarisácia", 71.

them Slovak and their national customs. Third, in the *schools*, since the current situation demanded that the parents had to send their youngsters abroad to get high school education. The issue of the Slovak gymnasium, and the lack thereof, respectively, must have reminded Šrobár of his own discrimination in the Magyar and German gymnasiums that contrasted his happy times in Přerov. His otherwise sober, quiet and fact-oriented tone became slightly angry and very determined at the same time:

"Therefore, it is now the duty of every Slovak family which does not want its children to be uprooted, morally suffocated, their spiritual facilities drowned instead of developing, to send them to Czech schools, where they shall be protected against this three-fold evil."[399]

Concluding his article Šrobár added a claim that reminds us of Daxner's efforts: he called for collecting funds to finance a Slovak gymnasium. Needless to say that this collection was not successful.

Realism did not only mean to apply sober, issue-related and scientific thinking to political matters – it also included self-criticism. In his article *Lessons learnt from our mistakes* Šrobár was hard on the Hlasists, including himself; they, so he thought, had failed to evaluate their activities and possibilities, thereby allowing their enemies to blacken their efforts and reputation:

"We are not to blame for the fact that mistakes and weaknesses were found, but it is unfortunate that *our enemy* found out about our weaknesses *before we did.* ... The second cardinal mistake was that the *conscious and unconscious lie* became the crucial actor in Slovak political and public life. We were mistaken in our beliefs that we had gained success and the sympathy of the powerful; we had illusions that we could fulfil our wishes, and that is why we lost our energetical approach and the fight for the peoples' rights. They erected entire legends ... and we were, like children, smugly falling asleep and becoming lazy in our work and fight."[400]

Although the Hlasists understood themselves as a non-political group that was willing to co-operate with everybody who agreed with their direction, Šrobár spoke in this article about the political fight and the successes they were missing. Naïveté was a further factor he thought the Slovak Realists had to take into account. They had concentrated all their efforts on their political success and were now disappointed. A small and weak nation could simply not put all its hopes on one card, since it would

---

[399]   Šrobár, "Maďarisácia", 73.
[400]   Šrobár, "Poučenia z chýb"", in *Boy o nový* ..., 120-121.

loose all its strength if it were to fail. One had to diversify one's efforts to various fields. However, nobody could hinder them not to organise themselves financially, to send their children to Czech schools and to care about the distribution of good books and journals[401]. *Czechoslovakism* was one of the cards he set his hopes on.

VI. 2. Political legitimating

VI. 2. 1. Czechoslovakism

"Prague was quiet, somewhat closed. My friends kept telling me that the hotels, coffee houses, editorial offices and the streets were full of detectives and spies. ... At Dr. Herben's house I met with some members of the Maffia. I had no idea back then that the persons I had the honour to meet were so influential. They asked me about the conditions in Slovakia, about Pest, ... I stressed the following: 'We do not have teachers, we lack middle schools and the professors to run them, ... For 10 to 15 years they have assimilated entire towns, for 20-30 years to come, Slovak villages shall remain only islands in a Magyar sea. ... If you leave us out of your first declaration, the international community and our government will notice and leave us to rot with the Magyars, which will be our national death.' Švehla listened to me attentively and, after I had finished, told me in a clear and determined voice: 'We shall not leave you, we will certainly include you to our declaration.' ... Up to my trip there was no connection of Slovakia with Prague. We promised ourselves that we would inform the public about our common line of action."[402]

If Šrobár's political education in Prague made him an adherent of Masaryk's Realism, he was equally convinced of the feasibility of the professor's political plans that foresaw the sovereignty of a common state of the Czechs and Slovaks. *Political Czechoslovakism* meant to fight the empire's ruling nations by sketching a common state and legitimate it with historical arguments. Šrobár always openly admitted to the significant influence of Masaryk's thought; he followed the only person interested in the fate of the Slovaks in the 1890s with personal respect and a critical und unimpassioned reason. The chronology of *political Czechoslovakism* is thus telling: Masaryk wrote already in 1905 about the common future of the *Czechoslovak nation*:

---

[401] Šrobár, "Poučenia ... ", 123.

[402] Šrobár, *Pamäti* ... , 77-78. Antonín Švehla (1873 – 1933), member of the *Maffia*, the circle of Masaryk's adherents that founded the Revolutionary Committee in 1918 in Prague; Czechoslovak politician, Minister President from 1922 to 1929 and member of the Agrarian party. Jan Herben (1857 – 1936), was a Czech literate, journalist, senator and also involved in the independence movement during the war.

"Just think how we consider Bohemia, Moravia, Silesia and, finally, Slovakia as separate units! Two million Czechs [*dva miliony Čechů*] live in the Hungarian kingdom! ... We won't give up *a third of our nation*."[403]

In 1902, Šrobár had spoken of a *Czechoslovak mutuality* or *reciprocity* [vzájomnosť československá], determining the relations between the two national groups as historical and cultural-linguistical[404]. One should not fall for the unfeasible or adhere to a utopia, so Šrobár, since a political union was impossible. The Slovaks had been a part of the lands of the Hungarian Crown and it was their duty to protect the integrity of their state. Although the Czech and Slovak reciprocity was of a historical character, it would be damaging to the Slovak cause to speak of 'one literary and written language' or to follow a course of unification [splynutí][405]:

"It is a pure and blunt romanticism to ignite an unfeasible idea or an utopia ... and this romanticism will bring us only unnecessary persecution from the powerful enemies and aggravate our fight for the rights of the Slovak people."[406]

Any mentioning of a so-called unity in linguistic terms, that is of "one common written language" [o jednom spisovnom jazyku][407], would be too materialistic and therefore morally and sociologically inappropriate – Slovak was, after all, a language of its own. Furthermore, Ján Kollár, the father of *literary reciprocity* [literárnej vzájomnosti], had held that every Slavic dialect should rejuvenate and improve itself by the exchange and contact with the other dialects, but this did not mean to absorb them or be absorbed. True reciprocity respected the existence of all Slavic dialects that enriched the language of the Slavs[408]. It was, so Šrobár, absolutely unnecessary and damaging to focus on the task of one written language:

"You would prove to have a bad knowledge of the psychology of a nation [psychologiu národa], if you assumed it possible to take away this or that language or to stop the nation

---

[403]   Tomáš Garrigue Masaryk, "Prostsředky národa malého," in *Ideály humanitní* (Praha: Melantrich, 1991), 85-88; 87; italics by me.

[404]   Šrobár, "Vzájomnosť československá!" in *Boj o nový...* 168-173; 169. The article was first published in *Hlas IV* (1902): 289.

[405]   Šrobár, "Vzájomnosť...", 169.

[406]   Šrobár, "Vzájomnosť...", 169.

[407]   Šrobár, "Vzájomnosť...", 170.

[408]   Šrobár, "Vzájomnosť...", 170.

with other means to use this or that language. ... What kind of reciprocity do we need today?"[409]

A Czechoslovak reciprocity that deserved the name in the true sense of what Kollár had suggested, should improve its inner strength in the schools, religious affairs, literature and the social and economic spheres. Only a union of a close spirit, mutual help and love that extended to the entire population and was not limited to the intellectual elite would benefit both branches [kmenov]. Therefore, a Panslavist programme had to be rejected:

> "We Slovaks had been hypnotised by the Panslavist programme of Danilevskii's 'Rossiia i Evropa' into such a deep slumber that we are terrified to remember the precious time that was lost for all national Slovak forces ... because not all of our powers are yet awake and ready to act, and, after a long slumber, the soul of our nation has not yet fully healed."[410]

Using the historical and socio-cultural myth of the 'slumber' the Slavic nations had undergone before they started to 'revive' their languages and cultures in the early 19th century, Šrobár stressed the importance of exchange. To succumb to a common written language would only replace the Magyar dominance with the Czech. It was therefore irrational and un-Realistic to promote a Czechoslovak reciprocity that was *de facto* a hidden domination by the brother nation. In this sense, Šrobár's political interest was close, but not identical to the goals of the organisation *Československá jednota* that was founded in Prague in 1896 and represented various factions of progressive, anti-clerical and democratically minded intellectuals[411]. The political situation in the years prior to WWI was such that "Slovak politics were continuously oscillating between the needs of unity and the naturally given differences."[412] While he first considered political Czechoslovakism as infeasible and also unwanted, he would soon change his mind.

Before he was convinced that political liberty was only possible in a common state, Šrobár acted and wrote like the Slovak patriot he considered himself to be: Learning from the more developed Czechs, but always to the prospects of his nation, which needed new impulses for its national politics. By 1907, however, he was in full

---

[409]   Šrobár, "Vzájomnosť...", 171.
[410]   Šrobár, "Vzájomnosť...", 173.
[411]   Ivan Dubnička, "Vavro Šrobár a čechoslovakizmus", in *Kultúrno-politický profil...*, 105-135; 122.
[412]   Kováč, *Dejiny...*, 159.

support of the prospects of a common state, as he writes in the preface of his memoirs
Liberated Slovakia, published in 1928:

> "After a couple of days I met again with Seton-Watson ... Saying good-bye, he asked me:
> 'What is your programme in terms of a state?' The question surprised me ... After a while,
> immersed in quiet thoughts, I answered: 'Great Moravia, with the Czech lands, Moravia,
> Silesia with Slovakia and Pannonia. ... this happened seven years before the outbreak of
> the Great War and eleven years after 'Great Moravia' was called the 'Czechoslovak
> state'."[413]

The quote above illustrates how Šrobár used the historiographical icon of *Great
Moravia* to justify the future state. The Great Moravian Empire existed in the 9th
century and entailed territories settled by Czechs in today's Southern Moravia and
Slovaks in Western Slovakia; it was, however, historically not correct to name it the
first common state, as both the 19th century Czech and Slovak historiographies did[414].
Šrobár was somewhat acquainted with Sasinek's works, since he mentioned the
maximalist claim of the eccentric historian that included Pannonia to Slovakia. He
referred to him in his article *The Slovak National Party and its programme* to
demonstrate the nation's painful lack of self-awareness and historical knowledge:

> "Here are a couple of examples: the nation has no knowledge about the empire of
> Svatopluk; the attempts of Mr. Sasinek to prove the existence of a Slovak political
> independence [politickú samostatnosť] ... were recognised only hesitantly; the
> Memorandum, at least as we remember it, was the latest of the basic claims that were
> publicly known and, finally, the congress of the nationalities in Pest could not come up
> with one national and important programme, as it existed only on paper, from the very first
> day of its emerging."[415]

Šrobár was not a trained historian; he avoided adding lengthy historical analysis to
his basic statements. He wanted his readers to understand the appalling depths of
national clumsiness, repeating the three points of the Realist movement, thereby

---

[413]   Šrobár, *Osvobodené Slovensko. Pamäti z rokov 1918 – 1920,* (Praha: Čin, 1928), 7, 8. Robert
Seton-Watson (1878-1951) was the first British professor of Central European history and
personally acquainted with Masaryk and Šrobár. His expertise was critical for the British
governmenent's support of the foundation of Czechoslovakia. For more information see
http://www.history.ac.uk/makinghistory/historians/seton-watson_robert.html; accessed 8 June
2009.

[414]   Kováč, *Dejiny...,* 29, 172. See also Kováč, *Slováci* ... for a more detailed analysis of Great
Moravia and its legitimating function for the Chechoslovak state.

[415]   Šrobár, "Slovenská národna strana a jej program", in *Boj o nový* ..., 136-142. The article was
first published in *Hlas IV* (1902): 48.

putting them into opposition to the passivity of the *National party:* the Slovak national programme had to be a. Christian, b. democratic and c. progressive[416]. As regards the aspect of Christianity, it is interesting to analyse his thoughts about religion and the clergy prior to WWI. They are connected to his Czechoslovakism and his goal of the democratic common state. I disagree with Dubnička, who links Šrobár's anti-clericalism, in a wider frame, to the liberalism of the 19th century[417]. I shall present my views on the *triumvirate of Czechoslovakism –anti-clericalism / religion – democracy* in the following subchapter "Political religion or religious politics?". The concept 'liberalism' had different meanings in Frankfurt, Prague and Budapest; its facets of atheism and anti-clericalism should be dealt with more precisely. I hold furthermore that it is impossible to make a sharp division between the three concepts *czechoslovakism – anti-clericalism / religion – democracy* in Šrobár's thought. Therefore, I shall conclude this subchapter on Czechoslovakism with two quotes from Šrobár's memoirs of the crucial events in October 1918. He was released from the Cegléd prison, owing to his contacts and the fact that his son was ill with typhus. He came back to Slovakia, observing how the war was affecting even the most modest activities of the people:

> "I took the earliest train to Slovakia. The trains were late and the journey never lasted as long as then. But during the entire trip I saw the signs of the end of the war and the breakdown of the state. The train guards avoided the travellers, and the soldiers from the front created the greatest anarchy, not listening to anybody. Common soldiers threw out passengers from the II class and took their seats. ... Openly, people spoke about defeats, desertions and the horrors our platoons were subject to at the front. The restaurants, full of soldiers, were dirty and neglected. Everywhere, the people were timid and the aristocrats only whispered."[418]

Once Šrobár arrived in his native Ružomberok, he took care of his ill son. He dates the following interesting psychological experience on the 24 October 1918.

> "Around the 24 October an unclear and vague unrest caught me. ... I had a vague premonition that something is about to come, that something important is to happen, something grand and unimaginable, something our nation had not experienced in its history. ... On Monday 28 of October I got off the train at 10 in the morning at the state railway station. ... I made my way to the editorial office of the Nar. Listy, where I met Štefánek. ... 'We have been waiting for you since three days.' ... 'Me? I told nobody about

---

[416] Šrobár, "Slovenská národna...", 139.
[417] Dubnička, "Vavro Šrobár a ... ", 121.
[418] Šrobár, *Pamäti* ... 245.

my trip to Prague.' 'Well, anyway, we have been waiting for you.' ... We went to meet our friends. ... In front of the Obecny dom there was a huge crowd. We entered. ... I read the telegram ... I informed the nation that we finally had our government, our independence and our state. Through the whole night and the following days we put down the [institutional, add. JB] requirements of the state."[419]

The future plenipotentiary minister for Slovak affairs did not impose himself to the government position; due to his acquaintance with the members of the *Maffia*, the Prague circle in close contact with the exile government that had negotiated with the allies, he was one of the few Slovaks ready to run the country. Until the day he died, he would prove that he was a Slovak politician who understood in depth the differences of politics on a Czechoslovak and a Slovak level. Šrobár was, most probably, the only guarantee for Masaryk and Beneš to integrate Slovakia in political and intellectual terms. While the common state was one issue, there was another most pressing problem – the dominance of the clergy.

VI. 2. 2.   Political religion or religious politics?

We have mentioned above that the concepts *czechoslovakism – anti-clericalism / religion –democracy* form a triumvirate that cannot be divided. Let me now clarify my point.

First, I hold that Šrobár's anti-clericalism was not a consequence or influence of 19th century liberal thought, but originated in his patriotism. I have found no passage in his texts where he addressed liberalism in a positive way, all the more since the Magyar *assimilationist Liberalism* was not exactly an attractive set of ideas for a Slovak patriot. While his religious belief originated in his childhood and 'survived', albeit somewhat damaged, the rationalism and scientific education acquired in Prague, his anti-clericalism rooted in rationalism and his political goal of a Czechoslovak democracy. Šrobár's anti-clerical views had thus nothing to do with liberalism, but were a consequence of his democratic thought; he considered democracy the best possible expression of humanity in political and social institutions. If sovereignty was ever to be achieved, or so he must have thought, the constitution had to be a modern democratic one that protected the rights of the minorities, granted equality of gender and individuals, abolished the privileges of the

---

[419]   Šrobár, *Pamäti* ... 245, 247, 248-9. Anton Štefánek (1877 – 1936), Slovak journalist and politician, member of the Hlasists and from 1908 to 1918 editor of the Prague *Národní Listy*.

aristocracy and clergy and provided social security and welfare. Unlike Magyar rule, the democratic constitution would furthermore instigate economic progress and establish an educational system that targeted exactly the values the clergy had helped to firm up in the minds of the population: the lack of critical thought, superstition, devoutness to the regime and its representatives and the lack of personal and national self-awareness.

Second, his anti-clericalism mirrored, to some extent, Masaryk's *rational theism*, that is the idea that imagining the world without God is irrational[420]. Masaryk, however, had a clearer vision of how to integrate faith into modern politics, since he had converted to Protestantism in his early twenties, owing to his critique of the Catholic clergy. He spoke of *sub specie aeternitatis* and *love of the other,* addressing eternity as the last horizon of human reason. Whatever faith or lack thereof an individual adhered to, mankind shared the values of humanity. Everybody, save perhaps a psychopath, would admit that first, humanity meant to live in a human world, and second, that it required some distinct values. Every society needed guidelines such as not to kill, to steal or to lie, to regulate social behaviour. *Sub specie aeternitatis* meant further that human reason was limited; it could not go beyond a distinct horizon or a borderline dividing the physical world from the metaphysical. Šrobár's anti-clericalism led him into a phase of religious doubt. His aversion to the clergy, which might have increased through his psychological impressions of Hlinka, must have evoked serious doubts about the authority of Catholicism in the modern age. While in prison in Cegléd, Šrobár and a Serbian prisoner, an artist, had long talks about religion, faith, the future and the meaning of life:

"– And you, doctor, do you believe in God? Wait, don't answer right now, I have to confess ... I am watching you already for some time and now, when you went to look after the patients, I asked myself: Does he believe in God? ... If I told you that I do, you would not believe me, if I said I do not believe, you would not understand me. – I really don't understand you. – Read what stands in the scripture: God is Love. Others say: God is Wisdom, Perfection, the Truth, the Word, the Being, the Cosmos and so on. ... Which of

---

[420] Excellent on Masaryk's rational theism are Dalibor Truhlar, *Thomas G. Masaryk. Philosophie der Demokratie* (Frankfurt a. Main: Peter Lang, 1994) and Otakar A. Funda, *Tomáš Garrigue Masaryk. Sein philosophisches, religiöses und politisches Denken* (Bern: Peter Lang, 1978). For a good introduction to rational theism, theism and atheism see http://plato.stan ford.edu/entries/pragmatic-belief-god/ accessed 17 July 2009.

these words can determine what we have to think? Was there ever, is there or will there be a person who can express in one word all aspects of the concept of God so that we can understand it? ... –Why should mankind never be capable of understanding Life, Love, and God? – We reached the sphere of the Unimaginable, the Absolute. And here, in this sphere, we have no orientation. We lack the means, because our senses are insufficient. The man of our times knows just that which he can comprehend with his reason, and reason depends on information and the data of our thoughts."[421]

Religion in a collectivist sense as *institutionalised faith* presented an intellectual problem to him. How to establish the much needed values of Christianity, equality and tolerance in a democracy without the clergy's experience in instruction? Under the imperative of fraternity as the love for the next, how to effectively convince the population that a constitution granting the freedom of conscience, hence religious tolerance, did not equal an atheistic state? Bolshevism was the terrifying example of atheism. And, in regard of the particularities of the Czechoslovak democracy: if Christianity was the system of belief that created the nations' social and moral values while the clergy's power had to be significantly reduced, how to effectively prevent radical individualism that would lead to an atomised society? How to create and protect social cohesion under the conditions of a modern democracy? Masaryk was dealing with the same problem; he thought about the creation of a Czechoslovak National Church, similar to the Anglican Church. As the role model or blueprint for the National Church he foresaw the Protestant moral values of the Hussite movement. The National Church was never realised; much to Masaryk's chagrin, the people started to revere him in a personal cult, referring to him as *tatínek* (*Daddy*, *Väterchen*). While Šrobár and Masaryk considered the Catholic clergy as a hierarchy tightly connected to the illegitimate rule of the dynasty, from which it profited, Šrobár was in search of a "political religion" that could unite critical reason with pure, unaltered and unhindered belief. After attending a Serbian Orthodox mass, he wrote in his prison diary:

"It seemed to me that this god is spiritually closer to me than the Roman 'deus' with his marble-like Latin. I did not pray, but I felt how a certain mystical (religious) power entered my soul, enlivening and honouring it. ... We intellectuals ... do not know what faith is to the simple man. ... It is a fundamental fortress on earth ... It is the teaching of the absolute truth ... The intellectual has the philosophical treatise, ... critical scepticism, he has classical music, songs, painting, congresses and lectures of the savants. ... We intellectuals

---

[421]   Šrobár, *Pamäti* ..., 52, 54.

still lack a religion [náboženstvo]. But, when will we have it and, what if it will never exist for the intellectual class? ... We too need a religion to worship – but, until today, no genius has been born to establish it in such a way that we could believe in it with the soul of the common man."[422]

Šrobár identified religion as the main problem of Slovakia. Just a few months before the fall of the empire, in an atmosphere he described as "the quiet before the storm", he thought about his nation's most pressing problem: It was the religious question. The Slovaks had no sense of being a nation, because the masses used to identify themselves as Catholics and Lutherans. The confessions had divided the people and, while they believed in a pure, direct and decent manner, their faith included also the superstition of pagans, fetishism and fatalism[423]. His critique of the Catholic clergy expressed some of the reasons why Protestantism had emerged:

"Priests, who served God 'in the spirit and the truth' – do rarely exist. ... I think that the Church seminaries are the hotbed of that fall of the Slovak Catholic clergy, where materialism, exaggerated ambition, hatred and physical self-torture originate. ...That is why the Catholic clergy is magyarised in language and spirit. ... Not one of them stood up against the criminal theft of the voice and organ of God's house."[424]

Religion was to Šrobár a spiritual need and he considered it a fundamental pillar of the Czechoslovak democracy. Democracy was the political expression of the Christian love of the next and Czechoslovakism not just a strategy to leave Hungary, but the only way that would ensure Slovakia's autonomy. His religious doubts originated in his incapability to stop reasoning in exchange for a system of belief that had an answer to all questions. I think that Šrobár was simply too intelligent to fall for another authoritarian-totalitarian ideology, such as Bolshevism or National Socialism. He would have never rejected scientific rationalism and scepticism, but he missed the spiritual security of uncontested and unchallenged belief. Uncontested faith had been a spiritual home that had offered a meaning of life and a relief from solitude and injustice, which critical rationalism could never fully replace. In his search for a balance between reason and spirit he spoke about the need of a "political religion" that would provide a metaphysical safety to counter the harsh reality. Czechoslovakism, the *small works* and his tasks to build the democracy would

---

[422] Šrobár, *Pamäti* ..., 135-136.
[423] Šrobár, *Pamäti* ..., 176.
[424] Šrobár, *Pamäti* ..., 176-177.

provide him at least with the possibility to realise his view of politics as a moral task. How did he conceive of democracy and what should democratic Slovakia look like?

VI. 2. 3. Democracy

"The three-fold power is composed of 1. the Legislative power, that is the power that makes the laws; 2. the executive power, that is the government that oversees the compliance with all legislation, the internal order and the defence of the country; 3. the judicative power. We call these three institutions the powers of the state."[425]

If the Realists had had a fulminant beginning, which made them well known among the intellectual elite, the Republic's motto *Czechoslovakism equals democracy* led to the autonomy they had wished for. Šrobár wanted to make it perfectly clear that the Czechoslovak democracy meant a new dawn for Slovak politics. In 1914, he had compared Slovak politics to a huckster in a grocer's shop:

"This type of our politicians does not have an opinion: he does not care at all whether he belongs to the Slovak or the Magyar party; whether he is a member of the Slovak clergy, a progressive, a socialist, a conservative; whether he belongs to the side of Hurban, or Štefánik or Hlinka or dr. Šrobár; whether he publishes in the Národnie Noviny, the Denník, or the Robotnické Noviny – to our type – everything is the same. ... Today, he is a burning Slovak nationalist, tomorrow he will vilify them in public ... belief, church, religion – it is all the same to him. He is whatever you want him to be: Lutheran, Catholic, Jewish, Muslim ... This Hungarian politician is like a good businessman in a small town, like a huckster in a grocer's shop. He offers everything: rum, laces, grease for the wheels, bread, soap and garlic, whatever you desire. He has not much, but everything."[426]

Work, courage, honesty, commitment, responsibility, ethics and ideals were certainly honourable babble for simpletons, so Šrobár ironically, but not for a huckster to trade with. Furthermore, this type of corrupt and unprincipled politician could not be changed; he was immune to education, study and even verbal violence. The political bazaar that ruled in Slovakia prevented the nation from educating itself toward a sense of critical civil responsibility. The characteristic trait of lacking a clear goal and a realistic programme for social and political agency added up to the exaggerated interest for materialistic values. In Slovakia, there were Socialists, Conservatives and

---

[425]   Šrobár, *Vláda ľudu v demokracii*, 3 vol. (Bratislava: Práca, 1920); vol. I, 56-57.

[426]   Šrobár, "Politický kramár", in *Boj o nový...*, 272-278; 274. The article was first published in *Prúdy V*, č. 7 (1914).

Progressives like in other civilised nations[427], but the divide was still too large, which allowed the Clerical party to gain momentum.

Like Masaryk, who promoted the values of democracy by publishing small and affordable booklets designed to help the citizens understand the new politics, Šrobár published three booklets titled *The rule of the people in a democracy* (*Vláda ľudu v demokracii*). After two chapters on the Czechoslovak Republic, its founding idea and the history of the Slovaks prior to 1918, he wrote a detailed summary of the origins of the democratic idea, the divide of the legislative, judicative and executive powers, the sensible relationship of liberty and equality and the values of the democratic citizen. In the chapter about religion in a democracy he stressed the importance of the *freedom of conscience*:

> "What do 'the triumph of the truth [víťazstvo právdy] and the right to freedom of conscience mean? It means that man has the right to live and express what he considers the truth [čo poznal za právdu]. In every democracy there are fundamental rights that protect the freedom of conscience. According to the law, a Catholic, a Lutheran, an Orthodox, a Muslim, an Israelite and so on has the right to publicly commit himself to his religion in a state, where the majority of the populace adheres to a different faith."[428]

Religion and the right to openly express one's faith was one issue; another one was the influence of the Catholic clergy – or any other hierarchy that claimed absolute knowledge and a leading position because of that knowledge. Šrobár stressed that some groups that misunderstood or, worse, rejected the Christian principle of true equality had abused the imperative of love of the next. According to the Christian egalitarianism, to love the next involved to love and respect also the creed of the other, regardless of his social standing. The clergy, however, was not the only group to blame. Freedom of conscience and tolerance in practise had to extend to any system of belief, whether it was a religious one or a scientific:

> "And this applies not only to the field of the religious truths but also to the realm of the worldly sciences [svetských nauk]. The records of the martyrs of mankind include not only those who suffered for the religious truths, but also those who sacrificed their lives for the laws of nature [zákony prírody], openly expressing the truths of natural sciences, achieved through extensive study and immense work. ... If we insisted on the opinion that we have

---

[427] Šrobár, "Politický kramár", 276-277.

[428] His mentioning of 'the triumph of the truth' was an allusion to Jan Hus' motto 'the truth shall prevail' [pravda vítězí], which Masaryk revitalised, making it the spiritual and political symbol of the Czechoslovak democracy; Šrobár, *Vláda ľudu...*, vol. II, 24.

already achieved all truths, either the spiritual and religious ones or the scientific, societal and political, the development of mankind would falter. It would be impossible to further improve its status, accommodate the needs and crimes, liberate the enslaved and relieve mankind from hard labour."[429]

After some pages about progress and backwardness, in which Šrobár was not shy to criticise the nation, including himself and using the we-form, he proceeded to the essential issue of the religious feelings of the individual in a democracy. In the times of transition from aristocracy to democracy, when political authority changed in a revolutionary manner, it was impossible to get rid of all institutions at once. As much as the *ancien regime* had been based on the citizens' discipline and religious feelings, as fundamental were these civil virtues for the new state. The modern times made people forget about the harmony of reason and feelings, sense and sensibility, the balance of rationality and morality. In his critique of pure materialism and, subsequently, bolshevism, Šrobár referred to the Belgian economist and political thinker Émile Louis Victor de Laveleye (1822 - 1892). He quoted further the famous political theorist Alexis de Tocqueville (1805 - 1859) to stress the critical necessity of the social virtues that derived from religion, on the one hand, and the civic discipline required for a democracy, on the other.

> "Laveleye sketches life in an atheistic state as follows: '... if every religious thought [náboženská myšlienka] was purged from the nation's soul, morality [mravnosť] and the very thoughts of self-sacrifice [myšlienka sebaobetovania] and duty [povinnosti] would disappear at the same moment. ... If everything is broken into pieces, that is institutions and traditions, if, under the rule of democracy, the social order is changing from day to day and if there is an endless coming and going of those in power, then the people stop feeling connected [viazanými] to the political or the religious authorities ... The masses have lost their religious belief and ceased to hope for one world ... they are eager to establish, at any price, even by violence, a better order [lepší poriadok] ... From this follows the universal need to *publicly declare an independent moral codex to the people* [*aby bola hlásaná ľudu samostatná mravoveda*]'."[430]

Having substantiated his point with a reference to a distinguished economist and political thinker of his times, which he did in the experienced fashion of Realism, Šrobár continued with a quote from the famous author of *Democracy in America*:

---

[429] Šrobár, *Vláda ľudu...*, vol. II, 25.
[430] Šrobár, *Vláda ľudu...*, vol. II, 34, 35. Šrobár does not provide more detailed references about his quote from Laveleye. I assume that it originates in Laveleye's text *Essai sur les formes du gouvernment dans les socitétés modernes*, published in 1872.

"Tocqueville says strikingly: 'I doubt that man could bear being completely detached from religion and enjoy the political liberties to their fullest. And I am convinced that if man does not believe, he lives in slavery, and if he lives in freedom, he believes."[431]

Faith and the social and moral values derived from it were the civil glue that kept the state together and made it function. A religion supportive of the democratic state should be egalitarian and strengthen the civil virtues; it would endanger the state if it were opposed to the "ideals of the nation, which adheres to it"[432]. Šrobár added a few paragraphs on the virtues of the Hussite movement, which served as an example of a truly national religion. His thought that "the Hussite church had entirely touched the spirits and the hearts of the Czechoslovak nation [celého ducha i srdce československého národa] and had therefore united the people in one will and one wish [ľud sjednotila v jednej túžbe a v jednom cite]"[433] was historically not quite correct, but an important theorem of the Czechoslovak nation-building theory. While Hussitism could not be revived anymore, one should nevertheless pay attention to the dangers of the hierarchical traditions of the Catholic clergy. Šrobár used the term "religious hatred" [náboženská nesnášanlivosť] to describe the clergy's potential damage:

"Led by religious hatred they generally abuse the blind and uneducated people and also those who turn religion into politics. We call these persons clerics [klerikálmi]."[434]

A nation living in religious hatred and guided by fanaticism presented a threat not only to its own existence and freedom, but also to the peace, life and freedom of other nations. Therefore should every Slovak, who loved the freedom and independence of his home country, rejoiced that they had shaken off the Magyar yoke and enjoyed the people's rule, protect himself from the clerical poison. Furthermore, Šrobár's brief texts informed the reader about the importance of work, social welfare, the equal status of women and the dangers of alcoholism.

In his function as plenipotentiary minister of Slovakia, he was responsible for establishing the new democratic politics and institution building. Already in 1918, the first Slovak gymnasium opened in Skalica and a network of middle schools extended

---

[431] Šrobár, *Vláda ľudu...*, vol. II, 35, 36. He does not indicate the source of the Tocqueville quote.
[432] Šrobár, *Vláda ľudu...*, vol. II, 36.
[433] Šrobár, *Vláda ľudu...*, vol. II, 37.
[434] Šrobár, *Vláda ľudu...*, vol. II, 44.

over the country in a short time[435]. Pressburg was renamed Bratislava, where the Comenius university was founded in 1919. The *Matica slovenská* reopened in 1919 and was of crucial importance to the support of culture and instruction in the natural sciences, before the technical university emerged in the last years of the Republic. The building of educational institutions revealed a most pressing problem: the lack of Slovak teachers and instructors[436]. The lack of trained personnel led to the immigration of Czechs, who occupied important positions in the state institutions. Also, many more Slovaks than before had now the opportunity to study in Prague, while a system of bourses, stipends and private foundations allowed poor students to achieve a university degree.

In his public lecture *Politický problém Slovenska* (*Slovakia's political problem*), held on 26 March 1926 in the stock exchange in Prague, Šrobár gave a detailed account of his government's achievements in the first years of the Republic. In his introductory notes he presented Slovakia's history and the phases of the national development in the 19th century to the Czech audience. After a brief summary of the strike and the short fighting against the invading Hungarian troops, he highlighted the difficulties of establishing the new political order. The tactical semi-loyalty of the Catholic clergy and members of *Hlinka's Peoples Party* HSĽS was an important factor for a better understanding of the Slovak conditions. The clergy and the party were first enthusiastic about his ministry, expressing their support of the new government in their meeting in the autumn of 1919 in Žilina[437]:

"The meeting was crucially important for many reasons. Some one hundred and twenty Roman-Catholic priests attended, among them the current representatives of the People's Party Hlinka, Juriga, …, Jehlička aso. In the meeting, delegate Juriga suggested to abolish the celibacy of the priests, to make Slovak the liturgical language of the Catholic church. And these gentlemen unanimously supported the separation of the church and the state. Today, one cannot remind these gentlemen of that meeting, since they postulate the exact opposite …"[438]

---

[435]   Kováč, *Dejiny...*, 196.

[436]   Kováč, *Dejiny...*, 196.

[437]   Šrobár, *Politický problem...*, 12.

[438]   Šrobár, *Politický problem...*, 12-13. Ferdiš Juriga (1874 – 1950), politician and former Slovak delegate to the Hungarian assembly; František Jehlička (1879 – 1939), professor of theology and politician, who organised Hlinka's trip to the Paris peace conference in August 1919; Kováč, *Dejiny...*, 171, 174, 182.

In January, prior to the meeting with the clergy, a deputation of five had paid him a visit in his ministry in Žilina. Among them were Jehlička, Hlinka, two members of the HSĽS and Karol Medvecký, the advisor for religious affairs at Šrobár's own ministry. On behalf of the deputation, Jehlička demanded to appoint Hlinka as the first Slovak patriarch.

> "I was taken aback by the fact that a professor of theology would demand from the minister for Slovakia a mandate of such authority [takovou velkou pravomoc] that no government in the world enjoyed, with the exception of the Roman Curia. We got into a heated discussion about the ministry's authority, and Mr. Jehlička pressed me in a very loud voice to establish it [the patriarchate, add. JB]. I explained to him that I do not have that power, neither the government nor the president of the Republic; we worldly persons were establishing a worldly order, not a church hierarchy. ... To found a patriarchate would bring our Republic into a tremendous conflict with Rome and the international community, while we had already enough conflicts, shortages and unrest here in our homeland."[439]

After having defeated the troops of Bela Kun, the situation of the schools was a pressing task. Šrobár addressed the current critique of the so-called "Czechisation of Slovakia" as unsubstantiated, since it was not based on the detailed knowledge of the situation. There was no Slovak middle school before 1919; on his call for applications, only twenty Slovak professors replied. Most of them, however, did not speak Slovak fluently, as they were of Slovak origin, but had emigrated and lost contact to the country's culture and customs. He faced the shortage of instructors in the pragmatic and rational fashion of the Realists:

> "Besides the twenty, there were no qualified professors. And we needed some five hundred professors for the Slovak gymnasiums! I would like to know whence to get these five hundred professors. ... And today, our autonomists are yelling at the Czech professors who, in difficult times, committed themselves to the education of the Slovak youth in the gymnasiums."[440]

The dire economic and social conditions involved also the issue of the Slovak peasants, who prior to independence had worked as agrarian *Gastarbeiter* in Hungary and the United States of America, destinations now closed to them. The social hierarchy that stemmed from the times under Magyar rule, however, was his utmost concern. Šrobár explained to his Czech audience nothing else than what he had so fiercely criticised in his booklets about democracy: the current conditions, the

---

[439] Šrobár, *Politický problem...*, 13, 14.
[440] Šrobár, *Politický problem...*, 18.

political and socio-economical origins of these conditions, the potential threats to the Republic and possible solutions. In that, the title of his lecture *The political problem of Slovakia* seems, at first sight, somewhat modest, as one has the impression that there were many more problems, in educational, economical, sociological, socio-psychological, clerical and political aspects. On a second and more thorough glance, however, Šrobár identified the main problem: the *legacy of Magyarisation*, visible in the autonomy claims of the separatist movement and promoted by the increasing opposition against the Republic's political order. The masses perceived the new regime as favouring *Czech centralism* and were being incited by the conservative elite, which was eager to protect its privileges:

> "In Slovakia, there are some two thousand notaries, three thousand church teachers, one thousand and five hundred Roman-Catholic priests, some thousand higher administrators and thousands of lower. These gentlemen meet on a regular basis, remember fondly the golden times under Magyar rule and hammer away at the Republic, the Czechoslovak nation and the state. I think it was in those circles where the following rhyme emerged: 'When there was 'kezét csókolom' (I kiss your hand), there was bread even under the table; now it is 'má úcta (my honour) and no bread in front of our mouths.'"[441]

The *administrative dualism*, supported by the Czech side, presented a further problem; Slovakia was organised along the *župy*, which lacked the legal basis to unite in order to gain the local autonomy Moravia and Bohemia enjoyed. The people could not understand why Bohemia and Moravia enjoyed decentralisation from Prague, while the Slovak counties did not. The discrepancy in the administration, along with the uncritical *Czechophobia*, the poverty and economic shortages were leading the people to join the separatism of the Martinists. Adhering to the Russophile and Panslavist ideology Vajanský had been cultivating, major parts of the nation viewed their identity based on those fundamental ideological aspects that distinguished them from the Czechs. Concluding his lecture, Šrobár addressed a common misunderstanding:

> "The Czech public thinks that the relationship of Hlinka and me is the main issue in Slovakia. But that is not the point. It would be too personal and simplicist. If I tried to formulate our relationship in a brief sentence, it would sound like this: It is the hatred of the leader of a political party that is directed against the Czechoslovak progressive modernity

---

[441]   Šrobár, *Politický problem...*, 32. The rhyme in original Slovak: "Keď bolo 'kezét csókolom' (ruce líbám) bolo chleba i pod stolom, a keď je teraz 'má úcta', niet chleba ani pre ústa."

and its programme. Hlinka is a man of the dark age, a fanatic, a priest [středověký fanatický člověk, kněz]."[442]

Šrobár's assessment of Hlinka's psychological make up and the potential danger he posed seems to us like a prophetic view of Slovakia's future – which is very easy to say *ex post*. Since Czechoslovakia was a modern democracy committed to the values of pluralism and tolerance, there was no legal possibility for the government to alleviate the leader of HSĽS or to somehow get rid of him. Šrobár concluded his lecture with a synthesis of the socio-psychological stereotypes of the two nations, ascribing to the Czechs their work driven by the facilities of human reason [české rozumové práce] and to the Slovaks their sensitive-emotional disposition [slovenského citového hnutí][443]. By doing so, Šrobár, driven by his best intentions to unite the Slovaks and the Czechs, actually helped to cement, at least in parts, the legacy of Vajanský's national characteristics in the minds of the Czechs and Slovaks. In his efforts to enlighten the Slovaks, fight the conservative clergy and plant the roots of a humanist, democratic and progressive-modern thinking, he was not aware that he was re-enforcing the mutual stereotypes each nation had from the other – sense against sensibility, the opposition of the Czech sense against the Slovak sensibility. As a convinced democrat, a minister responsible to the government and a Slovak nationalist, he had a deep understanding for the conditions in Slovakia. If his warnings were ignored, then there were also no legal means to prevent Hlinka's party from gaining the political following it would. Šrobár described the conditions in Slovakia after 1926 in an honest and fact-based fashion, in the best tradition of the Hlasists. In 1931, his reports sounded more optimistic.

In his short text *Kultúrny pokrok na Slovensku* (*The cultural progress in Slovakia*)[444], published by Robert Seton-Watson and prominent Slovaks, Šrobár highlighted the improvements made in the thirteen years of the Republic's existence. Slovakia had established all the institutions of a modern democracy: gymnasiums, theatres, independent clubs and civil associations. The economy was recovering. Prior to the Great War, famines had broken out in the *župy* of Orava, Trenčín, Spiš, Liptov, Zemplín, Užhorod and Horehronie; there were no famines on record for the

---

[442] Šrobár, *Politický problem...*, 34.
[443] Šrobár, *Politický problem...*, 35.
[444] Šrobár, "Kultúrny pokrok na Slovensku", in *Slovensko kedysi a teraz* (Praha: Orbis, 1931), 104-111.

last ten years[445]. The government had introduced laws for the protection of the workers and the unemployed in cases of sickness and invalidity, while new social rights secured the existential minimum and a pension plan. The housing shortage was almost resolved, because the government had financially supported the building of new houses. The total sum of that investment amounted to one hundred million crowns in Slovakia and some milliard crowns in the entire Republic[446]. The building of new railway lines and the repair works of roads and streets integrated the communities on the countryside. A land reform abolished the century old system of the Magyar magnates and enabled the peasants to buy a share of land; the foresight to timely adopt the law on land reform had effectively stopped the spreading of the Bolshevist ideology[447]. Also, the educational system was developing in the right direction:

> "Today, the Slovak nation has more than two thousand students, around twenty thousand high school students and about a quarter of a million pupils in the national schools. That is an immense development of modernisation and enlightenment in Slovakia."[448]

Apart from the new theatres, sport associations emerged such as the national *Sokol*, the worker's *Jednota* and the Catholic *Orolstvo*. Others were committed to social care; the association of Slovak women *Živena* had an enormous merit for health care, the upbringing of children, questions of hygiene and the equal status of girls and women in society[449]. In regard to the political development, Šrobár stressed that the Magyar minority amounting to six hundred and fifty thousand citizens had sent their elected twelve members of parliament to Prague already twice, while the three hundred thousand Slovaks living in Hungary enjoyed no representation and lacked educational institutions instructing in their mother tongue[450]. Furthermore, Slovak was the language of communication in Slovakia and enjoyed equal status with Czech. The foreign propaganda of the alleged oppression of the Slovaks had to be rejected as malicious defamation that counted on the common ignorance and lack of information.

---

[445] Šrobár, "Kultúrny pokrok...", 104-105.
[446] Šrobár, "Kultúrny pokrok...", 105.
[447] Šrobár, "Kultúrny pokrok...", 106.
[448] Šrobár, "Kultúrny pokrok...", 108.
[449] Šrobár, "Kultúrny pokrok...", 108.
[450] Šrobár, "Kultúrny pokrok...", 109.

If Šrobár was proud of the achievements of the government, he saw also clearly that Slovakia was a young state and needed time to further develop.

"The Czechoslovak nation built itself a new state, the democratic Republic. We are immensely grateful to the four great nations in the West and the South that made it possible for us to live in the spirit of our traditions, our culture and our historical past. France, England, America and Italy shall forever be our benefactors. ... We are bound to do everything for the good of the nations living in our state. ... at the top of our state stands a man whom the world honours and appraises. He is our guarantee to continue on the right path ... What we strongly demand for now are peace and quiet to fulfil our national and international mission."[451]

In many respects, Šrobár was a man of the 19th century who had experienced the absence of justice, equality and political morality. His efforts for the Republic and the improvement of the conditions in Slovakia were impressive. Like Masaryk in Bohemia, he could not garner a wide following in Slovakia; the theoretical approach of the Hlasists-Realists and their perception of national politics were too intellectual, withdrawn and alien for the masses. Insisting on the equality of both nations, Šrobár was a democrat and a nationalist, in the positive sense of national consciousness that rejects chauvinism. He was no liberal, but a Realist and faithful Christian. I deem it fair to call him the founder of modern Slovakia within the context of Czechoslovakism. One could say that the moral aspects and the mission to build the modern nation had a conveying effect on the discrepancy he felt between reason and faith. It would, however, be exaggerated to say that Czechoslovakism was his political religion.

Šrobár was a principal figure in Slovak politics; also thanks to his efforts, Slovakia was integrated into Czechoslovakia. He certainly deserves more public and scholarly attention than the silence surrounding him until today. Compared to the reverence Milan Rastislav Štefánik enjoys, Šrobár's efforts for the nation are almost forgotten. Let me conclude with a quote from Edvard Beneš, who mentioned Šrobár just once in his memoirs:

"Very important was the co-operation with dr. Vavro Srobar, around whom the secret political movement emerged in 1943 that included all parties (even the Communists). He was in steady contact with us, sent us vitally important news and informed us in detail

---

[451] Šrobár, "Kultúrny pokrok...", 110-111.

about the plans of a Slovak uprising. The uprising started in September 1944 with the London exile government's full military and political support."[452]

---

[452]   Edvard Beneš, *Paměti II. Od Mnichova k nové válce a k novému vítezství* (Academia: Praha, 2008), 391.

Vavro Šrobár – life in brief

(Pseudonym: V. Lieskovan)

9 August 1867	Born in Lisková, district of Ružomberok in northern Central Slovakia.
1878-82	Went to the gymnasium in Ružomberok, where the language of education was Hungarian, which he did not speak.
1882-83	He continued his education at the German gymnasium in Levoča.
1883-86	Attended the gymnasium in Banská Bystrica and finally graduated from the gymnasium in Přerov in Moravia. Because of his nationality, Šrobár could not graduate at a gymnasium in Upper Hungary.
1888-98	Studied medicine at Charles University in Prague.
1896-99	Chairman of the national student circle *Detvan.*
1898-1904	Founded the revue *Hlas* (*the voice*) and was its chief-editor. *Hlas* was the first journal of young intellectuals who opposed the conservative politics of the Slovak National Party. Šrobár was familiar with the political thought of Tomáš Garrigue Masaryk (1850 - 1937) and personally acquainted with the future founder of the Czechoslovak Republic.
1907-08	Sentenced to prison for his political activities.
1909	Published Ľudová obrázková zdravoveda (Illustrated guide to public health)
April 1915	Involved with the beginnings of the agrarian movement in Slovakia, he acted as representative of *Maffia*, the domestic underground organisation of the *Council of the Czechs and Slovaks*, which lobbied in exile for independence. Masaryk, Edvard Beneš (1884 - 1948) and the Slovak astronomer and general Milan Rastislav Štefánik (1880 - 1919) led the exile organisation.
1 May 1918	Šrobár proclaimed the Slovak nation's right to self-determination in a common state with the Czechs. On his return, the Hungarian authorities arrested him for his participation in the illegal

	congress of the oppressed nationalities of the k.k. empire, which had taken place in May in Prague. He stayed in prison until the beginning of October.
28 October	Co-opted as Slovak chairman of the National Council and signed the law on the internal administrative and political order of the Czechoslovak state.
November	He founded the Slovak provisional government and became the first Czechoslovak minister of health, a position he kept until 1920.
December	He was also appointed the Slovak minister of information. This position, which he held until 1920, enabled him to contribute significantly to the establishment of the Czechoslovak government in Slovakia.
1918-25	He was a member of parliament, first for the Slovak Club, then for the Agrarian Party.
1920	Šrobár led the ministry of public health and physical education as well as the ministry of unification of laws and organisation of information.
1921-22	Appointed minister of education and national enlightenment.
1922	Published *Pamäti z vojny a väzenia (Memoirs from war and prison)*.
1923	He submitted his post-doctoral thesis in social medicine at the Comenius university in Bratislava.
1925-35	Represented the Agrarians in the Senate and acted as chairman of the Agrarians' club in the Senate from 1925 to 1929.
1928-32	Publication of *Oslobodené Slovensko I–II (Liberated Slovakia)*.
1935	Appointed as tenured professor for the history of medicine at the medical faculty of Comenius University in Bratislava.
1937	Retired from academia and politics.
1939-45	During WWII, Šrobár kept a low profile, but worked underground for the the Czechoslovak antifascist opposition.
1944	Co-chairman of the Slovak national council.
1945-46	Appointed minister of finance in re-established Czechoslovakia.

1946	Founded the *Strana slobody* (Freedom Party), which supported the Communist Party. Published *Z môjho života* (*From my life*).
January 1948	Until the Communist *coup d'état* in February, he acted as minister of unification of laws.
1948-50	Appointed minister of unification of laws in the Gottwald government and member of the executive council of the communist-controlled National Front. Šrobár tried to continue Beneš's political line in Slovak affairs.
6 Dec. 1950	Died in Olomouc in Moravia. His body was later transferred to the St. Martin cemetery in Bratislava.

Conclusion

1. The autonomy of the *okolie*

Slovak political thought in the subject period of 1861 to 1914 included various plans, ideas and suggestions – all of which came to nothing, with the exception of Realism and Czechoslovakism, a movement and set of ideas that originated in Masaryk's Czech nation-building theory. The main reasons why Slovak politics did not bring about any successes were, on the one hand, the Magyar programme of state-building and, on the other, Vienna's indifference. With the failure of the 1848 revolution, the leaders of the national movement did have some substantiated hopes for the *okolie*, the *autonomy* within the framework of the kingdom. That window of opportunity, however, was very small and closed as soon as Austrian-Prussian disunity began to dominate Vienna's politics. The *Ausgleich* of 1867 destroyed the most modest hopes for autonomy. The constitution of the compromise would provide the project of Magyar state-building, the Magyar political nation, with the legal basis to assimilate the non-Magyar nationalities to such extent that there was not a single Slovak gymnasium left in Upper Hungary in the 1880s.

2. Sovereignty

Sovereignty was therefore not only a highly unrealistic idea: none of the six intellectuals claimed for sovereignty, with the exception of Šrobár, who would react to a changing political environment that made sovereignty a possibility. They were aware that their nation was not ready yet – the Slovaks had no army, their economy was basically limited to agriculture and they certainly lacked trained personnel that could have a run a state administration. In terms of political thought, sovereignty was also an *alien concept* to those thinkers who adhered to the *Romanticism* of Kollár and Štúr, namely Francisci and Daxner. As an expression of national individuality and to counteract the universalism of the Enlightenment, Romantic thought conveyed the idea that institutions were nothing but stiff and lifeless artificial buildings that oppressed the spirit and soul of man. The spirit of Slovak nationhood should not be 'stained' by rationalistic elements such as governmental institutions or administrative issues. While this anti-universalist view was the fundamental approach to the national identity of Kollár and Štúr, Francisci, Daxner and Sasinek fought for the language rights, which became a political issue because of the assimilation. Vajanský's Romanticism contained a further element: it was inextricably connected with the *Panslavist idea*, which rejected Western political philosophy in general (which Romanticism did not, as it was a Western idea, born as a reaction against Napoleonic rule and the universalism of the Enlighenment), despised of individualism and praised the greatness of the Russian Empire in particular. All of the six but for Vajanský engaged for the language: Francisci, Daxner, Palarík, Sasinek and Šrobár fought the assimilation, but from different perspectives.

3.   Method and philosophical influence

Their political argumentation mirrored their *method*. Francisci, the diplomat and Daxner, the lawyer, used pragmatic arguments to convince their readers that the *okolie* was the national political goal. They also went into great efforts to prove that activities such as founding a newspaper, fund-raising and the free legal support of citizens charged with anti-patriotic activities would strengthen the nation. Both were adherents of Štúr and influenced by their experiences of the 1848 revolution. National identity was to them the usage of their language in schools and institutions of higher education. Daxner, the lawyer, formulated the text of the memorandum and defended the lyceum in Veľká Revúca. Although Palarík was of the same generation, he opposed the *okolie*, condemned it as pre-mature and suggested supporting the Magyars; once they would have successfully fought Vienna's centralism, the way toward a Hungarian multi-national federation would be free. The rebellious priest's liberalism was very close to *Palacký's Liberalism and Austroslavism*, because of his support of the ruling Magyars and their political programme. For Sasinek, the eccentric historian, the *okolie* was more or less a thing of the past; nevertheless, he considered the language rights still as a sign of nationhood, all the more as they had been granted in the past. But he added a further important element to the definition of nationhood: As long as the Slovaks did not know their own *history*, they would neither be free, nor a nation. History was a huge arsenal, and historical argumentation the nation's sharpest weapon. The sensitive poet Vajansky chose literature and art, dogmatically condemning any political activities as they would mean to leave the only path toward true nationhood – which he had defined as art and literature in his own *canon*. For the masses, the only way of resisting the assimilation was passivity and obedience to the intellectual elite. The elite's task was to create art, a national literature as sign of nationhood and civilisation. Šrobár was the only one trained in natural sciences; he concentrated his efforts on the poor socio-economical conditions that came along with the low level of education. His method was as pragmatic as that of Francisci and Daxner: he tried to do his best to change the poverty and misery. He was also, due to his personal acquaintance with Masaryk, the only one who adopted the method of the *small works*.

All of the six *narodovci* shared the significant *philosophical influence* from Western thought. All were familiar with Herder's Romantic idea of national individuality, which they had absorbed through the 'Slavic filter' of Kollár and Štúr. They were fully aware that natural law argumentation was the best weapon, since it legitimated the equality of nations and individuals, thus also theirs. Palarík, however, was the only one who refused to acknowledge natural law in politics. He adhered to the positive law of the kingdom, a consequence of his admiration for Montesquieu. Natural law belonged to the area of the national renaissance as the cultural rebirth of the nation. It should not be used to demand for political rights. The rebellious priest made also the clearest suggestions for a future constitution; his admiration for Montesquieu's separation of powers would only be shared by Šrobár some thirty years later. Daxner, the last *podžupan* of Slovak origin, held the highest government position prior to Šrobár's various ministeries after 1918. Yet, his wealth, contacts and reputation as a lawyer did not protect him from the increasing harshness of the assimilation. Daxner believed in justice granted by positive law and the equality of citizens in front of the law – he was shocked when learning that even the law could become an instrument of the assimilation. Although Vajanský had enjoyed the most expensive education, owing to his father's contacts and wealth, he was the only one who rejected Western political thought in an absolute dogmatism. His Panslavistic belief in Russia's leadership of mankind was indestructible. Young Vajanský had been sent to Lutheran schools in Prussia and travelled through Germany, while young Šrobár had often nothing to eat in his student years in Moravia and then Prague.

In terms of *egalitarianism*, the six *narodovci's* political thought is also very interesting: if we consider the equality of citizens established by the French Revolution as a forerunner for democracy, then only Vajanský and Sasinek rejected that proto-democratic egalitarianism. They did not consider equality as a moral value – on the contrary. Sasinek wanted to make it perfectly clear that only the Catholic catechism he was trained in would be capable of leading the nation, while the *uncrowned poet laureate* thought of himself as the authority of the nation. Both were elitist and anti-liberal to an extent, which was already old-fashioned in their times. With the exception of Šrobár, who was an adherent of Masaryk's Realism and established the Hlasist movement in Slovakia, all other five were not democrats. Daxner, Francisci and Palarík were certainly convinced of the Christian value of egalitarianism, but this did not mean that they promoted the universal right to vote. All six shared their belief in personal freedom as the opposite of slavery, which was one of the liberal claims of the 1848 revolution.

We can further say that their *religious adherence* did not significantly influence their thought. Vajanský was a Lutheran and praised the traditional and peaceful obedience of the Russian people, who had withstood Napoleon. His thought was diametrically opposed to Francisci and Daxner's nationalism. Palarík, Sasinek and Šrobár were Roman Catholics, but only Sasinek was conservative and anti-liberal to the bone. In terms of liberal values, Palarík was certainly the most modern thinker; his admiration for the Magyar Liberals led to the foundation of the *nová škola slovenská*, which divided the national movement into the adherents of the memorandum and those who considered a co-operation with the ruling Magyars the better option. Although Šrobár fought for democracy and certainly deemed ethnic and religious tolerance, market economy and scientific progress as fundamental, he was no liberal. His democratism originated in his nationalism. Occupied with improving the situation of the people, he despised Magyar Liberalism as the fundamental idea that led to the *uprooting* (*odrodílstvo*) of the non-Magyars.

Vajanský and Šrobár openly expressed their *anti-Semitism* in their texts. They disliked the collaboration of the Jews with the Magyar oppressors and their economic success as entrepreneurial and religious minority, but did not understand that the Jews were oppressed themselves. Unlike Vajanský, Šrobár was, later in the Republic, willing to change his views. Both did not call for violence against the Jews and refused to believe in the anti-Semitic fairy tale of the blood libel. The reason that the other four did not write about the alleged Jewish oppression was no proof that they did not hold anti-Semitic views. They simply did not express them, most probably because they did not share the experience of the latter two: the assimilation's most brutal power peaked in the 1890s and the two decades prior to WWI – when Sasinek, Daxner and Francisci were very old and Palarík already dead. Vajanský and Šrobár were in close contact with the people on the countryside, the former a national hero because of his poetry, the latter a doctor, who treated the sick in their huts.

3.1. Comparative chart

Thinker / political agency and thought	Francisci, the pragmatic diplomat	Palárik, the rebellious liberal	Daxner, the sober lawyer	Sasinek, the eccentric historian	Vajanský, the Panslavist poet	Šrobár, the Czechoslovakist
National identity	Slovak	Slovak	Slovak	Slovak	Slovak	Slovak
Political identity	Slovak	Magyar liberal	Slovak	Slovak	Slovak and Slavophile	Czecho-Slovak
Autonomy in the form of the *okolie*	Yes	No, too early; in support of the Hungarian liberals; anti-centralist = anti-Vienna	Yes	Unclear; autonomy guided by the Catholic Church	No longer relevant	No longer relevant
Sovereignty	No, not realistic	No, neither realistic nor feasible – nation requires higher level of education	No, not realistic	No, neither realistic nor feasible – nation should regain its former joint rule with the Magyars	Unclear; did not think in terms of statehood	Yes, as part of Czechoslovakia
Constitution	No specific suggestions	Yes, future Hungarian federation; opposed the constitution of 1867	No specific suggestions	Preference for 1848 constitution; no specific suggestions	Anti-constitutional; anti-institutional; national freedom is spiritual freedom	Modern democracy, including minority rights

Thinker / political agency and thought	Francisci, the pragmatic diplomat	Palárik, the rebellious liberal	Daxner, the sober lawyer	Sasinek, the eccentric historian	Vajanský, the Panslavist poet	Šrobár, the Czechoslovakist
Philosophical influence	Natural law; Kollár – Štúr; nationalism	Montesquieu and Herder – Kollár; positive law in politics, natural law in culture and nation; Palacký's federation; tolerance in political debate	Natural law; Kollár – Štúr; nationalism	Catholicism; natural law; Kollár – Štúr; nationalism	Literature; Panslavist belief in the liberation by Russia; anti-Nietzsche; anti-Western individualism	Kollár – Štúr; scientific Positivism; Masaryk's Realism and Czechoslovakism
Political principles	Pragmatism; 1848 liberalism; nationalism	Constitutionalism; Magyar liberalism; Slovak nationalism	Pragmatism; positive law as guarantee of civil rights; nationalism	Historical research; Catholic catechism	Political passivity; art constitutes identity; intellectual elitism	Enlightenment; education; anti-clericalism; natural sciences
Method	Management of finances; founding of *Pešťbudínské Vedomosti*; publishing	Publishing in various genres	Legal assistance; building of institutions of higher education	Publishing, teaching	Poetry; literature; critique; founding of *Slovenské pohľady*	Medical care; founding of *Hlas*; publishing; after 1918, executive political positions
Punishment for political activities	Imprisoned and sentenced to death in 1848; amnestied	Three weeks' house arrest at the Franciscan monastery in Esztergom.	Imprisoned and sentenced to death in 1848; amnestied; several charges; campaign against his son in the 1890s	Expelled to Austria in 1913	Imprisoned in 1893-1894; 1900-1901 (5 months); 1903 (2 months).	Imprisoned in 1908-1909; 1918
Religion	Lutheran	Roman Catholic	Lutheran	Roman Catholic	Lutheran	Roman Catholic

4.   Hypothesis

The hypothesis we set in the introduction reads as follows:

Why was Andrej Hlinka's People's party HSĽS the most successful after 1918, given the fact that a wide range of political opinions, ideas and intellectual currents existed prior to 1918?

The six patriots, who differed in their political thought and goals, were certainly significant for their nation in terms of identity, particularity and also, activities. They were, however, not successful in terms of the political support of the population. The popularity of HSĽS, which gained 34% of the vote in the parliamentary elections of 1925[453] and determined Slovakia's politics until 1945, can, to a very modest extent and under the greatest reservation, be explained by what one could call *the legacy of Vajanský*: an uncritical acceptance of authoritarian leadership, passivity in political decision-making and participation, the rejection of Western thought, perceived as *Czechoslovakist atheistic dominance* and the belief in the nation's spirit that was inextricably bound to Catholic faith. But Catholicism was a Western idea, which was not relevant for Vajanský. He identified the national spirit as peaceful, obedient, resisting shallow and petty activities on behalf of Western decadent materialism and atheism – the very values of Panslavism he so admired in the Russian people. It would not only be too simplicist and unfair, but also completely mistaken to blame the great poet for the regime of the *Hlinková garda* and the republic's collaboration with Nazi Germany. Slovakia was pressed into independence, and the political elite of what became the I. Republic did not have the intellectual strength to resist authoritarianism, the subsequent *Führer* principle and the pro-active murder of the Jewish citizens. The course of autonomy HSĽS pursued was in part a consequence of Czechoslovakism and the perceived dominance by the 'atheistic' Czechs, respectively; on the other hand, one could say that the populist rhetorics of the party appealed to some of the conservative values the Catholic Church had defended in the past: discipline, obedience, dogmatic belief and the rejection of Enlightenment rationality, ethnic, national and religious tolerance and egalitarianism in politics.

---

[453]   Kováč, *Dejiny* ..., 189.

Whether the claims for autonomy were justified in regard of the Pittsburgh treaty, is a different matter.

What we can say for sure now is that, with the exception of Šrobár, none of the *narodovci* exercised a significant political influence. They were, however, of crucial importance for their nation's intellectual and political history. All of them endured imprisonment and discrimination for their national identity. Some were wealthy and occupied government positions, while others lived in perennial financial distress, but always found time and energy to raise funds for books or newspapers. Some dared to criticise the national movement, others contributed to it, making it grow stronger. Some adhered to Western political philosophy, other rejected it, hoping for Russia to liberate the Slavs. Some adhered to Russian political thought, others admired Montesquieu; some rejected Nietzsche, Kant and the entire Western philosophy, condemning it as decadence. Others found answers in Czech political thought. All of them pursued the most basic civil rights such as equality of citizens, an unbiased judicial system, freedom of expressing oneself in one's mother tongue and freedom of opinion. They shared the peaceful, continuous and law-abiding engagement; some of them were forgotten, while others are still remembered today in Slovakia. Of all six, only Francisci, Palarík and Vajanský have 'made it' to the Internet[454]. All of them, however, are still being ignored by international academia and the wider public. There are no translations available of their memoirs, poetry and novels. My investigation shall hopefully change that painful ignorance a bit. Let me conclude this study with a quote from one of the six patriots that illustrates the core values of the national movement from 1861 to 1914:

"Hatred, of whatever contents and origins, is a sign of backwardness and low spirit. The Slovak people are so sensitive and devoted to all things that are grand and beautiful that we firmly believe that it will choose the way to its own good and education, which is the way toward freedom, fraternity and progress."[455]

---

[454] http://zlatyfond.sme.sk/autori; accessed 6 July 2009.
[455] Šrobár, *Vláda ľudu...*, kn. II, 46.

Bibliography

"Memorandum národa slovenského." In *Z prameňov národa. Na pamiatku stodvatsiateho piateho výročia vzniku memoranda slovenského národa z roku 1861.* Martin: Matica slovenská, 1988.

"Nationalitätenkarte der österreichisch -ungarischen Monarchie nach den Sprachen-, bzw. Konfessionserhebungen vom Jahre 1910". Appendix of *Die Habsburgermonarchie 1848–1918.* Vol. III.

150 years of the Slovak cooperative movement. Victories and defeats. Bratislava: Reetas-Renesans, 1997.

Arendt, Hanna. *The Origins of Totalitarianism.* San Diego, New York, London: Harcourt Brace & Company, 1973.

Baer, Josette. *Slavic Thinkers or the Creation of Polities. Intellectual History and Political Thought in Central Europe and the Balkans, 19th Century.* Washington D.C.: New Academia Publishing, 2007.

Baer, Josette. "Czech national identity – an exit factor from Totalitarianism?" In *Totalitarismus und Transformation.* Göttingen: Vandenhoeck & Ruprecht, 2008.

Baer, Josette. "Montesquieu in Upper Hungary? Jan Palarík's Slovak constitutionalism and its failure." In *Czech and Slovak Culture in International and Global Context.* Halama Publications: České Budějovice, 2008.

Baer, Josette. "National Emancipation – not the Making of Slovakia. Ľudovít Štúr's Conception of the Slovak Nation." *Postcommunist Occasional Papers 1,* no. 2, 2003, http://www.stfx.ca/pinstitutes/cpcs/studies-in-post-communism/

Baer, Josette. *Politik als praktizierte Sittlichkeit. Zum Demokratiebegriff von Thomas G. Masaryk und Václav Havel.* Sinzheim: Pro Universitate, 1998.

Baer, Josette. *Preparing Liberty in Central Europe. Political texts from the Spring of Nations 1848 to the Spring of Prague 1968.* Stuttgart: ibidem, 2006.

Béder, Ján. "Tajný spolok slovenských radikálov." *Mladá tvorba 2,* č. 12 (1957): 374-377.

Beller, Steven. "Jewish entrepreneurship and identity under capitalism and socialism in central Europe: the unresolved dilemmas of Hungarian Jewry." In *Essential outsiders. Chinese and Jews in the modern transformation of Southeast Asia and Central Europe*. Seattle: University of Washington Press, 1997.

Beller, Steven. "The Hilsner affair. Nationalism, Antisemitism and the individual in the Habsburg Monarchy at the turn of the century." In *T. G. Masaryk (1850 – 1937). Thinker and Critic*, vol. II. London: MacMillan and School of Slavonic and East European Studies, 1990.

Beller, Steven. *Rethinking Vienna*. Berghahn: New York, 2001.

Beller, Steven. *Vienna and the Jews. A cultural history*. Cambridge, New York: Cambridge University Press, 1990.

Beneš, Edvard. *Paměti II. Od Mnichova k nové válce a k novému vítezství*. Academia: Praha, 2008.

Berlin, Isaiah. "Herder and the Enlightenment." In *The Proper Study of Mankind. An Anthology of Essays*. London: Pimlico, 1998.

Berlin, Isaiah. "The Apotheosis of the Romantic Will. The Revolt against the Myth of an Ideal World." In *The Proper Study of Mankind. An Anthology of Essays*. London: Pimlico, 1998.

Bettelheim, Bruno. "Freedom from Ghetto Thinking." In *Freud's Vienna and other Essays*. New York: Vintage books, 1989.

Bokeš, František. "Dnes." In *Štefan Marko Daxner. Život a dielo v dokumentoch*. Osveta: Martin, 1976.

Bokeš, František. "Slovenské národné hnutie a memorandum." In *Memorandum v slovenskej literature*. Bratislava: Slovenské vydavateľstvo krásnej literatúry, 1961.

Bokeš, František. *Dokumenty k slovenskému národnému hnutiu v rokoch 1848 – 1914*. 3 volumes. Bratislava: Historický ústav Slovenské akademie ved, 1965, 1972.

Botto, Juliuš. *Jan Francisci. Nakres životopisný*. Matica Slovenská: Rimavská Sobota, 1922.

Botto, Juliuš. *Životopis Štefana Marka Daxnera*. Rimavská Sobota: Matica Slovenská, 1922.

Bremer, Thomas. *Zwischen Kreuz und Kreml. Kleine Geschichte der Orthodoxen Kirche in Russland*. Freiburg: Herder, 2007.

Brock, Peter. *The Slovak National Awakening: an Essay in the intellectual history of East Central Europe.* Toronto, Buffalo: University of Toronto Press, 1976.

Čechová, Františka. "Štúrovci v mladej Európe." *Historická revue 14*, č. 4 (2003): 20-22.

Červeňák, Andrej. *Vajanský a Turgenev.* Bratislava: Vydavateľstvo Slovenskej akadémie vied, 1968.

Chirot, Daniel and Anthony Reid, eds. *Essential outsiders. Chinese and Jews in the modern transformation of Southeast Asia and Central Europe.* Seattle: University of Washington Press, 1997.

Chizhevskii, Dmitrii. "Hegel bei den Slowaken." In *Hegel bei den Slawen.* Darmstadt: Wissenschaftliche Buchgesellschaft, 1961 (2).

Danilevskii, Nikolai Y. *Rossiia i Evropa.* Moskva: Kniga, 1991.

Daxner, Štefan Marko. "K našim dejom." *Národnie Noviny VIII*, č. 64, 3. 6. 1882.

Daxner, Štefan Marko. "Národnie školy." *Pešťbudínske Vedomosti III*, č. 17, 27. 2. 1863.

Daxner, Štefan Marko. "Politika je obrana záujmov." *Peštbudínske Vedomosti I*, č. 9, 16. 4. 1861.

Daxner, Štefan Marko. "Poznámky." In *Pamäti slov. ev. a. v. gymnasium a s nim spojeného učiteľského semeniska vo Veľkej Revúci.* Ružomberok: Tlačov Karla Salvy – nákladom vydavateľovým, 1889.

Daxner, Štefan Marko. "Slovenský Demokratismus." *Pešťbudínske Vedomosti VIII*, č. 36, 5. 5. 1868.

Daxner, Štefan Marko. *Hlas zo Slovenska.* Pest: Trattner-Károlyi, 1861.

Daxner, Štefan Marko. *Slovenská otázka od konca 18. Stoletia.* Turčiansky Sv. Martin: Náklad kníhtlačiarský účastinárskeho spolku, 1912.

Deák, Istvan. *Assimilation and nationalism in East Central Europe during the last century of Habsburg rule.* Pittsburgh, PA: University of Pittsburgh, 1983.

Dubnička, Ivan. "Vavro Šrobár a čechoslovakizmus." In *Kultúrno-politický profil Vavra Šrobára.* Nitra: Kulturologická spoločnosť, 2005.

Eliáš, Michal, ed. *Listy Jána Francisciho 2 (1851-1902).* Martin: Matica Slovenská, 2004.

Encyklopédia Slovenska VI. Bratislava: Veda, 1982.

Fadner, Frank, L. *Seventy Years of Pan-Slavism in Russia: Karamzin to Danilevskii, 1800-1870.* Washington: Georgetown University Press, 1962.

Felák, James, R. *At the Price of the Republic: Hlinka's Slovak People's Party, 1929-1938.* Pittsburgh: Pittsburgh University Press, 1994.

Fond Vavra Šrobára. Slovenská Národní Knižnica SNK, Martin, sig: 173 D 28.

Fond Vavra Šrobára. Slovenská Národní Knižnica SNK, Martin, sig: 173 P 15.

Francisci, Ján. "Janko Podrimavský." In *Iskry zo zaviatej pahreby.* Bratislava: Tatran, 1977.

Francisci, Ján. "Severoslovania v Uhrách, t.j. Slováci a Rusíni, a krajinský snem uhorský." In *Memorandum v slovenskej literature.* Bratislava: Slovenské vydavateľstvo krásnej literatúry, 1961.

Francisci, Ján. "Vlastný životopis." In *Vlastný životopis. Črty z doby moysesovskej.* Bratislava: Slovenské vydavateľstvo krásnej literatúry, 1956.

Funda, Otakar A. *Tomáš Garrigue Masaryk. Sein philosophisches, religiöses und politisches Denken.* Bern: Peter Lang, 1978.

Gasparík, Mikuláš. "Ján Palarík – bojovník za prava a reč ľudu." In *Za reč a práva ľudu: kultúrnopolitické články.* Bratislava: Slovenské vydavateľstvo krásnej literatúry, 1956.

Goerdt, Wilhelm. "Teil II Russland und Europa." In *Russische Philosophie. Grundlagen.* Freiburg, München: Karl Alber, 1995 (2).

Herder, Johann Gottfried. *Outlines of a Philosophy of the History of Man,* transl. from the German *Ideen zur Philosophie der Geschichte der Menschheit* by T. Churchill. New York: Bergman Publishers, 1980.

Hobsbawm, Eric. *Age of extremes: the short twentieth century, 1914 – 1991.* London: Michael Joseph, 1994 .

Hobsbawm, Eric. *The age of empire 1875-1914.* New York: Pantheon, 1987.

Hoensch, Jörg, K. *Geschichte Böhmens.* München: Beck, 1987.

Holec, Roman. *Poľnohospodárstvo na Slovensku v poslednej tretine 19. Storočia.* Bratislava: Veda, 1991.

Hollý, Karol. "Negácia událostnej histórie a historický optimizmus: Historická ideológia Svetozára Hurbana Vajanského, (1881 – 1897)." *Historický časopis 57*, č. 2 (2009): 243-269.

Holotík, L'udovít. "Der österreichisch-ungarische Ausgleich und die Slowaken." In *Der österreichisch-ungarische Ausgleich 1867. Materialien (Referate und Diskussion) der internationalen Konferenz in Bratislava 28.8.-1.9. 1967.* Bratislava: Verlag der Slowakischen Akademie der Wissenschaften, 1971.

Holotík, L'udovít. "Die Slovaken". In *Die Habsburgermonarchie 1848–1918.* Vol. III, Die Völker des Reiches. Wien: Österreichische Akademie der Wissenschaften, 1980.

Hroch, Miroslav. *Das Europa der Nationen. Die moderne Nationsbildung im europäischen Vergleich.* Göttingen: Vandenhoeck & Ruprecht, 2005.

Hroch, Miroslav. *Die Vorkämpfer der nationalen Bewegungen bei den kleinen Völkern Europas: Eine vergleichende Analyse zur gesellschaftlichen Schichtung der patriotischen Gruppen.* Prag: Acta Universitatis Carolinae, 1968.

http://mirimen.com/co_beo/Lamanskij-Vladimir-Ivanovich-2009.html; accessed 5 June 2008.

http://philosophy.eserver.org/kant/metaphys-of-morals.txt ; accessed 1 July 2009.

http://plato.stanford.edu/entries/critical-theory/; accessed 29 June 2009.

http://plato.stanford.edu/entries/nietzsche/; accessed 2 July 2009.

http://plato.stanford.edu/entries/pragmatic-belief-god/ accessed 17 July 2009

http://plato.stanford.edu/entries/rights-human/; accessed 4 June 2008.

http://plato.stanford.edu/search/searcher.py?query=messianism; accessed 27 June 2009;

http://search.freefind.com/find.html?id=5355294&pageid=r&lang=de&mode=ALL& query=Messianismus&Find=Suche; accessed 27 June 2009

http://www.britannica.com/eb/article-9055045/natural-law; accessed 3 June 2008.

http://www.britannica.com/EBchecked/topic/192308/eschatology/247643/Messianis m#ref=ref846793; accessed 27 June 2009.

http://www.britannica.com/EBchecked/topic/324824/Bela-Kun; accessed 10 June 2009.

http://www.history.ac.uk/makinghistory/historians/seton-watson_robert.html; accessed 8 June 2009.

http://www.lexexakt.de/glossar/naturrecht.php; accessed 3 June 2008.

http://www.luno.hu/mambo/index.php?option=content&task=view&id=7890; accessed 23 April 2009.

http://www.marxists.org/archive/kun-bela/index.html; accessed 10 June 2009.

http://zlatyfond.sme.sk/autori; accessed 6 July 2009.

Ján Kollár a slovanská vzájomnosť. Geneza nacionalizmu v strednej Európe. Bratislava: Spoločnosť' pre dejiny a kulturú strednej a východnej Európy SDKSVE, 2006.

Juríček, Ján. *Vajanský. Portrét odvážného.* Bratislava: Obzor, 1988.

Kacírek, Luboš. *Nová škola slovenská a jej snahy o modernizáciu slovenskej spoločnosti.* Bratislava: SAV, 2007.

Kamenec, Ivan and Eduard Nižňanský, eds. *Holokaust na Slovensku: Prezident, vláda, snem SR a štátni rada o židovskej otázke.* Zvolen: Klemo; Bratislava: nadacia Milana Šimečka, židovská náboženská obec.

Kamenec, Ivan. *Po stopách tragédie.* Praha: Archa, 1991.

Kann, Robert A. "The Austro-Hungarian Compromise of 1867 in Retrospect. Causes and Effect." In *Der österreichisch-ungarische Ausgleich 1867. Materialien (Referate und Diskussion) der internationalen Konferenz in Bratislava 28.8.-1.9. 1967.* Bratislava: Verlag der Slowakischen Akademie der Wissenschaften, 1971.

Kann, Robert A. *A History of the Habsburg Empire 1526-1918.* Berkeley: University of California Press, 1974.

Kann, Robert A. *Das Nationalitätenproblem der Habsburgermonarchie,* vol. I Das Reich und die Völker. Graz, Köln: Böhlau, 1964 (2).

Kann, Robert A., and Zdeněk V. David. *The peoples of the Eastern Habsburg Lands, 1526-1918.* Seattle: University of Washington Press, 1984.

Katus, Lászlo. "Die Magyaren." In *Die Habsburgermonarchie 1848–1918.* Vol. III, Die Völker des Reiches. Wien: Österreichische Akademie der Wissenschaften, 1980.

Kodajová, Daniela. "Slováci na slovanských zjazdoch – sny, realita a sklamania slovenského rojčenia (1848, 1867, 1908, 1910)." In *Stredoeurópske národy na križovatkách novodobých dejín 1848-1918*. *Zborník venovaný prof. PhDr. Michailovi Danilákovi, CSc. k jeho 65. Narodeninám*. Prešov, Bratislava, Wien: Filozoficka fakulta Prešovskej university, Spoločnosť pre dejiny a kultúru strednej a východnej Európy pri SAV v Bratislave, Österreichisches Ost- und Südosteuropa-Institut in Wien, 1999.

Kohn, Hans. *Pan-Slavism: Its History and Ideology*. New York: Vintage Books, 1960.

Kollár, Johann. *Ueber literarische Wechselseitigkeit zwischen den verschiedenen Stämmen und Mundarten der slawischen Nation*. Pesth: Trattner-Karolyi, 1837.

Kořalka Jiří. "Nationsbildung und nationale Identität der Deutschen, Österreicher, Tschechen und Slovaken um die Mitte des 19. Jahrhunderts." In *Ungleiche Nachbarn. Demokratische und nationale Emanzipation bei Deutschen, Tschechen und Slovaken (1815-1914)*. Essen: Klartext Verlag, 1993.

Kořalka, Jiří. *František Palacký (1798-1876): Životopis*. Praha: Argo, 1998.

Kostický, Bohus. *Nová škola slovenská*. Bratislava: SAV, 1959.

Kováč, Dušan a kol.. *Muži deklarácie*. Bratislava: Veda, 2000.

Kováč, Dušan. "Philosophie und Mythologisierung der slowakischen Geschichte." *Österreichische Osthefte 35*, no. 4 (1993): 517-536.

Kováč, Dušan. "Popoluška slovenskej historiografii – vlastné dejiny." *Historický časopis 52*, č. 2 (2004): 233-237.

Kováč, Dušan. *Dejiny Slovenska*. Praha: Nakladatelství Lidové Noviny, 2007.

Kováč, Dušan. *Slováci. Češi. Dějiny*. Bratislava: Academic Electronic Press AEP, 1997.

Kučera, Matúš. "Koncepcia slovenských dejín v diele F. V. Sasinka." In *Franko Víťazoslav Sasinek. Najvýznamnejší slovenský historik 19. Storočia, 1830-1914*. Martin: Matica Slovenská, 2007.

Kusý, Ivan. *Zrelý Vajanský*. Bratislava: Tatran, 1992.

Lässig, Simone. "Introduction: Biography in modern history – modern historiography in Biography." In *Biography between structure and agency. Central European lives in international historiography.* New York, Oxford: Berghahn books, 2008.

Lauček, Daniel Záboj. "1872-1881. Budeme teda trpieť za vec našu." In *Štefan Marko Daxner. Život a dielo v dokumentoch.* Osveta: Martin, 1976.

Leikert, Jozef a kol.. *Kultúrno-politický profil Vavra Šrobára.* Nitra: Kulturologická spoločnosť, 2005.

Leikert, Jozef. "Životné a politické postoje Vavra Šrobára do roku 1918." In *Kultúrno-politický profil Vavra Šrobára.* Nitra: Kulturologická spoločnosť, 2005.

Lipták, Ľubomír. "Elitenwechsel in der bürgerlichen Gesellschaft der Slowakei im ersten Drittel des 20. Jahrhunderts." In *Bürgertum und und bürgerliche Gesellschaft in der Slowakei 1900-1989.* Bratislava: Academic Electronic Press AEP, 1997.

Lipták, Ľubomír. "Slovak political parties, societies and political culture up to 1914." In *Changes of changes. Society and politics in Slovakia in the 20th Century.* Bratislava: Academic Electronic Press AEP, Historický ústav SAV, 2002.

Macurek, Josef. "The Achievements of the Slavonic Congress." *The Slavonic and East European Review,* 1947/48, no. 26, 329-340.

Mannová, Elena. "Entwicklungsbedingungen bürgerlicher Schichten in der Slowakei im 20. Jahrhundert." In *Bürgertum und bürgerliche Gesellschaft in der Slowakei 1900-1989.* Bratislava: Academic Electronic Press AEP, 1997.

Marsina, Richard, and Peter Mulík, eds. *Franko Víťazoslav Sasinek. Najvýznamnejší slovenský historik 19. Storočia, 1830-1914.* Martin: Matica Slovenská, 2007.

Masaryk, Tomáš G. "Prostství národa malého." In *Ideály humanitní.* Praha: Melantrich, 1991.

Masaryk, Tomáš G. *Česká otázka. Naše nynejší krize.* Praha: Svoboda, 1990.

Mikuš, Joseph A. "Slovakia within the kingdom of Hungary (907-1918)." In *Slovakia. A Political and Constitutional History (with Documents).* Bratislava: Slovak Academic Press, 1995.

Montesquieu. *The Spirit of the Laws.* Cambridge: Cambridge University Press, 1989.

Moritsch, Andreas, ed. *Die slawische Idee.* Bratislava: Slovak Academic Press, 1993.

Mruškovič, Viliam. "Neznámy list 'vzájomnostných novín.'" *Literárny archív 27*, č. 90 (1994): 37-54.

Otčenáš, Michal. "Vedecko-organizačná a bádateľská činnosť F. V. Sasinka." in *Franko Víťazoslav Sasinek. Najvýznamnejší slovenský historik 19. Storočia, 1830-1914*. Martin: Matica Slovenská, 2007.

Palacký, František. "Idea státu Rakouského." In *Radhost. Sbírka spisůw drobných z oboru řeči a literatury češské, krásowědy, historie a politiky*. Praha: B. Tempsky, 1873.

Palacký, František. *Geschichte von Böhmen: groesstenteils nach Urkunden und Handschriften*. Prag: Kronberger & Riwac, 1836-1867.

Palarík, Ján. "Buďme svorní, krajania uhorskí!" *Priateľ ľudu I*, č. 1 (1861): 2-3.

Palarík, Ján. "Čo máme očkakávat od konštitúcie uhorskej pre našu národnosť a čo nám teraz predovšetkým treba?" In *Memorandum v slovenskej literature*. Bratislava: Slovenské vydavateľstvo krásnej literatúry, 1961.

Palarík, Ján. "Na dorozumenie." in *Za reč a práva ľudu: kultúrnopolitické články*. Bratislava: Slovenské vydavateľstvo krásnej literatúry, 1956.

Palarík, Ján. "Národnie sobectvo zkáza národa." *Slovenské Noviny II*, č. 54, 20. 5. 1869.

Palarík, Ján. "Návrh zákona o rovnoprávnosti národov v Uhrach, od vätšiny výboru snemového vypracovaný." *Priateľ školy a literatury III*, č. 35 (1861): 269-272.

Palarík, Ján. "Nová škola." *Slovenské Noviny I*, č. 36, 24. 3. 1868.

Palarík, Ján. "O vzájemnosti slovanskej. Úvahy politicko-literárne." *Lipa III* (1864): 277-297.

Palarík, Ján. "Účel Austrije pod centralismom a dualismom." *Slovenské Noviny I*, č. 42, 7. 4. 1868.

Palarík, Ján. "Účel Austrije pod centralismom a dualismom." *Slovenské Noviny I*, č. 38, 28. 3. 1868.

Pašiak, Ján. "Bürgertum im Kontext der Siedlungsentwicklung." In *Bürgertum und bürgerliche Gesellschaft in der Slowakei 1900-1989*. Bratislava: Academic Electronic Press AEP, 1997.

Pearson, Roger. *Voltaire Almighty. A life in pursuit of freedom.* London: Bloomsbury, 2006.

Pichler, Tibor. "Dejiny a pohyb ideí v slovenskom politickom myslení", *Filozofia 58,* č.10 (2003): 684-698.

Pichler, Tibor. "Nationaleiferer oder Bürger. Institutionalisierung als Problem." In *Bürgertum und bürgerliche Gesellschaft in der Slowakei 1900-1989.* Bratislava: Academic Electronic Press AEP, 1997.

Pichler, Tibor. *Národovci a občania: O slovenskom politickom myšleni v 19. storoči.* Bratislava: Slovenská Akademie Věd SAV, 1998.

Pius, Miroslav. *Ján Francisci-Rimavský a vrcholná fáza slovenského národného obrodenia.* Bratislava: Národné osvetové centrum, 1997.

Plaschka, Richard G. "The political significance of František Palacký." *Journal of Contemporary History 8,* no. 3 (1973): 35-55.

Podrimavský, Milan. *Slovenská národná strana v druhej polovici XIX. storočia.* Bratislava: vydavateľstvo slovenskej akadémie vied, 1983.

Poliakov, Leon. *Moscou, troisième Rome: les intermittences de la mémoire historique.* Paris: Hachette, 1989.

Polla, Belo, ed. *Matica slovenska a narodnostna otazka.* Martin: Matica slovenská, 1997.

Rapant, Daniel. *Dejiny slovenského povstania r. 1848-49. Diel prvý. Slovenská jar 1848.* Turčiansky sv. Martin: Matica Slovenská, 1937.

Rapant, Daniel. *Ilegalná Maďarizácia 1790-1840.* Turčiansky Sv. Martin: Matica Slovenská, 1947.

Rapant, Daniel. *Slovenské povstanie 1848-1849,* I, dokumenty. Turčiansky Sv. Martin, 1950.

Rawls, John. *A Theory of justice.* Cambridge, MA: Belknap Press of Harvard University Press, 1971.

Sasinek, František, V. "Čo nieje a čo je 'Matica Slov.'?" *Národnie Noviny,* č. 32, 15. 3. 1873.

Sasinek, František, V. "Či absolutism alebo konštitúcia?" *Národné Noviny III,* č. 39, 30. 3. 1872.

Sasinek, František, V. "Haňba XIX. storočiu!" *Národnie Noviny VII*, č. 11, 27. 1. 1876.

Sasinek, František, V. "Historické právo." *Pestbuďinské Vedomosti V*, č. 58, 21. 7. 1865.

Sasinek, František, V. "Ján Palarík (Nekrolog)." *Národnie Noviny I*, č. 116, 11. 12. 1870.

Sasinek, František, V. "Liberál." *Katolické Noviny XXV*, č. 6, 8, 9, 1894.

Sasinek, František, V. "Memorandum a protesty." *Peštbudinské Vedomosti I*, č. 40, 2. 8. 1861.

Sasinek, František, V. "Memorandum a protesty." *Peštbudinské Vedomosti I*, č. 41, 6. 8. 1861.

Sasinek, František, V. "Millenium." *Národnie Noviny XXII*, č. 141, 1. 12. 1891.

Sasinek, František, V. "Patriotismus." *Národné Noviny III*, č. 121, 10. 10. 1872.

Sasinek, František, V. "Poddanstvo v Uhorsku." *Kalendár Národni II*, (1894): 130-147.

Sasinek, František, V. "Rovnoprávnosť." *Pestbuďinské Vedomosti VIII*, č. 53, 3. 7. 1868.

Sasinek, František, V. "Škola a maďarisácia." *Národnie Noviny IX*, č. 128, 31. 10. 1878.

Sasinek, František, V. "Sociálná otázka." *Katolické Noviny XXV*, č. 10, 14, 21-23, 1894.

Sasinek, František, V. "Uhor a Madar." *Slovenský Letopis I*, (1876): 96-111.

Schorske, Carl E. *Fin-de-Siècle in Vienna. Politics and Culture*. New York: Vintage, Random, 1979.

Škultéty, August Hor. *Pamäti slov. ev. a. v. gymnasium a s nim spojeného učiteľského semeniska vo Veľkej Revúci*. Ružomberok: Tlačov Karla Salvy – nákladom vydavateľovým, 1889.

Šolle, Zdeněk, *Masaryk a Beneš ve svých dopisech z doby pařížských mírových jednání v roce 1919*. Vol. I. Praha: Archiv AV ČR, 1993.

Šrobár, Vavro. "Kultúrny pokrok na Slovensku." In *Slovensko kedysi a teraz*. Praha: Orbis, 1931.

Šrobár, Vavro. "Kus svetla.", *Národnie Noviny XXIII*, č. 92, 9. 8. 1892.

Šrobár, Vavro. "Maďarisácia." *Hlas I* (1898): 65-73.

Šrobár, Vavro. "Naše snahy." *Hlas I* (1898): 1-6.

Šrobár, Vavro. "Nečekaná návšteva detektiva Duliškieviča u Dra Šrobára." In *Boj o nový život*. Ján Párička: Ružomberok, 1920.

Šrobár, Vavro. "Počiatky slovenského obrodenia." In *Boj o nový život*. Ján Párička: Ružomberok, 1920.

Šrobár, Vavro. "Politický kramár." In *Boj o nový život*. Ján Párička: Ružomberok, 1920.

Šrobár, Vavro. "Poučenia z chýb." In *Boj o nový život*. Ján Párička: Ružomberok, 1920.

Šrobár, Vavro. "Slovenská národna strana a jej program." In *Boj o nový život*. Ján Párička: Ružomberok, 1920.

Šrobár, Vavro. "Voľnosť, rovnosť, bratstvo." *Národnie Noviny XXV*, č. 135, 15. 11. 1894.

Šrobár, Vavro. "Vzájomnosť československá!" In *Boj o nový život*. Ján Párička: Ružomberok, 1920.

Šrobár, Vavro. *Oslobodené Slovensko. Pamäti z rokov 1918-1920*. Bratislava: Academic Electronic Press, 2004.

Šrobár, Vavro. *Osvobodené Slovensko. Pamäti z rokov 1918 – 1920*. Praha: Čin, 1928.

Šrobár, Vavro. *Pamäti z vojny a z väzenia*. Praha: Náklad Gustav Dubského, 1922.

Šrobár, Vavro. *Politický problém Slovenska*. Praha: Svaz národního osvobození: Praha, 1926.

Šrobár, Vavro. *Vláda ľudu v demokracii*. 3 vol. Bratislava: Práca, 1920.

Šrobár, Vavro. *Z môjho života*. Praha: Fr. Borový, 1946.

Šrobárov sborník k 70. Narodeninám. Bratislava: Štefánikova spoločnosť, 1937.

Štúr, Ľudovít. "Dôležitost volenia rozličneho stavu pre nas" (1846). In *Dielo v piatich zväzkoch*. Bratislava: Slovenské vydavatelstvo krasnej literatury, 1954-56; vol. I, 1954.

Štúr, Ľudovít. "Ponosy a žaloby Slovanóv" (1843). In *Dielo v piatich zväzkoch*. Bratislava: Slovenské vydavatelstvo krasnej literatury, 1954-56; vol. I, 1954.

Štúr, Ľudovít. *Das Slawenthum und die Welt der Zukunft*. ed. by Jozef Jirášek. Bratislava: Šafaříková společnost, 1931.

Štúr, Ľudovít. *Slovanstvo a Svět Budúcnosti*. Translated by Adam Bžoch. Bratislava: Slovenský Institut Mezinárodnich Studii, 1993.

Sutherland, Anthony X. "Studies into the intellectual history of Slovak nationalism (1500s-1914)." *Slovak Studies XXV* (1985): 69-145.

Svetoň, Ján. *Obyvateľstvo Slovenska za kapitalizmu*. Bratislava: Slovenské vydavateľstvo politickej literatúry, 1958.

Szarka, Lászlo. "The Slovak National Question and Hungarian Nationality Policy before 1918." *The Hungarian Quarterly 35*, no. 136 (1994): 98-114.

Szücz, Jenö. "The three historical regions of Europe." *Acta Historica Academiae Scientiarum Hungaricae 29*, no. 2–4, (1983): 131-184.

Truhlar, Dalibor. *Thomas G. Masaryk. Philosophie der Demokratie*. Frankfurt a. Main: Peter Lang, 1994.

Urbán, Otto. "Die tschechische Frage um 1900." *Österreichische Osthefte 32*, no. 3 (1990): 427-43.

Urbán, Otto. *Česká společnost 1848–1918*. Praha: Svoboda, 1982.

Vajanský, Svetozár Hurban. "Anarchia ducha." *Národnie Noviny XXXI*, č. 32, 17. 3. 1900; č. 46, 30. 3. 1900.

Vajanský, Svetozár Hurban. "Cár osvoboditeľ." *Národnie Noviny XII*, č. 32, 17. 3. 1881.

Vajanský, Svetozár Hurban. "My budeme tichí, ale vytrváme." *Národnie Noviny V*, č. 139, 24. 11. 1874.

Vajanský, Svetozár Hurban. "Novinárska vojna." *Národnie Noviny X*, č. 100, 28. 8. 1879.

Vajanský, Svetozár Hurban. "O nihilizme." *Národnie Noviny X*, č. 42, 10. 4. 1879.

Vajanský, Svetozár Hurban. "Parlamentarismus." *Národnie Noviny XX*, č. 25, 28. 2. 1889.

Vajanský, Svetozár Hurban. "Protikresťanské theorie." *Národnie Noviny XXIX*, č. 248, 29. 10. 1898.

Vajanský, Svetozár Hurban. "Slavianska popelka." *Národnie Noviny IX*, č. 140, 28. 11. 1878.

Vajanský, Svetozár Hurban. "Umenie a národnosť." *Národnie Noviny XVII*, č. 115, 5. 8. 1886.

Vajanský, Svetozár Hurban. "Vnútorní nepriatelia." *Národnie Noviny XXIX*, č. 64, 19. 3. 1898.

Vajanský, Svetozár Hurban. "Zradili ľud." *Národnie Noviny XXXI*, č. 36, 27. 3. 1900.

Vajanský, Svetozár Hurban. *Nálady a výhľady*. Kníhtlačiarsko-účastinársky spolok: Turčiansky Sv. Martin, 1897.

Vajanský, Svetozár Hurban. *Ružomberský kriminálny process proti Andrejovi Hlinkovi a spoločníkom*. Turčiansky Sv. Martin: Kníhtlaciarsko-účastinársky spolok, 1906.

Vajanský, Svetozár Hurban. *Zápasy a hľadania v zrkadlení času. Život a dielo v dokumentoch*. Martin: Osveta, 1985.

Verba, Sidney. "Conclusion: Comparative Political Culture." In *Political Culture and Political Development*. Princeton: Princeton University Press, 1965.

Vietor, Martin. "Die Beschaffenheit der Ausgleichsgesetze." In *Der österreichisch-ungarische Ausgleich 1867. Materialien (Referate und Diskussion) der internationalen Konferenz in Bratislava 28.8.-1.9. 1967*. Bratislava: Verlag der Slowakischen Akademie der Wissenschaften, 1971.

von Gogolák, Ludwig. "Die historische Entwicklung des slovakischen Nationalbewusstseins." In *Die Slowakei als mitteleuropäisches Problem in Geschichte und Gegenwart*. München: Oldenbourg, 1965.

von Gogolák, Ludwig. "Ungarns Nationalitätengesetze und das Problem des Magyarischen National- und Zentralstaates." In *Die Habsburgermonarchie 1848–1918*. Vol. III.

Walter, Friedrich. "Kaiser Franz Josephs Ungarnpolitik in der Zeit des Neoabsolutismus." In *Der österreichisch-ungarische Ausgleich von 1867*. München: Oldenbourg, 1968.

Wandruszka, Adam, and Peter Urbanitsch, eds. *Die Habsburger Monarchie 1848-1918* vol. III. Die Völker des Reiches. Wien: Österreichische Akademie der Wissenschaften, 1980.

Záček, Joseph F., ed. *East European Quaterly 15*, no. 1 (1981).

Zurbuchen, Simone. *Naturrecht und natürliche Religion. Zur Geschichte des Toleranzbegriffs von Samuel Pufendorf bis Jean-Jacques Rousseau*. Würzburg: Königshausen & Neumann, 1991.

Index

A

assimilation X, XV, XVI, 2, 7, 11, 13, 19,
28, 29, 32, 82, 87, 88, 90, 96, 127, 146,
152, 153, 156, 165, 170, 179, 183, 184,
191, 192, 193, 199, 226, 227, 229
Ausgleich X, 3, 7, 20, 21, 23, 57, 61, 68,
70, 78, 79, 80, 83, 87, 90, 93, 98, 127,
129, 141, 154, 225
Austroslavism 15, 83, 226

C

Cisleithania XV
constitutionalism XIV, 63, 65, 70, 77, 78,
81, 83, 140
contextual biography 32
Czechoslovakism XIII, XIV, 1, 10, 34,
38, 167, 179, 180, 186, 191, 201, 203,
205, 209, 210, 219, 225, 231, 232

D

definition 10, 25, 34, 37, 57, 73, 132, 140,
155, 166, 167, 226

H

Hegel, Georg Wilhelm Friedrich 9, 11,
35, 57, 58, 127, 171
Herder, Johann Gottfried 10, 11, 35, 43,
57, 76, 78, 82, 83, 127, 146, 227, 231
Hlinka, Andrej 30, 39, 123, 176, 177,
182, 184, 185, 190, 207, 210, 214, 215,
216, 217, 232
Hobbes, Thomas 36, 63, 71, 84

K

Kollár, Ján 9, 10, 12, 57, 64, 89, 96, 141,
155, 165, 183, 202, 203, 225, 226, 227,
231
Kováč, Dušan XI, XVI, 31, 95

L

language law 7, 35
language rights 3, 9, 20, 58, 76, 82, 90,
128, 132, 133, 151, 167, 226
Liberalism 7, 35, 47, 63, 69, 70, 135, 138,
139, 152, 153, 163, 180, 193, 205, 206,
226, 228, 231

M

Magyarisation XIV, XV, 2, 3, 7, 8, 11,
13, 23, 25, 26, 34, 38, 50, 57, 59, 65,
81, 87, 98, 105, 135, 137, 170, 183,
198, 199, 216
Martin XIV, 18, 19, 38, 54, 61, 70, 85,
90, 97, 104, 130, 137, 138, 148, 149,
152, 175, 176, 177, 179, 183
Martinists 152, 184, 191, 192, 193, 195,
196, 197, 216
Masaryk, Tomáš Garrigue XIII, XIV,
XV, 1, 10, 29, 35, 38, 41, 181, 182,
183, 186, 187, 190, 194, 195, 201, 206,
207, 208, 211, 219, 221, 225, 227, 228,
231
Memorandum X, XIII, XIV, 3, 16, 18, 19,
31, 38, 51, 61, 68, 87, 89, 90, 91, 100,
104, 127, 128, 131, 137, 138, 139, 146,
152, 153, 154, 179, 184, 204, 226, 228

ibidem-Verlag / *ibidem* Press
Melchiorstr. 15
70439 Stuttgart
Germany

ibidem@ibidem.eu
www.ibidem-verlag.com
www.ibidem.eu

GPSR Authorized Representative: Easy Access System Europe, Mustamäe tee 50, 10621 Tallinn, Estonia, gpsr.requests@easproject.com

www.ingramcontent.com/pod-product-compliance
Lightning Source LLC
Chambersburg PA
CBHW071717120626
46550CB00001B/277